QUAKERS
IN
CALIFORNIA

QUAKERS IN CALIFORNIA

THE EFFECTS OF 19TH CENTURY REVIVALISM ON WESTERN QUAKERISM

David C. Le Shana

with foreword by
D. ELTON TRUEBLOOD

*Long Beach
CA 69*

THE BARCLAY PRESS
Newberg, Oregon 97132

Published in cooperation with
the Board of Publications
of
California Yearly Meeting of Friends Church
on the
75th Anniversary
of the Yearly Meeting
June, 1969

Printed in the United States of America

*For Becky
and for
our children*

Foreword

ALTHOUGH THE WORD QUAKER is known to most people in America, there is widespread confusion and misunderstanding about the significance of the term. Many think of the Quaker Movement as something confined, historically, to the seventeenth century or confined, geographically, to the eastern seaboard of the United States. David Le Shana's careful historical study can be helpful in overcoming such misconceptions. When he writes of Quakers he deals, also, with the American Far West. It is not likely that any thoughtful reader can study this book and continue to think of Quakerism as merely antique.

There is no chance of understanding the Quaker Movement without recognizing its close association with the westward trek. Rufus M. Jones was, perhaps, the first to see this clearly, with the consequence that one of his most eloquent chapters in **The Later Periods of Quakerism** is called "The Great Migration." For many contemporary American Quaker families, the history of three centuries is that of a slow journey from England to California or Oregon, with stops on the way in North Carolina, Ohio, Indiana, and Iowa or Kansas. It was a sharp surprise to me when I realized that, in my particular inheritance, I was the first person in over 300 years to go against the stream and to move east.

California Quakerism is important, partly because it represents the climax of one historical process. The Friends of California and Oregon, with whom David Le Shana has been closely associated, stand at the end of a line. There may be other migrations, but there will be no further chapter in this particular story.

It was almost inevitable that California, at the end of the Quaker trek, should involve all of the major variations that Quakerism has produced in three centuries of growth and change. At one time, the city of Pasadena was the home of three strong Friends congregations, each representing a distinct branch of the Quaker tree. It is part of the merit of the present scholarly work that it does equal justice to the various variations of Quaker thought and experience. While David Le Shana makes no effort to deny differences, he presents each variation fairly, as demonstrated by his treatment of the Friends of San Jose.

California Quakerism is of national interest today for several reasons, the greatest of which is the fact it has produced the thirty-seventh President of the United States. It is not possible to understand President Nixon apart from his deep early involvement in the California Quaker story. The Quakerism of California gave him his early spiritual nurture and, through Whittier College, his most formative educational experience. That this nurture was not identical with Quaker nurture in some other areas is a point on which some people appear to be ignorant, but about which information should lead to understanding.

If there is any tendency to minimize the Quaker life of the West Coast, this error may be corrected by recognizing the fact that the only men of Quaker culture who have been elected President have come from that area. Most of Herbert Hoover's early years were spent in Oregon, while California was his home until after the death of his wife. All of Richard Nixon's early years were spent in California. There he grew up to manhood, closely associated with contemporary Quakers, many of whom are still alive. Americans need to know the character of the life of which their two Quaker Presidents are products.

I am grateful to David Le Shana for the careful research that lies behind this volume and that tells me a great deal I did not otherwise know. He has shown that it is possible to be both scholarly and clear. It is a pleasure to know his historical work is now available to the ordinary reader and that its publication coincides with his election to the presidency of George Fox College.

—*D. Elton Trueblood*

vi

Preface

FOR OVER 300 YEARS, the Religious Society of Friends has been a part of the American religious scene, participating in and contributing to the history and culture of the nation. From its hesitant beginnings in the Massachusetts Bay Colony, through periods of colonial expansion and influence, through days of struggle for national freedom and identity, to the present moments of concern within an affluent society, Quakerism has had an influence all out of proportion to its size.

The first Quakers known to have set foot on American soil were two women, Ann Austin and Mary Fisher, who appeared in Boston harbor on July 11, 1656, having come from the island of Barbados for the purpose of continuing the testimony of Quakers against the religious formalism of the English Puritans. Their deportation, however, only encouraged others to come to the colonies. With the arrival of George Fox in Maryland in 1672, the movement to America was given new impetus. The purchase of one-half of New Jersey in 1674 from Lord Berkeley by two Quakers and the establishment of William Penn's "Holy Experiment" in Pennsylvania firmly rooted the presence and participation of Quakers in American life.

The history of Quakers in America has been characterized by a pioneering spirit, due partially to the initial and motivating zeal of their faith, and due in part to the spirit of the new world —a spirit characterized by the vision of greater and newer expansion. Along with others in the early colonies, a perceptible shift in population to the south and west took place. The shifting of the War of the Revolution to the south caused the migrations to that region soon to cease, and the Quakers now turned their faces to the west.

For the next century, the westward migration continued as Quakers poured into western Ohio and eastern Indiana, and then on to the great plains of Iowa and Kansas. The movement did not stop, however, until Quakers had reached the shores of the Pacific. Today, about 150,000 Quakers in America are scattered from the Atlantic to Hawaii and from the Gulf of Mexico to Alaska.

The "last chapter" in the westward movement of Friends has been "written" in the past seventy-five years. In 1895, the California Yearly Meeting of Friends Church was established with a membership of 1,166 people in two quarterly meetings. Six years earlier, the College Park Association of Friends was formed in San Jose, eventually becoming one of the forerunners of the Pacific Yearly Meeting of the Religious Society of Friends.

Today, these two Quaker bodies continue to exist in California and are the subject of this study. These two yearly meetings reflect wide and divergent views on ecclesiology, theology, and social concerns in contradistinction to the unity of spirit and purpose exhibited when Quakers first landed on American soil and began their westward movement.

It is my purpose to examine these two groups in the light of their history and to point to the exigencies of revivalism in America, especially the period of religious awakening in the mid-nineteenth century, as being a primary factor in the disunity experienced by western Quakers.

I am deeply indebted to a large number of people who have made this study possible: my professors at the University of Southern California, where this study was first written as a doctoral dissertation; the members of the First Friends Church, Long Beach, California, who encouraged me in the undertaking; and, above all, my wife and family, whose love and patience made the task worthwhile.

I am particularly grateful to various Friends in California, especially the Board of Publications of California Yearly Meeting, who have made this publication possible as part of the observance of the Seventy-fifth Anniversary of California Yearly Meeting.

The sources for this study have been varied and are listed in the footnotes. Collections were also researched at a number of Quaker colleges. I am grateful for the kind assistance and suggestions of the librarians at these institutions.

The story of Quakers in California is, of course, just beginning. It is my hope that this study will help produce for Friends an understanding and appreciation of their differing roles and contribution to modern American society and will encourage a deeper involvement in the work of the Kingdom of God.

—*David C. Le Shana*
George Fox College
Newberg, Oregon

June, 1969

Contents

The Background
of American Quakerism

GEORGE FOX HAS left an indelible mark upon the religious history of the world. An unusual man, called a "religious genius" by some historians,[1] he has excited a variety of notions concerning his life and ministry. Quakerism, however, which resulted from his personal encounter with God, has continued to impress upon the world its concepts of the worship of God, the practice of the presence of God, and its concern to meet the needs of humanity in the name of God.

As we begin a study of Quakerism in western America, it is important to recognize the beginnings of the Quaker movement and the background it supplied for American Quakerism. Early Quakerism was a "movement of ordinary men,"[2] men and women who were filled with the intensity of personal experience with God and actualized this experience in everyday living. This radical inward experience provided both the motivation and the continuity to a movement that spread from the north of England, throughout the British Isles, to the Continent, to the colonies, and around the world.

The Advent of Quakerism

The Founder of Quakerism

George Fox was born in July, 1624, in the English hamlet called Drayton-in-the-Clay, located in the heart of the Midlands, in Leicestershire.[3] His parents were Christopher and Mary Fox, both Puritans. His father was a church warden and was, by trade, a weaver. William Penn said of Mary Fox that she "was a woman accomplished above most of her degree in the place where she lived."[4] George was a serious-minded boy, sensitive and mature beyond his years. Although he had little formal schooling, he was not uneducated. He read much, for his later writings show a wide interest, and during his lifetime he acquired an extensive library. He was, nevertheless, essentially religiously-minded; indeed, he knew the Bible so well that he could quote large portions of it from memory.[5]

During his teen-age years, a great uneasiness came upon him so that he could no longer stay in the warm and familiar fellowship of his home and family, but felt it necessary to travel about among persons of reputed knowledge.[6] He plied them with questions about sin and salvation only to find that they had no answers for his need. "I went to many a priest to look for comfort," wrote George Fox, "but found no comfort from them."[7] It was in 1647, at the age of twenty-three, that this period came to an end with an experience upon which the whole of the Quaker message was to hinge. George Fox later wrote concerning the experience in his **Journal**:

> And when all my hopes in them and in all men were gone, so that I had nothing outwardly to help me, nor could tell what to do, then, oh then, I heard a voice which said, "There is one, even Christ Jesus, that can speak to thy condition," and when I heard it my heart did leap for joy. Then the Lord did let me see why there was none upon the earth that could speak to my condition, namely, that I might give him all the glory; for all are concluded under sin, and shut up in unbelief as I had been, that Jesus Christ might have the pre-eminence, who enlightens, and gives grace, and faith, and power. Thus when God doth work who shall let it? And this I knew experimentally. My desires after the Lord grew stronger and zeal in the pure knowledge of God and of Christ alone, without the help of any man, book or writing. For though I read the Scriptures that spoke of Christ and of God, yet I knew him not but by revelation, as he who hath the key, did open, and as the Father of life drew me to his Son by his spirit. And then the Lord did gently lead me along, and let me see his love, which was endless and eternal . . .[8]

From this time on Fox had a realization of God such as few men in any time have experienced. Indeed, from the intense struggles of this one man have emanated influences that have profoundly affected the world's thought. Consciousness of inherent sin, futility of all earthly agencies to redeem, a personal and inherent ability to perceive God—these constituted the message that George Fox brought to the world. It was in Jesus Christ that Fox found the answer to his personal needs and the motivation for the incendiary movement that resulted. Fox wrote:

> And I found that there were two thirsts in me, the one after the creatures, to have gotten help and strength there, and the other after the Lord the Creator and his Son Jesus Christ. And I saw all the world could do me no good. If I had a king's diet, palace, and attendance, all would have been as nothing, for nothing gave me comfort but the Lord by his power.[9]

Fox preached these ideas with all of their power and freshness to a people already torn with many dissensions. With outstanding rapidity his teachings spread throughout England, and for a time it seemed as if the faith of the whole nation would be shaken.[10]

Many books have been written about the personality of George Fox. Rufus Jones has emphasized his role as a "positive mystic," as one who seeks "to realize the presence of God in this finite human life."[11] Others have attempted psychological studies[12] and personality investigations,[13] but perhaps the best description is that which was made by William Penn:

> He was a man that God endowed with a clear and wonderful depth, a discerner of others' spirits, and very much a master of his own. . . . And his ministry and writings show they are from one that was not taught of man, nor had learned what he said by study. He had an extraordinary gift in opening the Scriptures. He would go to the marrow of things and shew the mind, harmony, and fulfilling of them with much plainness, and to great comfort and edification. . . . But above all he excelled in prayer. The inwardness and weight of his spirit, the reverence and solemnity of his address and behavior, and the fewness and fullness of his words, have often struck even strangers with admiration, as they used to reach others with consolation. The most awful, living, reverent frame I ever felt or beheld, I must say, was his in prayer.[14]

The Historical Setting

During these beginnings of Quakerism, England was under the reign of the Stuarts. Henry VIII had been dead for a hundred years, and many changes had taken place in English life during the ensuing century. The absolutism of Charles I was now in sharp conflict with the chartered rights of Englishmen; and the mighty Church of England was doing all in its power to subdue the rising spirit of Puritanism. The tyranny of the sovereign had been challenged by the demands of popular liberty, and religious intolerance was being countered with an insistent demand for freedom of worship. In 1640, Charles I began a nine-year quarrel with the Long Parliament, a quarrel that twice erupted into civil war and concluded only in 1649 when a Puritan-dominated Parliament sent him to the scaffold. The claim of the sovereign to the divine right of kings was abrogated, and England was declared a Commonwealth.[15]

In addition to the political upheavals, England was experiencing confusion in religious and ecclesiological matters. Numerous sects arose in the nation. There were Cavaliers—the people of privileged power—and Roundheads, Presbyterians and Independents, Separatists and Puritans, Familists and Seekers. In the midst of the turmoil of contending and conflicting factions in religion, Quakerism was born.

It is most important to note, however, the Puritan setting of which early Quakerism was an essential part. In a recent and definitive study, Professor Hugh Barbour has written:

> The Quakers were also puritans. . . . Most of their insights in ethics and worship were in fact the same as those of the puritans. Even characteristically Quaker teachings were often puritan attitudes pushed to severe conclusions. Early Quakerism showed its unique power in many areas, yet, in describing their faith, Friends mainly used ideas and phrases which they shared with "spiritual puritans" of the time.[16]

The Puritan movement was at least a century older than Quakerism and has undoubtedly been the greatest religious movement in English history.[17] "The heart of this movement was an experience of the sovereignty of God"[18] and the Puritan "living in a world polarized into positive and negative, good and evil, by the tension of God's presence—found himself set apart from other men."[19] He was a stranger in an indifferent world, but "his citizenship in the heavenly city did not make him other worldly, for this world itself would be transformed into the New Jerusalem by God's power."[20]

The idealism and concerns of Puritanism became the inheritance of early Quakerism. The urgency for a pure church, the concerns for social justice and spiritual inspiration, the expectation for God to rule both church and state, the simplicity of life and the development of economic and business ethics, the emphasis upon worship—these were the strands from the Puritan movement that were woven into the fabric of Quakerism. "Early Quakerism arose in this setting and only gradually came to develop a character of its own."[21]

England was thus well prepared to receive the message of the Quakers. The English Reformation had molded the times into a receptive mood. About the middle of the seventeenth century great crowds gathered to discuss religious questions in the marketplaces, in churches, and in the great open fields. There was also a widespread knowledge of and interest in the Scriptures. A greater freedom to read the Scriptures resulted in the use of the little Geneva Bible, published in 1560, in many English homes. Fifty years later, the Authorized Version was published in 1611 and enjoyed wide favor among English-speaking people. John Richard Green consequently observed:

> England became the people of a book, and that book was the Bible. . . . Elizabeth might silence or tune the pulpits; but it was impossible for her to silence or tune the great preachers of justice and mercy and truth who spoke from the book which she had opened again to her people. . . . The whole temper of the nation felt the change. A new conception of life and of man superseded the old. A new moral and religious impulse spread through every class. . . . The great problems of life and death . . . pressed for an answer, not only from the noble and scholar but from farmer and shopkeeper.[22]

George Fox took advantage of these opportunities. The great religious gatherings afforded him a platform to propagate his religious ideas; and his extensive knowledge of the Scriptures made it possible for him to appeal strongly to the masses of the people.[23] Large numbers of earnest and seeking individuals could find no satisfaction in the established religious groupings of their day. Some called themselves "seekers." They were not a sect and had no characteristic literature, but they were those Separatists who denied the existence of a true church or ministry, and waited upon God in prayer, anticipating a return of the church to the apostolic pattern. It was from them that the Quaker movement began to draw a great number of followers.[24]

A leading English Quaker at the turn of this century concluded:

> The reason why so many of the "seekers" attached themselves to George Fox was that he seemed to be the "apostle" they were looking for: a man who could "in the spirit give visible demonstration of being sent." He was able to convince them that he had really found what they were seeking; that God had really spoken to him as He spoke to the ancient prophets. And, as they came under Fox's influence, he led them into the same first-hand experience that he himself enjoyed, so that they found their leader and teacher was not Fox but Christ.[25]

This was probably the real significance of the early movement of Quakerism, an intense consciousness of a direct and personal relationship with God, through Jesus Christ, whose Spirit was ever present to be man's Guide and Teacher. It perhaps would be helpful at this point to discuss briefly the nature of early Quakerism.

The Nature of Quakerism

The beginning of the Friends movement is generally considered to be a part of the Protestant Reformation. Historically, the Reformation extended from Martin Luther's posting his ninety-five theses for debate in Wittenberg in 1517 to the Peace of Westphalia, which closed the Thirty Years War in 1648. The fact that George Fox began preaching in 1647 relates the movement chronologically to the Reformation.[26]

Friends, with others, professed freely their belief in salvation through Christ by grace and faith alone, in the authority of the Scriptures, in the universal priesthood of believers, and in the spiritual nature of the church. Hence, on the basic doctrines they stood in the midst of the Protestant forces in the seventeenth century.[27]

A second fact which shows the relation of the Society of Friends with the Reformation is that George Fox and the early

Quakers understood themselves as carrying the Reformation to its logical conclusion in the spiritual interpretation of the Gospel of Christ in the New Testament. Friends interpreted Christianity as a practical and spiritual religion, rejecting all outward ordinances. Elbert Russell writes in the introduction to his **History of Quakerism,**

> If, therefore, Quakerism was organically related to contemporary history, it should be by its chronological position the final development of the English Reformation, the most protestant phase of Protestantism.[28]

Quakerism, then, was held by the "Publishers of Truth" as being the practical interpretation and application (doctrines and testimonies) of the Christian faith. George Fox believed that the seventeenth century Christian should live in the same spirit and power in which the first century apostles lived. The title of William Penn's book, **Primitive Christianity Revived in the Faith and Practice of the People Called Quakers,**[29] is a good illustration of the importance that early Friends ascribed to New Testament Christianity. The faith and practice of early Friends was centered in the Christ of the Holy Scriptures and was not based on human reason and speculation.

Friends believed:

> that God, through Christ, hath placed a principle in every man, to inform him of his duty, and to enable him to do it, and those that live up to this principle are the people of God, and those that live in disobedience to it are not God's people, whatever name they bear or profession they may make of religion.[30]

This principle they called "the light of Christ within" or other scriptural terms, but never the current impersonal expression "Inner Light."

Belief in this Light was at the very heart of the Quaker faith.

> This was not a variable, haphazard illumination, peculiarly infallible for each person, but, shining dimly in some and more strongly in others, it was identified with the Light that shone supremely in Jesus.[31]

It was not any light, but the Light of Christ, and if individual guidance showed a course of action contrary to the teaching of Jesus, it was rejected. Sidney Lucas writes:

In practice, the Quaker theory of Inward Light was clothed less with the purity of the first century than with the Puritanism of the seventeenth century, for the Quakers' interpretation of the Light was naturally affected by the environment in which they lived. They compared the Inward Light to the candle in a lantern; we can see now that although the light was clear, the lantern was of Puritan pattern and the glass colored by prejudice. Fox reflected the times in his strong religious objection to bells, music, pictures, candles, games, images, bishops, festivals, maypoles, and Roman Catholics.[32]

The outward applications of their inward beliefs were called "Testimonies." The Puritan upbringing of many early Friends predisposed them to accept without much question the Testimonies that Fox and other leaders declared necessary to demonstrate the "Truth."[33] These Testimonies fall into four main categories: (1) Worship, (2) Truthfulness, (3) Simplicity, and (4) Social Concerns. Whether as an objection to conscription, fashion, oaths, and ritual, or as an urge toward social improvement, prison reform, and peacemaking, the Testimonies were public demonstrations of the Quaker belief in the "Light of Christ within." This Light was the "mainspring of action behind all the Testimonies, inspiring man's life and giving him faith and courage to withstand persecution."[34] A brief description of these categories of Testimonies will help to clarify some of the issues that later arose within the Society of Friends.

Worship. The Meetings for Worship became the center for the later organization of the Quaker movement.[35] Early Friends were concerned to revive the New Testament concepts of worship. Corporate worship was felt to be necessary, for Quakers held that something was done in a common act that could not be done by individuals, resulting in a heightened awareness of God and His will for the life of both the individual and the Society. The worship of early Christians was marked by two distinct elements: spontaneity, which produced a vitality; and obedience, the involvement of the individual within the group.[36]

George Fox wanted to recover this vitality and reality in worship, and so the early Quakers gathered together, listened and waited for the Spirit's leading, and were obedient to it. In their worship they discovered a double freedom—the freedom to use words, and the freedom from the necessity of uttering words.[37] This freedom was based upon holy obedience, and it is this that supplied the central experience of worship. There was no complete worship without complete obedience; consequently the early Quakers held that no preacher or leader could do worship for them. Robert Barclay writes in his **Apology**:

When the saints are met together, this Spirit is limited in his operations, by setting up a particular man or men to preach and pray in man's will, and all the rest are excluded from so much as believing that they are to wait for God's Spirit to move them in such things; and so they, neglecting that in themselves which should quicken them . . . and led merely to depend upon the preacher and hear what he will say.[38]

Worship became an act of holy dependence upon God; it was a matter of individual and corporate experience, not of mere speculation or observation. "The great work of one and all (in worship) ought to be to wait upon God; and returning out of their own thoughts and imaginations to feel the Lord's presence."[39] The meetings for worship were, therefore, held in a setting of silence so that "what was worthy in one person could reach out to the worth in others."[40] This was not silence for the sake of silence, but a corporate waiting upon the Lord. Barclay clearly writes,

For as our worship consisted not in words, so neither in silence, as silence; but in a holy dependence of the mind upon God; from which dependence silence necessarily follows in the first place until words can be brought forth, which are from God's Spirit.[41]

It is important that this understanding of worship according to Friends be kept in mind. In contradistinction to the popular notions, the basis of Friends worship is **not** silence, but holy obedience! This fact, though perhaps not widely understood or accepted even among Quakers, should be remembered when later in this study the division in western Friends centered upon the use or misuse of the silent meetings.[42]

Silence in the Meeting for Worship was not an end in itself; indeed, rightly understood, it could never be more than a means to an end. The heart of Quaker worship—whether in silent communion or praying, whether in the spoken messages of several individuals, or whether in the current use of pastoral sermons and congregational singing—the heart of Quaker worship was and is, holy obedience—a dependence upon the guidance of the Light of Christ within.[43]

Truthfulness. The Quakers felt that as Christians they were obligated to be truthful in all things, in matters of business as well as in conversation.[44] To take an oath in court that they would tell the truth implied a double standard, that less than truthfulness was acceptable on other occasions. The Quaker had only one standard, whether in conversation, in business or in the courts of law. "A refusal to take the oath, therefore, became one of the Quaker testimonies, to prove that he practiced first-century and not seventeenth-century Christianity."[45]

Simplicity. The Quakers kept the emphasis of their concerns upon the inner life and tended toward simplicity in the outward life.[46] It is not germaine to this study to do more than simply identify the fact that simplicity in daily life, in matters of speech, dress and name, became another important Testimony.

Social Concern. Many of the Testimonies, or practices and attitudes adopted because of religious convictions, were concerned with society and with man in his social setting.[47] The testimony against war and slavery, against extremely severe punishments, and especially capital punishment for a variety of offences; the testimony on behalf of civic and religious liberties, on behalf of equal rights for all races—these are a few of the Testimonies for which Quakers are well-known.

The Early Growth of Quakerism

It is impossible to recover a clear picture of the earliest gatherings of groups of Friends. George Fox refers to "meetings of Friends . . . gathered to God's teaching" as early as 1646-48.[48] Braithwaite feels, however, that the "beginning of propagandist work may be dated back to 1647, but not earlier."[49] It was not long, however, until the north of England experienced a Quaker awakening. Quaker groups often were started from separatist groups of Seekers on the fringes of strong Puritan areas. But, as Professor Barbour has indicated, Quakerism was not merely a reaction against Puritanism, but a new movement into new areas. He writes:

> In the North the frontier character made this an "awakening" among the unchurched not unlike the Great Awakening under Jonathan Edwards or the Kentucky camp meetings of the American Second Awakening. The similarity of early Quakerism in the North to John Wesley's mission among the English factory workers and miners has been noted.[50]

From the north of England, the "Quaker Galilee," the movement spread to the south, and soon London and Bristol became centers of Friends as well. As we note this early growth, it will be helpful to identify the organization that developed, and some of the key leaders of the movement.

Quaker Organization

Every religious movement has found it necessary to develop some kind of organization in order to give cohesiveness and continuity to the movement. This was no less true of Quakerism, for early Friends discovered that the awareness of the Spirit's guidance did not abrogate the need for human arrangements and organization. A simple but durable pattern emerged.

Monthly Meetings. The first "monthly meeting" appears to have been held in 1653 at Swarthmore with the purpose of taking care of the poor.[51] This meeting was probably held by the local leaders or elders. Before long the monthly meeting became the local administrative group and generally included local groups or meetings that were situated in a contiguous territory. Russell writes that the monthly meeting

> arose out of the needs of, and the demands on, the first Friends communities. It provided for the necessities of the traveling ministers and their families. . . . It looked after persecuted Friends . . . [and] the care of the poor . . . devolved upon it.[52]

Out of the local monthly meetings gradually developed both the later quarterly and yearly meetings.

Quarterly Meetings. Under the guidance of George Fox, existing monthly meetings were systematized, and following 1657 general or regional meetings were held. Sometimes these meetings were called "quarterly meetings." Gradually this latter term

came to be applied to the less frequent gatherings of Quakers
from a wider area. Russell comments,

> There was a tendency to make the county the unit for the quar-
> terly gatherings and for them to be concerned with the spread
> of the Quaker message, its social and religious applications,
> and the oversight of the ministry.[53]

George Fox devoted himself to the consolidation of Quakerism and the development of a strong corporate consciousness by
the establishment of the monthly and quarterly meetings. His
object was to reinforce the leadership among the Publishers of
Truth, and the sense of corporate unity which resulted turned the
Quaker movement into the Religious Society of Friends.

Yearly Meeting. The central organization developed gradually, and in 1660 the first general meeting on a national level was
held at Skipton. Fox called this a "yearly meeting."[54] The following year a general meeting was held for ministers in London, and
then again in 1666 and 1668. In 1671 it was decided to establish
a central meeting of representatives from the various counties,
but it was not until 1678 that such a meeting was held for members of the Society other than ministers. The latter date is given
as the establishment of the Yearly Meeting in London. Its function was at first advisory in character, although it soon became a
strong controlling influence in the life of the Society.

> To bring together from all parts of the country the men of
> most weight in the movement, for conference and for fellow-
> ship and the rekindling of vision, was a true way of developing
> a corporate life which should carry forward the Society in one
> common service.[55]

In reading the **Journal** of George Fox, it is evident that Fox
felt that the organizing of Friends into the various meetings had
for its purpose the strengthening and channeling of spiritual
vitality into the service of the church. In his book, **The Second
Period of Quakerism**, W. C. Braithwaite comments on the organizing work of George Fox. He writes:

> It was not in his view a step back into earthly things, but a
> step up into the life and order of the Gospel. This is shown by
> reiterated phrases in his **Journal**, which for convenience I may
> be allowed to summarize in modern language. In the first
> place, he saw that the true authority in the Church was not of

man, but was of God. The sovereign power was the power of God. Then it came to him that all the heirs of the gospel, both men and women, inherited its authority, and ought to be entering into their inheritance. It followed naturally that there was a true gospel order in church affairs—to be exercised by all spiritually-minded Friends met together to wait upon the Lord. . . . There is a simple directness about the arguments and conclusions of Fox which may well amaze us. Theories of government in Church and State were the burning issues of the age. But it is most unlikely that he had read or would have cared to read the **Ecclesiastical Polity** of Hooker, or the **Leviathan** of Hobbes. His statesmanship, like that of other prophets, depended upon revelation and moral insight. He felt the lack of authority in the Church, and came to see that it was there all the time, in the highest form, if only those who should be using it rose to their responsibilities.[56]

Early Quaker Leaders

The early converts to the preaching of George Fox were usually very humble men and women, often with little or no education. These early Quakers were harassed and persecuted for unwillingness to conform to the Act of Establishment. When the movement was in danger of being extinguished, Friends received into membership some of the most noted recruits and later leaders of the Society. Acquaintance with a few of these leaders will provide further background to this study.

Isaac Penington. Although he was first repelled by what he had seen and read of Quakers, Penington came under the strong influence of George Fox and publicly joined the Quaker movement in 1658. The Peningtons were of a high social position, and his writings and influence did much to strengthen the position of the Society.[57]

Thomas Elwood. Another Quaker writer who greatly served the Society was Thomas Elwood. A friend of the Peningtons, he served for a time as secretary to the poet, John Milton. Upon the death of George Fox, Elwood was given the task of editing the writings and the **Journal** of Fox.[58]

Robert Barclay. In 1666, another aristocrat joined the ranks of the early Quakers. Robert Barclay ranks as one of the most outstanding of all Quakers. A scholar of brilliance, he "lifted the controversy which had raged about Quakerism out of the realm of ignorant abuse into that of intelligent enquiry."[59] As a close companion with Fox, he traveled extensively on the Continent and to the colonies in the interest of Friends, but it was as a systematic theologian that he best served the Society.[60]

William Penn. Of singular importance to American Quakerism, William Penn is undoubtedly the best-known of all the early Quakers. His father was Admiral Sir William Penn, a man of noted ability and wealth, and close friend to King Charles II. In the year 1666, Penn cast his lot with the Quakers, to the anger of his father. Penn soon was writing and preaching on the behalf of the Quaker movement, and as a champion of civil liberty. His "Holy Experiment" in Pennsylvania opened the way for countless Quakers to seek a new home in the colonies and to help establish Quakerism in America.[61]

In addition to these men, called "Quaker Aristocrats" by D. Elton Trueblood, a host of others gave valuable leadership to early Quakerism and worked closely with Fox. Any such listing of names would have to include Francis Howgill, Edward Burrough, Margaret Fell, Richard Farnsworth, and William Dewsbury.[62] For our purposes, however, it is sufficient to note that the Quaker movement drew into the Society a wide variety of men and women who influenced the Society in its formative years.

The Expansion of Quakerism

In 1652, George Fox stood on top of Pendle Hill, close to the western border of Yorkshire. Before him spread the rolling countryside and the distant horizon of new territory. But to his inner eye, George Fox caught another vision. "And there atop of the hill I was moved to sound the day of the Lord, and the Lord let me see atop of the hill in what places he had a great people to be gathered."[63] From this day forward, Fox never lost sight of the vision of a gathered society of Friends. Throughout days of persecution and testing, he remained true to the "Heavenly Vision" and set about the work of gathering the Lord's people into a great Religious Society of Friends.

The early Quakers had a remarkable sense of mission: having found a personal encounter with Christ, they felt compelled

to share it with all who would listen. In 1654, Fox wrote that the
Lord moved

> upon the spirits of many, whom he had raised up and sent forth
> to labor in His vineyard to travel southwards, and spread
> themselves, in the service of the Gospel, to the eastern, south-
> ern, and western parts of the nation.[64]

With dedication and faith, the early Quakers began to witness to
the reality of an experience and encounter with God.

Expansion Throughout the Nation

In 1654, two-thirds of the English population was rural,
with few large centers or cities.[65] Only one-seventh of the population lived in the north of England,[66] where Quakerism had its beginning. It was a move of strategy, then, that compelled the
Quakers to move southward with their message and to make the
growing cities of London, Bristol and Norwich the centers of the
movement. Over sixty ministers were sent out from the north to
establish and propagate the faith. Called the "Valiant Sixty" by
Ernest Taylor,[67] these men gave impetus to the young movement
and soon "seekers" throughout England were becoming "finders."

The extreme persecution of the early Quakers is well-
known. The Quaker approach to the authority of the church and
of the civil government often caused magistrates and church
leaders to become antagonized. Their testimonies for the rights
of conscience, their customs based upon their convictions—all
these facts led to the imprisonment and persecution of large numbers of Quakers. Nevertheless, in spite of the great opposition,
Quakerism achieved considerable success throughout England
during the Commonwealth and Restoration periods. Persecution
tended to unite the early Quakers, and the movement gained a
cohesiveness. Lucas correctly observes:

> Under adversity Quakerism was tested, and Friends exhibited
> to the nation the strength of their conviction: more were con-
> verted to the Quaker way of life by seeing suffering nobly
> borne than by hearing sermons nobly worded. This demonstra-
> tion of the power of the inward life turned the scourge of per-
> secution into a triumphant instrument for proclaiming the
> Truth. The persecutor's pillory became the Quaker's pulpit.[68]

Expansion to the British Isles and the Continent

Quakerism did not experience as rapid a growth or as satisfactory progress in the other parts of the British Isles or on the Continent. In Ireland, the first meeting was established in 1654, and membership eventually grew to thirty thousand in the seventeenth century. A strong Presbyterian church afforded little opportunity for Quakers to make headway in Scotland, with the best reception for Quakerism, in both Scotland and Ireland, being found among the garrisons of English soldiers. In Wales, too, the growth of Quakerism was slow.[69]

On the Continent, Quakerism made small but important inroads. In 1655, Quakers began to witness and were supported by later visits by Fox himself, together with Barclay and Penn. Holland was the setting for the most substantial growth of Quakerism on the Continent, but even here little work of lasting value was accomplished.[70]

Further Attempts at Wider Expansion

The spiritual fervor of the early Quakers carried them to great distances as Publishers of the Truth, but without much success. Turkey was visited in 1657 by a small band of six; an attempt was even made to convert the city of Rome to Quakerism. Some Quakers were provided with epistles to the Emperor of China, the Kings of France and Spain, and even to the Emperor of Ethiopia, but the mission was never successful. Such schemes for the expansion of Quakerism were soon abandoned. "Outside England there was little support for the Quaker message in the Old World. It was in America that the energy and enterprise of the early Friends found fullest scope."[71]

Expansion to the New World

It was in the New World, first on the island of Barbados, and then in the colonies, that Quakerism made its greatest and most lasting impact. In 1655, Mary Fisher and Ann Austin reached the island of Barbados, a major point from which to reach the American continent. Mary Fisher had been a minister among Friends since 1652 and had suffered imprisonment and torture. Her companion, Ann Austin, was a mother of five children, and together they set sail for the Puritan stronghold of Boston in 1656 aboard the ship **Swallow**.[72] Their reception in the Massachusetts Bay Colony was less than cordial: their effects were searched, the books and tracts publicly burned; they themselves were subsequently imprisoned and searched for indications of witchcraft. After five weeks they were bound over to the captain of a vessel returning to Barbados and were expelled from the colony. Thus ended the first attempt of Quakers to establish the movement in America. The ship for Barbados set sail August 5, 1656, and may well have passed the inbound vessel from England, the **Speedwell**. On August 9, 1656, the **Speedwell** sailed into Massachusetts Bay with the first direct expedition of a group of Quakers from England. Under the leadership of Christopher Holder, the small band of eight Quakers (four men and four women) had sought the American shores for religious liberty, but after eleven weeks of imprisonment, their property was confiscated and they were returned to England.[73]

The Massachusetts Bay Colony, it must be remembered, had established under the leadership of John Winthrop a citadel of Puritanism.[74] The arrival of these few Quakers with their opposing views of church and state threatened the very basis of the government. This was considered an act of invasion and was treated as such. Consequently, on October 14, 1656, the first law was passed against the Quaker intruders, saying in part:

> Whereas there a cursed sect of haereticks lately risen up in the world, which are commonly called Quakers . . . this Court, taking into serious consideration the premises, and to prevent the like mischiefe as by the meanes is wrought in our native land, doth heereby order, and by the authoritie of the Court be it ordered and enacted, that . . . any Quaker coming into this jurisdiction shall be forthwith committed to the house of correction, and at their entrance to be severely whipt, and by the master thereof to be kept constantly to worke, and none suffered to converse or speak with them during the time of their imprisonment, which shall be no longer than necessitie requireth.[75]

The Quakers, however, were now accustomed to the possibility of imprisonment and persecution, and the new law only served to whet their desire to expand the Quaker movement and establish the Society in the New World. The ocean had been crossed, and the colonies presented the greatest hope and challenge to Friends. Here begins the westward movement of Friends, a movement which ultimately carries the Society to the far western shores of the New World.

Quakerism in America

In order to establish the later movements of Quakerism in America, it is important to recognize the background of the Society's struggle for identity and development by observing its growth and expansion in the New World. In this section of this chapter on "Backgrounds," we propose to examine briefly the development of American Quakerism through three distinct periods: The Formative Period, 1656-1701; The Middle Period, 1701-1827; and The Period of Conflict, 1827-1854. At this point in our study, we shall center our investigation on the first two periods, and shall discuss the third period, The Period of Conflict, in the following chapter.

The Formative Period, 1656-1701

We have already noted the hesitant and abortive beginnings of Quakerism in America. The barbarous "Cart and Whip Act" was utilized in the Massachusetts Bay Colony, but Quakers continued to persist in their efforts to propagate their ideas. Finally in 1658, the death penalty was invoked and in the following year four Quakers, including the woman, Mary Dyer, were hung on Boston Commons.[76] Before long, however, Charles II interceded and the death penalty was revoked. Floggings and whippings continued until 1677, and four years later the laws against the Quakers were repealed or suspended.[77]

Other colonies also felt the presence and heard the message of the Quakers. In 1657, a small group of Friends from the ship **Woodhouse** landed at New Amsterdam (New York) and still others settled at Newport.[78] It was in Rhode Island that the Quakers were given their most favorable reception, and though Roger Williams was "impervious to the message of the Friends" he was willing to allow them "to try their faith undisturbed."[79]

The Quaker expansion in the New World was given its greatest impetus by the arrival of George Fox in 1672 in Maryland. After a period of ministry there, he made his way overland to New England, arriving at the little Quaker "colony" in Newport in May, 1672. While he was in Maryland, he attended the establishment of the Baltimore Yearly Meeting and held his first meeting with a group of Indian chiefs. Some two months were spent among the strong Quaker centers of Rhode Island before Fox headed to the southern colonies of Virginia and Carolina. During the course of his trip to America, George Fox visited the most important Quaker centers, encouraging and stimulating further growth; he aided in the establishment of new yearly meetings; he quickened the impulse to missionary activities and initiated correspondence between Quakers of England and America.[80]

When Fox returned to England from America in 1673, he went directly upon his arrival to visit William Penn and may have introduced the idea of a Quaker colony in Penn's mind at this time.[81] This perhaps was the beginning of the next great phase in the Formative Period of American Quakerism, the establishment of Quaker colonies. In 1674, one-half of New Jersey was bought from Lord Berkeley by two Quakers, John Fenwick and Edward Byllynge. Five years later the second half of New Jersey was purchased from the widow of Sir George Carteret by twelve Quakers. Robert Barclay, the young Quaker apologist, was elected governor of the Quaker colony, although he never himself visited the territory. The two Jerseys were later united under a single Council of Proprietors. In 1861 a yearly meeting was established in Burlington, which became the forerunner of the influential and powerful Philadelphia Yearly Meeting.[82]

The major establishment of Quakers in the colonies came under the direction of William Penn. Penn had inherited extensive lands to the north of Maryland as the payment of a debt owed by Charles II to his father, Admiral Sir William Penn. Penn took the opportunity to create a "holy experiment" and established a colony on the basis of religious toleration. In a definitive study, Edwin Bronner identifies the deep feelings of Penn in regard to Pennsylvania:

First, he believed that God had been instrumental in granting him province in the New World. Secondly, and growing naturally out of his gratitude, he desired to use the gift from above to the glory of God. Finally, he hoped that the operation of his colony in accordance with the highest Christian ethic might serve as a model for mankind, to indicate by example what men may achieve on earth if they put themselves into the hands of God.[83]

Pennsylvania became the home for many who were oppressed because of their religious faith, and from the Continent, England, and neighboring colonies, individuals and groups came to share in the religious toleration and freedom of the new colony.[84] The actual vision of Penn's "holy experiment" never reached complete fruition, for Penn was forced largely to be an absentee governor and proprietor of his colony. Before he left his colony for the last time in 1701, however, Penn saw the establishment of a nucleus of committed Friends, whose continuing spirit and idealism influenced the province in later years. Pennsylvania itself became the stronghold of Quakers for the next one hundred and fifty years.

The Middle Period, 1701-1827

The Quaker movement in the colonies now entered a new phase. The Act of Toleration in 1689 brought an end to much of the persecution of the Society, and their meetings could be held without fear of arrest and imprisonment. Following the Formative Period, Friends began to give vital leadership in many areas of life and soon earned an enviable reputation for their thrift and honest business dealings.[85] The Society now turned its attention inwardly upon itself as it began to consolidate its gains and assume a position of respect in the various communities. The eighteenth century saw new changes among Friends, and these can be summarized briefly.

Age of Consolidation, 1701-1756. Thomas estimates that at the end of this period, Friends in America numbered about 50,000, perhaps more.[86] New buildings and the organizing of new meetings occupied the attention of many. The intervisitation by leading Friends from the Society in both England and America tended to consolidate the gains that had been made. The exchange of epistles and other correspondence between the various yearly meetings, and the distribution and circulation of tracts and writings of outstanding Quakers aided in developing a cohesiveness within the growing Society.

It was during this period that Friends took an active part in government and civil affairs. Although Friends lost control of New Jersey with the ascension of Queen Anne to the throne in 1702, Rhode Island was wisely governed by Quakers, for Friends constituted the largest religious body in the state during the early part of the eighteenth century.[87]

In Pennsylvania, Friends continued to control the Assembly until 1756, in spite of the growing interest and involvement of the many non-Quaker groups. It was also during this period that Friends began to be vocal concerning the wrongfulness of slavery, and John Woolman gave impetus to the movement by the expression of his concerns in New England in 1747.[88]

The first half of the eighteenth century also witnessed the beginnings of decline in the growth and forward impetus of the Society. Although academies and elementary schools were being provided, there was a general diminishing of the availability of educated leadership as compared with the earlier period.[89] But more important, and perhaps more disastrous, was the establishment of birthright membership. In 1737, the London Yearly Meeting declared that a man's family were to be considered members of the Society of Friends if he held membership. American Quakers also adopted these standards of membership and, like the Puritans of Massachusetts, emphasized membership by birth, and not by a conversion experience. "This road led downhill to an institutionalism that was both static and exclusive."[90]

Age of Quietism and Philanthropy, 1756-1827. As Quakerism became institutionalized, it entered into a period of quietism. Rules of church discipline were now emphasized and a crystallized "monument" was substituted for an aggressive "movement." The creative insight, the mobility, the freshness of the new movement almost entirely disappeared.[91] The Society became introspective and tended to the form of mysticism "which assumes that not only is unregenerate human nature corrupt, but even regenerated human nature is unreliable."[92] To be sure, Quakers developed an inner sensitivity and tenderness, but all too often the negative aspect of mysticism was so emphasized that meetings for worship became formalized into periods of complete silence, unbroken and without any spoken message.

This period also witnessed, however, the flowering of humanitarian concerns, and soon after the turn of the century many Quakers were influential leaders in the development of a "benevolent society." Interest in the Indians, aid to Bible societies, the antislavery movement, prison reform, the care of the insane— these were a few of the concerns of Friends in the latter half of the eighteenth century and the beginning of the nineteenth century.[93]

The Period of Conflict, 1827-1854

The Society of Friends in America now entered into a critical and disruptive period. The spiritual life of the Society was at a low ebb; the enforcement of the Discipline, the programs of social reform and philanthropy occupied the major concerns of the members, but little attention was given to matters of doctrine and evangelism. The deep separations that occurred within the ranks of the Society came as a result of division over matters theological as well as social, and disunity within the Society became evident on many fronts. Because it is important to note the separations that occurred in this period in more detail, for they form the immediate background of the critical separations that took place in the west during a later period, we will devote the following chapter to a discussion of the conflicts during this period. The Society of Friends now enters into the beginning of formal disunity.

Separations
within American Quakerism

THE RELIGIOUS SOCIETY of Friends had changed radically from the early days of its inception. The vast majority of the membership was now more concerned with the maintenance of certain outward standards; consequently, spiritual vitality and vigor was almost lost. The organization had become despotic, and the select group of ministers and elders tightly administered and enforced the Discipline. Wholesale disownments became common, not only for infractions of moral standards, but for breaking traditional customs of dress and behavior. Edward Grubb comments that "a spiritual despotism had settled down upon the Society of Friends, which had almost totally ceased to breathe the bracing air of liberty."[1]

In 1827 the first of many separations occurred within the ranks of Quakerism and disunity prevailed. Before identifying these separations, it will be helpful to note some of the factors that created the setting for separation.

Contributing Factors to Disunity

The low ebb of spiritual vitality has already been noted. The fervor and intense sense of mission had waned in the Society, which had become institutionalized. There was undoubtedly some ignorance as to the real nature of Quakerism, and the concern of reviving primitive Christianity that was so markedly evident in the early years of the movement was now gone. Because of their

fear of "creaturely activity," Quakers neglected the training of
their minds; indeed, their interpretation of the immediacy of
Divine revelation made religious instruction unnecessary.

More important, the reading and study of the Bible had fall-
en in widespread disuse. In contradistinction to the use that
George Fox and the first generation Quakers made of the Scriptures, the Friends of the early nineteenth century relied primarily upon the writings and interpretations of Quaker leaders and
did not develop a sense of judgment and discernment based upon
the Scriptures themselves. Consequently, as Grubb points out,
they became "easy prey of any persuasive preacher" who could
reinforce his argument from the writings of the early Quakers.[2]

The rigid administration of the Discipline undoubtedly
caused much dissatisfaction and led the way to internal strife and
separation. Extreme behavior by some members of the Society,
almost to the point of fanaticism, caused the intensification of
fears in the more conservative members, resulting in the development of still stricter bonds of traditional beliefs and practices.
Some Friends tended to become intolerant with those Quakers
whose views were not in strict accord with their own, and consequently the usual spirit of patience and love was often lacking
in dealing with the offender. The Discipline became the rule of
conduct, and its subsequent despotic administration led to open
conflict and disunity.

There is one other important factor which led to separation.
Samuel Janney, the Quaker historian, emphasized the role of
visiting English Quakers who traveled among many of the meetings of the Society of Friends. He cites, as an example, the
strong opposition of the English Quaker, William Forster, to
some trends in America and his insistence in 1825 that "a separation must and will take place in the Society in America."[3] Against
the strong emphasis that Janney makes of the English Quakers
as promoting separation, it perhaps would be more correct to
observe that the causes of separation were varied and numerous,
and that the visits and preaching of the English Quakers only
served to clarify certain issues and, at the most, precipitated a
separation that was already incipient.

The Great Separation, 1827-1828

The most serious division that has occurred among American Friends was also the first. The "evangelical revival" and the spread of Methodism in England had affected many Quakers in England. The concepts of the authority of Scripture and the depraved nature of man led to a new insistence on the necessity of personal conversion and an emphasis upon the Biblical teaching of salvation through Jesus Christ. Some of these Friends brought these concerns to America, together with the insistence on defending and propagating these views. But not only from England, but also from within its own ranks, American Quakers were confronted with evangelical Christianity. In 1795, Etienne de Grellet of Long Island underwent a transforming conversion experience and began to propagate the truths of evangelical Christianity.[4]

The major opponent to these views was a Long Island Quaker, Elias Hicks. Although the separatist group was later called Hicksite, it does not appear that Hicks considered himself to be the leader of a party, but rather as one who intensified the controversy that led to separation.

Elias Hicks was a man of "powerful build, commanding person, and indomitable will."[5] Logical and practical in his thinking, he had a wide and commanding influence among Friends, attracting many through his powerful preaching. Hicks insisted that "God is a Spirit," and since "spirit could only beget spirit," he concluded that Jesus Christ, the Son of God, was only a spiritual concept. The manifestation of God's Spirit alone was necessary to salvation, and thus Hicks further concluded that the atoning work of Christ, the Scriptures, the teaching of the church, were all unessential to salvation. The efficacy of the "Inner Light" became the touchstone of his doctrine.

Grubb is probably correct when he assesses the failure of Hicks to understand historical Christianity, or the development of the church as a body, or to realize the need in the church of a framework of sound theology.[6] Hicks was undoubtedly a child of the time, a product of the low state into which Quakerism had fallen.[7] His followers emphasized the freedom experienced by

one adhering to the leadings of the "Inner Light," and thus reacted against the restrictions of the Discipline.

The Occasion of the Great Separation

In 1823 the Meeting for Sufferings of Philadelphia Yearly
Meeting prepared a distinctly Orthodox doctrinal statement. Opposition was so great, however, that it was not adopted.[8] For
the next four years, the Yearly Meeting was involved in deep conflict and contention between the Orthodox and Hicksite groups.
Elias Hicks himself entered in controversy with visiting English
Quakers.

Finally in 1827, at the Philadelphia Yearly Meeting, matters
came to a climax. Under the leadership of John Comly, a follow-
er of Elias Hicks, attempts were made to control or dissolve the
sessions. When their efforts failed, Comly and nine others called
for a special meeting to organize a new and separate yearly
meeting in Philadelphia, declaring the necessity of "making a
quiet retreat from this scene of confusion."[9] But the retreat was
far from quiet, and the confusion was only compounded. A bitter
struggle ensued on every level of organization, in the quarterly,
monthly, and preparative meetings. Court cases and fights over
property, wholesale disownments of each other—these were all
part of the picture. Separation was now reality.

Results of the Great Separation

The conflicts of 1827-28 are rightly called the Great Separation among Friends. Over fifty percent of the Orthodox Quakers
followed the call of John Comly and became Hicksites. Grubb
points out that the membership following separation was approx-
imately two-to-one in favor of the Hicksites. However, in the
urban meetings of Philadelphia itself the situation was reversed.[10]
The urban and relatively well-to-do Quakers remained Orthodox,
while the rural, laboring class of Quakers more readily followed
the Hicksites. This was undoubtedly the reaction of a great mass
of Quakers to the despotic administration of the Discipline and
control of the Yearly Meeting by the relatively few urban leaders.

In 1828 separations occurred in New York, Ohio, Indiana,
and Baltimore Yearly Meetings along similar lines, and the dis-

unity experienced in Philadelphia now became the portion of the Friends Society at large. The door to separation and controversy was now open, and the ensuing years witnessed still further separations within the ranks of Orthodox Quakers in particular.

The Separation of 1845

The Great Separation strengthened the insistence of Orthodox Quakers upon the great Biblical truths of the person of Christ and His atoning sacrifice. In England, the "Beacon movement" resulted in new and corrective emphasis being placed upon an outward authority, the Scriptures, as well as upon the inward authority, i.e., the "Inner Light." One of the proponents of this evangelical doctrine was a leading Friend, Joseph John Gurney. An able student and scholar, he "put the Bible first as the authority for doctrine, but the Spirit first in the conduct of life and worship."[11] He introduced the critical study of the Bible among Friends and profoundly influenced the course of Quaker history and thought as a theologian.[12]

When Gurney came to America in 1837 to visit various Quaker meetings, substantial opposition arose to his views among Orthodox Friends in Philadelphia and Ohio Yearly Meetings. The leadership of the opposition was centered in John Wilbur of New England Yearly Meeting. Wilbur strongly opposed the new trends in Quakerism, especially the emphasis placed by Gurney upon the Scriptures. Wilbur had earlier, in 1832, confronted Gurney in England with the charge that his teachings were not according to the tradition of Friends, and now again he raised his voice in opposition. The conservatism of Wilbur finally led to a separation within New England Yearly Meeting in 1845, and the formation of a separate organization of Friends. Although only about 500 Quakers followed Wilbur into the new Yearly Meeting (the Small Body),[13] the separation was the cause for still further separations in other yearly meetings.

The Separation of 1854

All of the American yearly meetings recognized the "Large Body" in New England as the New England Yearly Meeting. In Philadelphia and Ohio, however, sympathy for John Wilbur was so intense that no decision on the matter of recognition could be made. In 1854 the issue between the Gurneyites and Wilburites came to a climax in Ohio. The debate centered upon the matter of appointing a new clerk; both sides had their candidate, but finally the pro-Wilbur group, actually a mediating group, maintained control. The Gurneyites withdrew and established their own organization. Although in this case the Gurneyites were the smaller of the two groups, they were eventually recognized fraternally by London Yearly Meeting as being consistent with their recognition earlier of the Gurneyite "Larger Body" in New England Yearly Meeting.[14]

Similar separations had now taken place in every Orthodox American yearly meeting, with the exception of Philadelphia and North Carolina. Philadelphia in effect, however, separated itself from other Orthodox yearly meetings when it decided in 1857 to abandon its recognition of the pro-Wilbur group in Ohio in order to avoid separation within its own ranks again. As a consequence, all epistolary correspondence ceased from Philadelphia to other American yearly meetings, and it gradually isolated itself from the rest of American Quakerism.[15] Such isolation existed only on an official level, for as we shall discover in the account of the westward movement of Quakerism, Philadelphia Yearly Meeting continued to affect profoundly the shape of American Quakerism, especially through its influential members and journals.

Separations had now deeply changed the course of the Society of Friends. The Hicksite Quakers had separated themselves from the Orthodox Quakers, and the Orthodox Quakers were later divided into two further camps: the conservative Wilburites, and the liberal, but evangelical and orthodox, Gurneyites. The stage is now set for the Great Awakening in American Quakerism.

3

The Great Awakening within American Quakerism

IN A SCHOLARLY study of revivalism in the mid-nineteenth century, Timothy L. Smith suggests that "the cutting edge of American Christianity after 1850 was the revival, adopted and promoted in one form or another by major segments of all denominations."[1] What was true of the Methodists, the Presbyterians, and the Baptists, was also true of the Quakers. Too often, studies of Quakerism have tended to leave unsaid the common features, the problems, the pressures, that the Society of Friends shared alike with the American church, in all of its denominated forms.[2]

Many Quaker writers, perhaps because of the enormity and complexity of their own studies, have neglected to show the interrelationship and the dialogues among denominations, the influences that molded the whole movement of American Christianity. As has already been stated, Quakerism has had an effect upon the world and the church in a most amazing fashion. But it must not be forgotten that Quakerism was, and is, the recipient of many influences from the various denominated groups of its time.

The Society of Friends has not only contributed to American Christianity, it has been greatly influenced by and has received much from American Christianity. Nowhere is this more clear than in the middle of the nineteenth century. The great religious awakenings that had moved across the life of the American church had previously done little to affect Quakerism. But

29

by 1854 Quakerism was open to the influences of American revivalism and, as a result, assumed an entirely different character. Rufus Jones spoke of the influence of revivalism by saying, "It closed one epoch and inaugurated another, and it began at the same time a new type of Quakerism."[3] The effect of revivalism upon Quakers assumes a crucial place in our understanding of western Quakerism. As we shall see in subsequent chapters, the revival movement among Friends, Quakerism's own "great awakening," led to the presence of two distinct types of the Society of Friends in California. It is important, therefore, that we examine carefully this awakening among Friends in the nineteenth century. First, however; we shall observe the phenomena of revivalism in American Christianity.

Religious Awakenings in the History of the American Church

It should be noted, by way of definition, that revivalism and awakening are not synonymous terms, as used in the context of this study. A religious awakening refers to a very complex religio-sociological event or group of events in which individuals become stirred and aroused concerning their own religious condition; and after resolving the personal nature of their concerns, they actually demonstrate significant change in their social behavior. On the other hand, the term revivalism denotes the use of various measures and techniques to confront the individual in society with his personal religious needs, promoting conversion and subsequent spiritual growth. Revivalism has not always precipitated an awakening, although the two are undoubtedly highly correlated. On the other hand, some may argue that religious awakenings have occurred in spite of the techniques of revivalism. In the history of the American church, at least three religious awakenings made their impact upon society.

The first awakening, often called the Great Awakening of American Christianity, occurred in the middle of the eighteenth century. The spark that kindled the fires of revival was ignited by a Dutch Reformed minister in the Raritan River Valley of New Jersey. Theodorus Frelinghuysen brought a deep disquiet to the religious routine of his congregation by his powerful preaching and emphasis upon strict discipline. Many conversions took place under his ministry, and by 1726 revival reached its peak and began to spread to other communities.[4]

The blaze was carried to the Presbyterians by William Tennent and his sons, and within fifteen years the revival had reached out to a wide area. The greatest impetus to revival and the religious awakening was undoubtedly the ministry of the Anglican evangelist, George Whitfield. Olmstead comments that "possibly more than any other man he brought widespread attention and support to Middle Colonies revivalism."[5] In New England, the Great Awakening was inaugurated by Jonathan Edwards in 1734.[6] By the time George Whitfield came to preach in New England in 1740, the harvest was ready. The evangelistic pattern of Whitfield and the theology of Edwards helped to mold the techniques and thinking of the American church for many years to come.

The first awakening was indeed a Great Awakening. A new spirit of independence was fostered; the colonies were united in a new fashion, and the religious awakening among a vast multitude of individuals was one of the factors that led the way to the birth of a new nation.

At the turn of the nineteenth century, American Christianity experienced the Second Awakening. The great expanse of the west had opened for settlement. The Northwest Ordinance of 1787 provided the needed impetus, and with the conclusion of the War of 1812, the new era of westward expansion was assured. The church was confronted with great masses of people upon the frontiers of society, and new and vigorous efforts were made to reach them for the Kingdom. Those religious groups that caught a vision of a national church and best accommodated their program to meet the needs of the frontier were the groups that emerged from this period as the strongest and largest in the new nation.[7]

Peter Mode has rightly called this process the "Americanizing of Christianity."[8] The churches that were willing to be "frontierized" greatly influenced the development of the new and growing communities of the west. It must also be remembered, however, that the activity of the church was not limited only to the geographical frontiers of the nation. In the urban settings of the east, a new and vigorous revival began to flourish. The religious stirrings of Yale College in 1802, under the leadership of President Timothy Dwight, activated similar awakenings in other centers of education.[9] But it was on the frontier that the most remarkable aspects of the Second Awakening occurred.

Under the revival preaching of a Scotch-Irish Presbyterian named James McGready, revival on the frontier came to its flowering in the camp meeting movement.[10] At the close of the eighteenth century, revival broke out in McGready's congregation in Logan County, Kentucky. In June 1800, it reached its peak at a protracted service at the Red River Church. The news of the success of the meeting spread rapidly and led to the inauguration the following year of the Cane Ridge camp meeting.[11] This colossus of the frontier camp meetings attracted over 20,000 people, and hundreds were reported to have been converted in what became an interdenominational enterprise.[12]

The frontier camp meeting became an important factor in the social, as well as the spiritual, life of the pioneers[13] and left a positive and religiously constructive influence upon American society for many years. Its greatest weakness lay in its appeal to the emotions. The Presbyterians reacted unsympathetically to the movement, but the Baptists and the Methodists made the camp meeting a time of spiritual harvest. By 1805, the camp meeting techniques had spread throughout the frontier, penetrating Kentucky, Tennessee, Ohio, as well as western New England, the old South, and western New York and Pennsylvania. During 1811, there were more than 400 camp meetings held in the United States.[14] The fate of many movements, however, became the lot of even the camp meetings; the spontaneity was replaced by formal organization and program, and the popularity of these outdoor revival campaigns diminished.

The national impulse for a benevolent society, which found its inspiration in the wave of revivals during the early nineteenth century, grew with intensity under the preaching of Charles Grandison Finney. More than any other man of his time, Finney was able to unite in himself the scholarly patterns of New England religion and the lay and pietistic emphases of the frontier.[15]

Finney was converted to Christianity just prior to his thirtieth birthday in 1821 and opened the first of his great revival campaigns in 1826. Although his methods were often attacked by his contemporary clergymen, Finney set a pace and standard for revivalists throughout the following decades. His powerful preaching, his deep conviction, and his clear logic made him one of the greatest evangelists to appear on the American scene.[16]

Revivalism in the United States continued to grow and deepen. Timothy Smith has well served the study of American church history by pointing out the resurgence of revivalism and its influence upon society during the years 1840-1865.[17] Instead of declining, revivalism continued to affect both the rural and the urban centers of America and led to the dramatic events of 1858 and the Third Awakening in American Protestantism.

In 1857, the stirrings of renewal within the American church were experienced in a new and dramatic way. Under the leadership of Jeremiah C. Lanphier, weekly prayer meetings and Bible studies were held on Fulton Street in New York City. These meetings were conducted primarily by laymen, and their popularity soon demanded their being held daily. Within months, thousands of people were crowding the meetings, which had now grown to twenty locations in New York City alone.

Coincident with this growth was an economic crisis, as the stock market suffered severe losses, and the nation turned to prayer. The news of the New York meetings spread rapidly throughout the nation, and before long every major city in the United States had a prayer meeting patterned after the Fulton Street meeting. The time had come for national repentance and an outpouring of the Holy Spirit. Revival and spiritual renewal moved across the country in a movement that was characterized by lay leadership and an urban character.[18]

As the interdenominational movement gathered momentum, it spread rapidly into the smaller towns and rural areas as well. Laymen took the leadership of the highly informal services, and a renewed emphasis was placed upon mass evangelism. The great revivalist of this period was himself a layman, Dwight L. Moody.[19] For two decades he preached throughout England and America and established himself as a man of God, declaring the riches of God's love. In contrast to the first two Awakenings, the Third Awakening was not dependent upon the reputation and effectiveness of outstanding clergymen, but was a spontaneous lay movement that greatly changed the character of revivalism in America. In addition, the new spirit of interdenominational brotherhood caught the imagination of many prominent church leaders. Old dogmatic pronouncements gave way to ethical concerns in the preaching of the evangelicals. Even theology took on a new emphasis as Arminian views regarding holiness and perfection replaced some of the old dogmas of Calvinism.

Quakerism had been largely untouched in the first two Awakenings. Quakerism's well-known mistrust of a "hireling ministry" and professional clergymen undoubtedly influenced the reaction to the clergy-led revivals of 1740 and 1800. During these earlier periods, the members of the Society of Friends had contented themselves with an exclusiveness, and they did not attend any religious meetings except their own.[20] By the middle of the nineteenth century, however, Quakerism was ready for its own Great Awakening. The waves of revival that swept across the American church this time profoundly affected Quakerism. The lay character of the Third Awakening found acceptance among Quakers; the emphasis upon informal prayer groups was not alien to the practice of Quakers; and as part of the American church, Quakerism was also in need of spiritual renewal. An editorial in the Philadelphia-published **The Friend** observed with interest:

> One of the striking features of this extraordinary movement is that it appears to have originated with the laity, and to have gone on increasing in force and interest, independent of clerical influence or interference; and that in some of the meetings, women appear to have taken a prominent part in the religious exercises. . . . There is much . . . of which we cannot approve . . . but many may thus receive impressions of good that will continue to grow deeper . . . and bring forth fruit unto holiness in circles and ways hid from public view.[21]

The spirit of revival among Quakers was marked by an evangelical fervor and spread from meeting to meeting, from yearly meeting to yearly meeting, until every area of the Society, with the exception of Philadelphia Yearly Meeting, felt its

ffects. This Great Awakening among Quakers had such pro-
)und consequences for western Quakerism that it is important
*e observe the movement in its beginnings, its growth, and its
:sults.

Beginnings of the Great Awakening in Quakerism

To Joseph John Gurney, more than any other Quaker in the
arly nineteenth century, must go the credit for bringing the
:sults of the "evangelical movement" in England to American
.uakers. The evangelical concern that he generated prepared
ie hearts and minds of many Friends and produced a receptiv-
y for revival. Friends did not need the evangelical movement
) rediscover experimental Christianity, yet Evangelicalism had
profoundly liberating effect. New interest was developed in the
erson and work of Christ. In contrast to the quietistic suppres-
on of intellectual activity as being "creaturely," Friends began
) think about their faith. Christian convictions and resulting
)cial concerns gave a common ground of meeting with other
vangelicals and soon many Friends ceased to be isolated as they
*ere drawn into organizational and personal associations with
on-Friends. Separations had left the Society in a deplorably
*eak condition and by 1860 it was prepared and ready for a
)iritual renewal.²²

The Great Awakening in Quakerism began first in the mid-
est. Small groups of young Indiana Quakers met for times of
)cial visiting, concluding the "apple eating and nut cracking"
ith prayer meetings. Allen Jay, of the Greenfield Monthly
[eeting, wrote in his **Autobiography**,

Thus in a quiet way, in this little Quaker community out by
itself on the prairie, during the years 1859-1860, began this
wave of revival work that a few years later began to spread
abroad over our branch of the church in various places. . . .²³

Although it is difficult to point with any certainty to a
articular place or person as being the beginning of revival, it is
)parent that the awakening took its particular form because of
ie influence of certain evangelical Quakers. Eli and Sibyl Jones
* New England Yearly Meeting were the outstanding examples
* this type of leadership. They had traveled extensively over-

seas on various missionary journeys to Europe and Africa, and
in 1860 visited Indiana Yearly Meeting and ministered effectively
among the Quakers there. Sibyl Jones had a remarkable gift of
preaching and her ministry marked as "clearly as any single
incident or event the beginning of the revival in the Society."
The 1860 sessions of the Indiana Yearly Meeting were note
worthy. The young people in attendance requested the privileg
of conducting an evening meeting for youth. The request wa
granted after much opposition, and more than one thousand per
sons attended the special service.[25] Hundreds of young peopl
prayed and testified. At the close of the Yearly Meeting, Siby
Jones expressed a concern to meet with those who had partici
pated in this great evening service, and from this after-meetin
developed a series of prayer meetings that fostered the Awak
ening among Friends.

The first revival in a Quaker meeting occurred in 1867 a
Walnut Ridge, Indiana.[26] A small group of members had bee
meeting informally for prayer and Bible study and had becom
so burdened with the need for spiritual renewal that they bega
to pray for a community-wide awakening. In these simple ser
vices, individuals came under conviction for their sins and bega
to seek forgiveness at appointed places for prayer.

The meetings grew spontaneously and increased in size an
power. Large groups of people began to drive in from the sur
rounding areas, and word of the revival began to spread. Man
Quakers, of long-standing membership, were converted and th
community experienced a religious awakening. What occurred a
Walnut Ridge was repeated, with a variety of means, in a larg
number of Quaker communities. Quakerism was now experienc
ing an awakening similar to what was taking place in othe
denominational groups.

Factors Contributing to the Great Awakening

The reasons for the Great Awakening in Quakerism ar
multifaceted and complex. We have already alluded to the emer
gence of Evangelicalism and the resultant opening to the wave o
revival that was sweeping across the country. But there wer
other factors, some of which were peculiar to Friends, that shoul

be noted. Undoubtedly, the years of controversy and separation had produced a concern among members of the Society to recapture the sense of unity and purpose that was so clearly exhibited by the first generation Quakers. The zeal for Bible study and the renewed interest in the Scriptures that had been inaugurated by Joseph John Gurney was continued by the development of Bible classes in the meetinghouses. Hannah Chapman Backhouse, cousin to Joseph John Gurney, is credited with starting and promoting Bible study classes among American Quakers.[27] This return to Scripture reading and study had an important part in preparing the way for revival.

The traditional isolation of Friends had been broken down in many ways. Individual Quakers had served in such interdenominational enterprises as the establishment of the American Bible Society and the antislavery movement. John Greenleaf Whittier wrote to his friend, Joseph Sturge, saying that the abolition cause "has destroyed all narrow sectarian prejudices and made me willing to be a man among men."[28]

The new and enlightened concern for education prompted the establishing of elementary schools. Often these schools were built adjacent to the meetinghouses and an effort was made to have such a monthly meeting school in every community. These schools laid the foundation for the public school system that was later developed in the states of Ohio, Indiana, Iowa, Kansas, North Carolina, and Tennessee.[29]

On the frontier these schools were often open to the children of neighbors who were not Quakers; and in some areas where Friends had no established schools, their enlightened concern for education allowed Quaker children to attend public schools conducted by non-Quakers.[30] This interaction among Quakers and non-Quakers, and the emphasis upon education, elementary as it was, helped to break down some of the old and traditional walls of isolation.

The nineteenth century witnessed the birth of the modern missionary movement. Following upon the influence of William Carey, who set sail for India from England in 1792, the American Board of Commissioners for Foreign Missions was established in

1810, the first in the United States. Before the middle of the century, numbers of Protestant denominations had caught the vision of a missionary program and were sharing in the great enterprise. A parallel movement can also be illustrated among certain individual Quakers. The birth of this missionary spirit prepared the way for the new epoch in Quakerism as men such as Thomas Shillitoe, Stephen Grellet, Daniel Wheeler, and James Backhouse took the Gospel to such widely scattered countries as Tasmania and Australia, South America, the West Indies, Africa, and the European continent.[31]

Another important factor leading to the Great Awakening in American Quakerism was the itinerant visits from England of concerned Friends. The direct and positive support given by Joseph John Gurney has already been noted. In addition, the visits of Benjamin Seebohm and Robert and Sarah Lindsey further prepared the way for revival. Benjamin Seebohm came to England in 1814 from Germany, becoming one of the major evangelical leaders.[32] His travels throughout America during the years of 1846-1851 gave continued impetus to Evangelicalism among Friends. Robert and Sarah Lindsey were from Yorkshire, as was Benjamin Seebohm.

In 1857, they began the most extensive itinerant ministry throughout America ever undertaken by Friends. Old Quaker communities were visited, as well as the new frontier settlements. Robert Lindsey was thoroughly evangelical in his preaching, and was a man of strong personal influence. As we will note in a later chapter, the Lindseys visited the rugged west and carefully recorded their impressions in a diary. Rufus Jones correctly estimates the value of the ministry of Robert Lindsey when he writes, "He must be regarded as an important factor in the transformation of American Quakerism."[33] All of these itinerant Friends brought their influence to bear upon the Society in America, rooted and grounded in the precepts of early Quakerism, but open to the religious and social reforms of the day.

In reading the accounts of the Great Awakening and from studying the memoirs and reminiscences of those Quakers who were part of this movement, one is made very conscious of the fact that it was a movement often generated and maintained by the Quaker youth. As has been noted, young people were responsible for the 1860 evening meeting at the sessions of Indiana Yearly Meeting. Allen Jay spoke of the young people gathering for times of social and spiritual fellowship. Nathan and Esther Frame point to the revival's inauguration among the youth. The young people of the mid-nineteenth century were not content with the old and inadequate ways of their elders. They found no barriers to attending the revival meetings in non-Quaker churches with their friends; often they themselves would be converted and would return to their own churches to testify to their spiritual experiences.

Throughout the country there now appeared young leaders with a new zeal and compassion for the work of Friends. Three of the most prominent were John Henry Douglas of Maine, David Updegraff of Ohio, and Allen Jay of Indiana. Douglas was undoubtedly the most dynamic of the new leaders and his ministry carried him from New England to the midwest and ultimately to California.[34]

David Updegraff was the most radical of the three; his conversion in a Methodist revival opened the way to an effective ministry in the midwest.[35] Allen Jay may be called the steadiest of these young leaders, having a remarkable ministry in Indiana and the neighboring states.[36] Dougan Clark, Luke Woodard, William Pinkham, and Esther Frame also contributed in a prominent way to the transformation in American Quakerism.

The Spread of the Great Awakening

Although the major impetus to revival seems to have occurred in the midwest, it wasn't long before the movement had spread throughout Quakerism. Rufus Jones writes, "The old sense of awe and restraint gave place to an era of freedom and spontaneity . . . nothing stemmed the current—the old order changed and the new came on apace."[37] One of the new tools devised for the spread of the evangelistic fervor was the General Meeting. In 1867, Indiana Yearly Meeting adopted a plan for a type of public service that resembled the meetings held by George

Fox and the early Quakers. Under the supervision of a Committee on General Meetings, a series of public meetings were held in various centers. The preaching was extemporaneous and without prearrangement, and paralleled frequently the type of meeting that had been held on Fulton Street in New York just ten years earlier.

One of the earliest of these general meetings was held in Chicago in December 1867, and many of the new leaders were present.[38] Rapidly the Indiana pattern was adopted by other yearly meetings. New York held a series of such public meetings in 1871-1872, and by 1873 the general meeting was in use in Iowa and Kansas.[39] Frequently, the general meetings were initiated by local groups who did not wait for the arrangements and supervision of the Yearly Meeting Committee. The Third Awakening had become a reality in the life of the American church, and this time the Quakers were not omitted from the revival movement. This became the time of Quakerism's greatest ingathering of souls since the days of George Fox.

Results of the Great Awakening

American Quakerism experienced a transformation during the two decades following 1860. Contacts with other denominations fostered new ideas and techniques. Although strong opposition was raised to many of the changes and the dangers of innovation were forcefully expressed by the older Quakers, a burst of new life was experienced. Old meetinghouses were modernized to the style of the period. Sunday schools were opened and the methods of worship were adapted to meet the needs of those who had not been raised as Friends. Many of the old Quaker customs were abandoned: the emphasis upon silence in worship, the use of plain dress and language, the wearing of men's hats during worship, and marriage after the manner of Friends without a presiding minister.

The revival techniques used so effectively by Finney and Moody were now used by Quaker evangelists. Updegraff, whose family had been intimate with Charles Finney, was the first to use an "altar of prayer" as a regular feature of his evangelistic meetings.[40] Personal work with those who responded to the invitation, opportunities to testify publicly to one's religious experiences—these were practices that Friends adopted in common with others.

Music and singing were introduced into the Meetings for Worship. Although congregational singing was not unknown among Quakers prior to the Great Awakening, it was during this time that it became an accepted, and indeed, expected practice in many of the evangelical meetings. After a period of hesitation, the piano and organ were also introduced into the churches.[41] In some cases such a move was necessary to keep the young people attending the services. In order to keep her children from attending the neighboring Methodist church, which had an organ in its sanctuary, one Quaker mother in West Branch, Iowa, privately purchased an organ for the Friends Meeting![42]

The most important innovation in Quakerism that came as a result of the Great Awakening was the introduction of the pastoral system. Prior to the revival, the old manner of worship in silence and the free ministry of the worshiper had become stagnated. The new spirit of renewal and the fervent evangelism of the times demanded a change. Although aspects of the pastoral idea had been with Friends from the beginning, the pastoral system was accepted by the majority in America as an appropriate and long overdue change. J. Wilhelm Rowntree made an extensive study of the problem and concluded that "the root cause of this new development was the failure of the ministry under the old order."[43] Writing for the **Friends Quarterly Examiner** in 1903, he said:

> The Quaker ministry, undisciplined by any adequate sense of the responsibility of mental effort, was, as a whole, and despite some magnificent exceptions, vague, ineffectual, rhapsodic. It did not grip, it was not virile, it wanted that specific quality which the application and concentration of the highest powers, illumined by a rich culture as well as by experience, and trained and consecrated to a noble office, alone could give. When the call to a wider service came, the ministry was unequal to the task.[44]

The pastoral system was a direct result of the revival among Quakers. The General Meetings had produced large numbers of converts, many of whom had no background or training in Quakerism. This fact, obviously welcome, led to the development of a concern for a vocal ministry to teach and retain the new converts. Most Quakers lived in rural and agrarian areas, and their full-time occupation of farming led them to set apart certain individuals as pastors. These new pastors were charged with the responsibility of not only giving oversight to the spiritual welfare of the meeting, but were also expected to conduct the Meeting for Worship, to help the new converts become grounded in the Scriptures and indoctrinated in the ways of Friends, and to guard against deviant behavior.[45] Those who introduced the pastoral system did not seem to have any deliberate intention of shattering the old Quaker traditions. As Grubb points out, "They sought to solve a pressing problem, and took the means readiest to hand—that of imitating the (apparently) more successful churches around them."[46] By 1880, the system had spread so rapidly that most of the orthodox, evangelical meetings had adopted it, first in the west and then in the east. Pastoral committees were established in each yearly meeting, making it their policy to see that each local meeting was supplied with a pastor. By the turn of the century, an estimated sixty-two percent of all Friends belonged to pastoral meetings.[47]

The Awakening had a still further positive result in the wave of interest in missionary endeavor. Every Yearly Meeting assumed a mission field: New England had Syria; New York had Mexico; Baltimore and Canada joined Philadelphia in a work in Japan; Ohio centered its attention on China and India; Indiana and Western Yearly Meetings also had a work in Mexico; Iowa took Jamaica, and Kansas looked toward Alaska.[48] The latter two Yearly Meetings also gave a missionary impulse to the migrations of Quakers to California.[49]

Revival in Quakerism brought many necessary and welcome changes, but in some areas it brought unnecessary difficulties, created division and made even deeper separations. The usual quiet of many of the meetings was disturbed by the excited utterances, the singing of hymns, and the calls for prayer and testimonies—to the deep distress of many of the older Friends. In some cases, the wedge between the old and new was driven beyond repair. The younger Quakers were enthusiastic about the new measures, while the older and more sober Quakers were slow to recognize the reality of new spiritual life if it did not function in the traditional and conventional channels. Edward Grubb writes:

> If on both sides there had been more sympathy and open mindedness, more insight and patience, things might have settled down, and new and outreaching life and love have been brought to the Society by the Revival, without serious loss to the "inwardness" of essential Quakerism. But each section was determined to have its way, certain that the other was wholly wrong; and so the Revival and its extravagences brought about a new crop of separations.[50]

The zealous evangelists of the revival frequently ignored the rich heritage of Quakerism and introduced radical changes too quickly, grieving many of the older Friends. Their lack of understanding and historical perspective caused many to turn their backs on the new movement and become more deeply entrenched in traditionalism. Others openly and strongly reacted against the revivalistic measures and led the way to further separation. A case in point is the division that occurred among Iowa Friends in 1877. Ten years earlier, in 1867, two Quaker ministers, Stacy Bevan and John S. Bond, held a revival meeting at the Bear Creek Meeting in Madison County. This public meeting was marked by emotional demonstrations, and an attempt to close the services was made by some of the more conservative members. This was the first serious contest between the two factions of Friends in Iowa.[51]

In the decade that followed, the revival or General Meetings became so prevalent in various parts of the Yearly Meeting that by 1872 a Yearly Meeting Committee was established to coordinate and control the revivalistic measures. This official recognition of revivalism marked the beginning of the end of unity in the Yearly Meeting.[52] In 1877, following an unusual demonstration of religious excitement in another meeting at Bear Creek, numbers of Friends abruptly left the service in protest of methods that were intolerable to them. Three months later, these offended Friends called a conference of the like-minded members of the Bear Creek Quarterly Meeting on May 5 in order to consider the

> present and sorrowful condition of our beloved and once favored Society, by relapsing into doctrines, forms and practices which we believe are inconsistent with our principles and profession and detrimental to the religious growth and prosperity of the Society.[53]

This conference of about sixty Friends appointed Zimri Horner as clerk, and after discussing at length "these and other declensions, both in doctrine and practice . . . with which we have no unity, being at variance and repugnant to our Christian principles,"[54] the conference made a clear and unmistakable call for separation:

> We believe the time has now fully come when it is incumbent upon us to disclaim the appointment of all the officers imposed upon us by the nondescript body now in the seat of church government, and replace them by those in unity with the doctrine, and in favor of supporting the ancient principles and testimonies of our Society. Seeing the walls of our Zion are much broken down, we solemnly appeal to the wisdom and judgment of all sound Friends to whom this may come, to seriously examine, and solemnly consider the things herein so briefly brought to view.[55]

The action of this conference led to similar separations in several monthly meetings and to a final breach in the Yearly Meeting when the dissident Friends organized, on September 7, 1877, the Iowa Yearly Meeting of (Conservative) Friends.[56]

The separation in Iowa Yearly Meeting provoked a similar action in Western and Kansas Yearly Meetings.[57] Various Friends journals in America and England carried full reports of events and the Society was made painfully aware of the divisions caused by revivalism.[58] However, not all Quakers who were opposed to revivalism were separatists. Numbers of Friends felt it their responsibility to stay within the established yearly meetings. Although they were in sympathy with the feelings of the separatists, their loyalties to the Society and to its welfare demanded that they remain within the yearly meeting. One such person was Joel Bean of Iowa. Joel Bean reacted sharply against the departure from traditional Friends methods and views that had come as a result of the Great Awakening. An outstanding leader, he served as clerk of Iowa Yearly Meeting in 1877 when separation occurred. In a letter to Rufus Jones, Joel Bean explained:

> I never encouraged separations nor had any part in them, believing for myself it was better to stand true to my convictions, and to suffer the consequences **in the body**, than to **separate from it.** At the same time, those beloved and true brethren who felt that the only course for them to maintain allegiance to our principles was in withdrawing from the "Friends Church," as it has come to be conducted, have ever had my sympathy. **I would never disown them, and I have never felt disowned by them.**[59]

By 1880, American Quakerism had undergone a transformation. The Great Awakening had brought reviving activity and renewed zeal. As it gained power, however, it became intolerant of dissent and Friends were divided again. During these years, another shift in the population of the Society of Friends took place, as more and more Quakers joined the trek to the far west and the shores of the Pacific Ocean. The revival movement in Iowa and Kansas Yearly Meetings resulted in the development ultimately of two distinct bodies of Friends in California.

The evangelicals, spurred on with missionary zeal and under the leadership of some of the most outstanding of the Friends evangelists, established the California Yearly Meeting of Friends Church. Other Friends, especially those under the leadership of nonseparatist Joel Bean, formed associations of Friends in California that ultimately led to the establishment of the Pacific Yearly Meeting of Friends. This thesis will be studied and developed in the following chapters of this book. Prior to a discussion of the migration of Friends to California, the next chapter will study the life and leadership of Joel Bean, who is primary and pivotal in our understanding of what later occurred among Quakers in the west.

4

Joel and Hannah Bean

IN A FOOTNOTE to his chapter on American Quakerism, in **The Later Periods of Quakerism**, Rufus Jones briefly describes Joel Bean as "a beautiful spiritual character, a saintly soul and a favored minister of the gospel."[1] Apart from this notation, Jones makes no identification of the personality or the important role that Joel Bean had in the formation of western Quakerism. The waves of revivalism that had profoundly affected the Society of Friends had brought not only renewal of spiritual vitality and vision, but as we have seen, they brought division and separation as well.

Joel Bean had attained a position of respect and leadership within the Society; but finding his voice too often in the minority among Iowa Friends, and while not wanting to separate from the Yearly Meeting, he found that by migrating to California he could still speak freely to the needs of Friends as he saw them. Joel Bean had always felt that the church should allow for great diversity of opinion and freedom of thought.

Revivalism in the west had dogmatized many of the beliefs of Friends and had suppressed opposition and silenced the resistance of many conservative Quakers. On the west coast, Joel Bean gathered around him a fellowship of other like-minded Quakers. This fellowship became the nucleus of a new body of Friends, and ultimately a new yearly meeting. There is no indication that he had ever wanted to form a separatist group; indeed, he spoke

47

often of his duty of staying within the body of Friends "to contend for the faith and suffer for it."[2] Yet the ultimate end of his cause was the formation of a new yearly meeting in California, separated from fellowship and vital communion with most orthodox Friends and, in many ways, innovators of ideas and practices that would have been foreign to Joel Bean.

It is important, therefore, that we examine the life and thought of Joel and Hannah Bean. Their reaction against the measures of revivalism and the "new look" of Quakerism resulted in the wide differences that can be found today in the two bodies of Friends in California, i.e., the California Yearly Meeting of Friends Church, and the Pacific Yearly Meeting of Friends.

1825-1860—Growth to Maturity

Joel Bean was born on December 16, 1825, in Alton, New Hampshire.[3] His parents were hard-working, birthright Quakers, John and Elizabeth Bean, and he grew up in what he later described as "an exceptionally happy childhood, in the midst of natural surroundings of surpassing beauty."[4] His paternal grandparents were descendants of John Bean, of the clan McBean of Scotland, who came to the colonies in 1660.[5] His maternal grandparents were also farmers of a strong Puritan ancestry; his great-grandmother Hill was a descendant of the Prescott family and of the colonial minister, Stephen Batchelder, whose posterity included such prominent New Englanders as Daniel Webster and John Greenleaf Whittier.[6] Joel Bean thus came of a stern Quaker and Puritan stock and was raised as a typical New Englander. His daughter described him in later years as being

> of slender, nervous build with clean-cut features, of logical mind, of reserved and quiet temper, with a quick sense of humor, a keen appreciation of natural beauty, and withal a mystic.[7]

A good education set the foundation for his clear and logical thinking and writing in later years. He attended district schools taught by "strict teachers," followed by "select schools" of higher grades. His parents then sent him to the Boarding School that Friends had established at Providence, Rhode Island.

During his early childhood, many of his friends were members of the Free-Will Baptist Church, which was the leading
religious body in the area. Even some relatives were Free-Will
Baptists, including an uncle who was a minister. The Bean children often attended the Baptist services when travel to the nearest Friends meeting was not possible, and through such contacts
Joel undoubtedly began to develop a generous and liberal spirit.
Joel Bean later wrote:

Most of our associations and friendships at this early period in
our lives were outside of the pole of our own Society. But the
religious training of our parents, and the books that we read,
and the general influence which Friends exerted upon us, were
such that I think no one of us was ever inclined to cast away
our birthright, or to undervalue it.[8]

When he completed school at Providence, Joel set out alone
in the spring of 1853 for the wide open spaces of the west. He
headed for Iowa, "a young pioneer to a new country," and found
a place to settle at Salem in Henry County. It was here that the
first Friends meeting was established, and later, the first quarterly meeting west of the Mississippi.[9] Joel Bean wrote of his
coming to the pioneer Quaker community, saying,

When the lot was found on which the light rested, as the place
for my future home, the prairie sod was broken and the little
cot built to which, after two years, I brought my mother.[10]

During these early years in Iowa, he established lifelong friendships with such men as Cyrus Beede, Alvin Hoag, and John Miller.
His sharp mind and quest for knowledge did not go unnoticed
among the settlers of the Salem community and he was invited
to be the teacher of a projected school. For six months, Joel Bean
taught the children of the area and quickly demonstrated his
ability to communicate and share knowledge with others.

In 1855, he sent for his parents from New England and
settled in a new home in West Branch, Cedar County, where another Friends meeting had been established. Soon all of his immediate family made the trek to Iowa and settled nearby. Three
years later, in 1858, Joel Bean was recorded as a minister by the
Red Cedar Monthly Meeting at the age of thirty-three.[11] This
meeting, like all of those in Iowa, belonged to the Indiana Yearly

Meeting. Teaching continued to be his occupation, and in this same year he was employed as teacher of a "select school."

In 1859, Joel Bean was married to a Philadelphia Quakeress, Hannah Elliott Shipley. Hannah had come to spend a summer with her sister in Iowa, and it was at her home that Joel and Hannah were introduced. Hannah was also a school teacher and together they discovered much of common interest and delight. Hannah was the daughter of Thomas and Lydia Shipley, prominent members of the Arch Street Meeting in Philadelphia. Thomas Shipley was an ardent abolitionist, and a founder of the American Antislavery Society and president of the Pennsylvania Society. Hannah's loving heart and cheerful spirit cemented her relationship with Joel, until on June 29, 1859, they were married in Philadelphia, "according to the good order used among us."[12] Upon their return to Iowa, they went to their little home in West Branch, where Joel's parents continued to live with them. Catherine Bean Cox wrote of her mother:

> Her fresh enthusiasm, her ready interest and sympathy in all of the activities of the pioneer community, and her sweet charm were instantly felt, and . . . in the little quiet meeting she spoke with the tenderness and feeling and aspiration that characterized her ministry. . . .[13]

Joel and Hannah entered eagerly into the busy life of the pioneer village. Joel was vice-president of the first bank, listened with interest to John Brown when he visited and spoke at a neighbor's home, and opened a private school. Together with Hannah they visited and encouraged many of the new Friends meetings and opened their own home to a class of Bible reading and study. Their influence and spiritual stature helped to make the West Branch Meeting a major center of Quakerism. In a letter to Rufus Jones, Joel Bean describes the growth of the meeting:

> My home was fixed at West Branch where the little houses of first settlers were beginning to dot the unbroken prairie. A small meeting, held in a broom-shop, had been started, of which Hannah B. Tatum was a beloved and gifted young minister. Her husband, David Tatum, was not then recorded. My first home was with them, and we were bound together in a life-long friendship. The meeting grew rapidly. Springdale, four miles

east, was a little older, and at that time larger. . . . Honey
Grove, a few miles north east, soon became a good sized meeting. . . . At Muscatine and neighborhood . . . there were soon
three meetings established. . . . These two groups of meetings
soon constituted Springdale Q.M. in Cedar County—the third
organized in Iowa. It numbered after a few years over 1000
members, and was one of the strongest in the State. Our meeting at West Branch became one of the largest meetings. . . .[14]

On Sundays, Joel was given the honor of sitting at the head of the
Meeting on the men's side, and his mother, Elizabeth, was accord-
ed the similar honor, sitting on the women's side of the meetinghouse. Hannah also usually sat in the raised seats that formed
the front of the meetinghouse.[15] Under the gifted leadership of
the Beans, the West Branch Meeting grew in strength and influence.

1860-1877—Years of Wider Service

Lydia was the first child born to Joel and Hannah Bean. In
1861, the young couple set out from Iowa with their baby to visit
friends and relatives in Philadelphia, and then to begin a journey
to Hawaii. When Joel was a young man of seventeen, he had a
concern to make a missionary trip to the Hawaiian Islands, then
called the Sandwich Islands.[16] Hannah had been fully informed
of this intent before their marriage, and now the way had been
opened to make the trip together. Indiana Yearly Meeting had
liberated the Beans according to the manner of Friends, and they
sailed from New York in June, 1861, arriving in Honolulu two
months later. This trip was significant in that it was only the
second recorded foreign missionary trip by American Quakers
and was preceded only by the visit of Eli and Sibyl Jones to
Africa in 1851.[17]

On the way to Honolulu they stopped briefly in San Francisco, little knowing that in twenty years California would be
their new home. For nine months they visited the various mission
stations on the islands of Oahu, Maui, and Hawaii. Their ministry
was warmly received and they were encouraged to remain. King
Kamehameha V and his wife, Queen Emma, entertained the
Beans, and the many missionaries urged them to open a school on
the island, but Joel and Hannah felt their ministry was completed

and so they began the long and difficult journey back to Iowa. Upon their return to Iowa, Joel opened a private school and taught for a number of years in the West Branch area.

For some time prior to this missionary journey, there had been expressed a growing concern for the establishment of a yearly meeting in Iowa. The monthly meetings up to this time were under the care of Indiana Yearly Meeting. Both Joel and Hannah gave important leadership in the organizing movement, traveling widely among the sparsely located Quaker settlements and assessing the feelings of the meetings. Finally, in the fall of 1863, the Iowa Yearly Meeting was organized and held its first meeting in the Spring Creek meetinghouse, near Oskaloosa.[18]

Joel Bean gave vital leadership to the young Yearly Meeting, serving as clerk and member of many committees. In 1867, he was appointed presiding clerk of the Yearly Meeting, an office which he held for the next five years. He also gave of his wise counsel during these years as clerk of the Meeting for Ministers and Elders.[19] The repeated demands that the Yearly Meeting made on his time and talent in the following years give evidence of the high esteem in which he was held. In the same year, 1867, a group of interested Friends subscribed $1,500 toward the construction of a building to be known as the "Friends Academy of West Branch."[20]

Joel and Hannah were engaged as teachers of the new academy and deeply impressed the students with their scholarship and piety. The academy had been in operation only a short time when the Friends were persuaded to rent the facilities to the town, and the first term of the public school was opened in 1869, with Joel and Hannah Bean remaining as teachers.[21]

By now the vision and concern for a wider ministry among Friends gripped the hearts of Joel and Hannah. Their trip to Hawaii had brought a new sense of world mission, and their work in the Yearly Meeting had developed a keener interest in the family of Friends. Although their farm provided only a meager income, the call to visit England and the home of Quakerism seemed clear. Their concern was shared with others, and a way was provided by those who recognized their gifts of ministry and felt a oneness with their mission. In 1872, therefore, Joel and Hannah left Iowa again, this time for England.[22] By now their family had grown to four, another daughter, Catherine, having been born in 1865. The two girls were left with their maternal grandmother, and the Beans entered into one of the more important periods of their life and ministry.

Their contacts with the rich heritage of Quakerism and with the influential English Friends of the day brought new influence into their lives. Discussions with Bevan Braithwaite, Thomas Hodgkin, and Isaac Sharp brought into clear focus the foundational truths of their faith and the distinctive principles of Quakerism. They visited and ministered in numerous meetings in England, Scotland and Ireland, and attended both Dublin and London Yearly Meetings.[23] Wherever they went, they captured the hearts of the English Friends. Their daughter Catherine later wrote of the trip:

It was characteristic of both Joel and Hannah Bean that they met it with the same sincerity and simplicity and open-mindedness and eager zest for life that had made them a vital part of a pioneer western settlement, had given them sympathetic insight into the needs and conditions of mission workers and of primitive peoples and had made them inspiring teachers of youth. A lifelong friend wrote, "Never were Gospel messengers more welcome and more useful." Their wide and varied ministry, Joel Bean's deep and fearless search for truth, his stand for freedom of thought and progress, his clear, forceful utterance, and Hannah Bean's wide interests and large-heartedness, her true spirituality, her charm and rare conversational gifts, found welcome in the homes of English Friends.[24]

The friendships that were formed in England during this period were steadily enriched in the ensuing years through correspondence and the visits of English Friends to the Bean residence. During a later period of difficulty and discouragement, these Friends brought support and encouragement to Joel. Upon their return to America, Joel and Hannah remained on the east coast. Their daughters were enrolled at the Friends Boarding School in Providence, and for two years, 1875-1877, Joel and Hannah joined the faculty of the school. During this interlude they entered into the literary life of New England and often visited with Whittier around his fireplace.[25]

In 1877, the Bean family returned to Iowa. The revival movement had spread by now throughout the various quarterly meetings. When the Yearly Meeting convened on September 5, 1877, Joel Bean was appointed as the presiding clerk.[26] Two days later, separation occurred within the Yearly Meeting and, as we have seen, the Iowa Yearly Meeting of Friends (Conservative) was organized.

Although Joel was a leader of conservative Friends, he was not a Separatist and remained within the parent body. The exigencies of revival had now taken their toll on the highest possible level. The recent years of discussion with conservative English Friends and with Friends in New England and Philadelphia Yearly Meetings had reinforced Joel's own feelings against the doctrines and practices that he felt had been inaugurated among Quakers by the overzealous evangelists of the Revival. The year 1877, therefore, marks the beginning of a new period in the life of Joel and Hannah Bean. Their disenchantment with revivalism had now become widely known, and the Beans entered into a time of conflict and controversy.

1877-1882—Years of Controversy

The changes in Quakerism in Iowa that took place in 1877 were due to many factors and forces that affected it both from within and without. The problems that paved the way for a religious awakening among Quakers across the country were true also of Iowa.

> The introduction of the Sunday or "First-Day Scripture Schools," the common patronage of the public schools, the adoption of evangelical methods of church activity, and the transition from the isolation of rural communities to modern social conditions and town life . . . [were]powerful factors in the breaking down of that conservatism which in the early days hedged the Friends about on every side.[27]

All of these forces interacted with one another, but the most prominent factor bringing change in Iowa, and to Western Quakerism, was the advent of revivalism.

One of the major evidences of the religious awakening among Friends was the revival spirit that appeared in many of the Quaker schools. In 1865, the students of the Center Grove

Academy, near Oskaloosa, formed "The Christian Vigilance Band" with the purpose of promoting revival.[28] The following year, a similar concern developed on the campus of Earlham College in Indiana. Allen Jay wrote that the revival spirit "broke out in Earlham College, when twenty young men were converted in one term, and before the end of the year almost the whole student body was swept into the movement."[29] In 1869, a revival-oriented student organization was also formed at Whittier College, in Salem, Iowa.[30] Spurred on by the youthful vitality and energy of these Friends, the old order was soon overturned and the new was instituted.

Joel Bean watched these developments with obvious concern. In his letter to Rufus Jones regarding the events of this period, he wrote:

The first activity of the movement in Iowa was imported from Walnut Ridge, Indiana. It was attended with a great deal of wild fire, and wrought sad havoc in a few localities. . . . It was attended with such excitement that women would fall down and roll upon the floor, as I saw in one meeting which I visited. The converts made extreme claims of perfection, so that some dear and valued members became so impressed with their superior Holiness, that they refused to shake hands with their old friends, who could not join them.[31]

The wholesome impulses and reviving activity of the new movement were readily accepted and welcomed by Joel Bean. But as the movement gathered momentum and the old order began to be drastically changed, Joel Bean strongly reacted on two counts. He was opposed, first, to the "change of methods."[32] As long as there was "no departure from Friends methods in religious meetings,"[33] Joel Bean shared in the vitality of the religious awakening. He wrote:

We were all united in those days in welcoming and cherishing the Divine visitation, the evident work of the Holy Spirit upon our people. The hearts of the young people around us in Iowa were tender, and receptive. They were loyal to our Society. They were habitual attenders of meeting, for worship and discipline, and interested in First-Day schools. Most of them gave promise of future usefulness, which has been fulfilled.[34]

When, however, the quiet of the meeting was broken by emotional outbursts and the innovations in worship and conduct were

thrust upon Friends by overzealous and sometimes tactless revivalists, Joel Bean reacted strongly and critically. In an article
written for the **British Friend** in 1881, he said:

> The present condition of our Society shows how far we have
> drifted out of our first course, and how radical are the changes
> into which we have been swept. A great movement has set in
> and borne the masses of our people along to consequences
> which they little anticipated, and which few of them see with
> entire satisfaction. It has been common to call it the "Revival
> Movement," and to denounce those who demur at any excesses
> connected with it as opposed to revivals and "opposed to the
> Lord's work." . . . Many who were amongst the readiest to
> welcome signs of revival in our Society, (using the word in its
> true sense), and who labored earnestly and devotedly to pro-
> mote it, have had to stand aloof from the movement, where it
> has adopted means which they felt to be hazardous and scatter-
> ing to the Church and defeating to the very object desired. . . .
> Those who saw the nature of the foreign elements introduced
> into the work, and the effects they must produce, when their
> cautions were unavailing and their judgment set aside, have
> had not only to grieve in consequence of the widening breach,
> but to feel their influence narrowed, and to feel that there was
> scarcely any place for them in the Church so dear to them.[35]

Joel Bean was not only dissatisfied with the changes in
Friends procedures, he was also deeply concerned, secondly, with
the "new basis of doctrine" that the revival seemed to promote.[36]
The necessity of passing through distinct religious crises—conversion, followed by the second experience of sanctification—the
emphasis upon a literal interpretation of the Bible, and the growing tendency toward creedal formulations were all opposed to
Joel Bean's concept of Quaker doctrine. His reaction to the "new
doctrines" led him into open conflict with others in the Society
and further alienated him from the revival movement. It is important, therefore, to understand the doctrines that were promoted by the revivalists.

The emphasis upon perfectionism during this period is a
recognized factor in American church history. Charles G. Finney
had earlier promoted the concepts of holiness,[37] and the Methodists widely influenced the church with their call to entire sanctification.[38] Such powerful Quaker revivalists as John Henry
Douglas, David Updegraff and Dougan Clark reintroduced the

concepts among Friends and taught "the theory of entire sanctification, instantaneously obtained by one act of faith alone."[39]
Enthusiasm for perfection in the Christian's life was characteristic of the entire evangelical revival during this period.

Foremost among the Quaker exponents of doctrine was
David Updegraff. He promoted a "four-fold gospel" of justification, sanctification, the Second Coming of Christ, and faith-heal-
ing. At the heart of his exposition was the stand that he took on
the experience of sanctification. Sanctification was distinct from
justification. The latter he said was a

> law term, and strictly refers to that Divine act by which a
> sinner is absolved from the guilt and penalty of his sin. It is not
> the acquittal of one who is proven innocent—but the pardon
> and forgiveness of one who confesses guilt.[40]

Entire sanctification, however, was an instantaneous work of
grace, allowing for "progress of expansion," and "cleansing from
the pollution, or the expulsion of inbred sin."[41] Updegraff concluded that "it deals not with the guilt of sin, but expels the inward proneness to it, the love of it, and gives power over tempta-
tion through the indwelling Holy Ghost."[42] This doctrinal emphasis of Updegraff was reinforced with the testimony of his
own personal experience. In 1869, he had come to a place of prayer and surrender. He said:

> Every "vile affection" was resolutely nailed to the cross. De-
> nominational standing, family, business, friends, time, talent
> and earthly store, were quickly and irrevocably committed to
> the sovereign control and disposal of my Almighty Savior. It
> came to be easy to trust Him, and I had no sooner reckoned
> myself "dead indeed unto sin and alive unto God," than the
> "Holy Ghost fell upon me," just as I supposed He did "at the be-
> ginning." Instantly I felt the melting and refining fire of God
> permeate my whole being. Conflict was a thing of the past. I
> had entered into "rest." I was nothing and nobody, and glad
> that it was settled that way. . . . I was deeply conscious of the
> presence of God within me, and of his sanctifying work.[43]

Dougan Clark[44] and Hannah Whitall Smith[45] also wrote extensively of this "second work of grace," and its teaching rapidly
became the focal point of the ministry of Quaker revivalists.

Holiness meetings, holiness camp meetings, and holiness preaching became a part of the revival movement among Friends. The
call for converts was often replaced with an invitation to the
Christian to experience God's sanctifying grace. As individuals
testified to such an experience, a wave of emotionalism often
swept over the meetings,

> and for a time there was grave danger that the apprehension
> of truth by the training of the mind and the slow moralization
> of the will by the practice of ordinary virtues and by the active
> formation of character might be overlooked and forgotten in
> the hope that all these things were the fruit of miracle.[46]

A further change in the doctrinal climate during this period
was the refutation by many of the Quaker revivalists of the "so
called doctrine of the Inner Light." In 1877, the Ohio Yearly
Meeting of Friends minuted a statement of opposition to the

> mystical views and expositions which appear here and there in
> certain of our members, in opposition to the plain scriptural
> doctrines of man's darkness and deadness in sin by nature and
> his redemption therefrom by the Lord Jesus Christ, whose shed
> blood is the alone means of cleansing the soul from all the guilt
> of sin.[47]

The following year this same Yearly Meeting, the body to which
David Updegraff belonged, issued an even stronger minute:

> We do not believe that there is any principle or quality in the
> soul of man, innate or otherwise, which, even though rightly
> used, will ever save a single soul. . . . And we repudiate the
> so-called doctrine of the inner light, or the gift of a portion of
> the Holy Spirit in the soul of every man, as dangerous, un-
> sound, and unscriptural.[48]

The reaction by conservative Friends was swift. John
Greenleaf Whittier spoke the sentiments of these Friends when
he wrote to the editor of **The Friend** in May, 1879:

> I have just seen a copy of "The Friend" of the 19th ult., and
> have read with more regret than surprise the extracts from the
> minutes of the Ohio Yearly Meeting for 1877 and 1878. They
> seem to me an entire abandonment of the one distinctive and
> root doctrine of our religious Society—that from which it
> derives all that is peculiar to it in doctrine and testimony, and
> which alone gives it a right to exist.[49]

The lines of demarcation were now clearly drawn for Joel Bean. By 1882, he was reacting strongly against the "new measures" and the "new doctrines" of the revival. He wrote widely and influentially. In 1879, the **Friends' Review** published his article on "The Light Within."[50] In this article, he posed the question, "Is there the light or Spirit of Christ in the soul of every man, which, if yielded to, brings salvation?" After citing the statements of Augustine, Thomas Chalmers, John Henry Newman, Joseph Cook, and Thomas Erskine, he concluded that the teaching of early Friends "while fully embracing the great evangelical doctrines of Christ's passion and atonement, at the same time directed all to the light and Spirit of Christ within."[51]

Two years later, he submitted an article to the **British Friend**, which was then reproduced and widely distributed. In this article, entitled "The Issue," Joel Bean wrote of the doctrines "which are preached and taught sedulously by a considerable class of our ministers, in common with a school outside."[52] He held that the revival movement "in its present phase, as exhibited in many of our meetings, is utterly diverse from essential Quakerism in almost every feature."[53] After critically questioning the "measures" and "doctrines" of the movement, he concluded:

> The statement of these facts might seem no better than detraction, if it were only to **expose our** condition, and I totally disclaim so ignoble a motive. It is to plead on their behalf the thoughtful consideration of judicial minds that I venture to arraign them to our notice. Let them not be summarily repulsed as overdrawn or untrue. We have had enough of such disposal of wisest warnings and expostulations. Whatever some in blind zeal may say, I trust the great body of candid Friends in America will regard the picture I have drawn as altogether within the bounds of truth.[54]

These two articles became the focal point of controversy and were later used as prime reasons for his being deposed as a minister and member of the Society of Friends. We will examine them at greater length later in this study.[55]

In 1882, Iowa Yearly Meeting reported a total membership of 9,348 individuals.[56] Much of the increase in growth in the previous decade had come as a result of the revival movement.[57] But

with the growth had come increasing dissension. Joel Bean wrote
of the movement:

> The revival movement was now pressed forward with a new
> impulse with this extreme Evangelicalism which denied the
> Light of Christ within, and the possibility of salvation by any
> other means than the preachng of the Gospel. . . . There seem-
> ed to be a concerted effort on the part of the leaders to commit
> the Society to these views. Yearly Meetings were packed with
> visitors to propagate these doctrines. And what must seem
> strange to future historians, almost all the Western ministers
> were drawn into the popular currents, and accepted them. For
> some years we heard few sermons from visiting Evangelists
> that did not warn and inveigh against the heresy of the Inward
> Light, or the presence of Christ in any but the converted
> souls.[58]

Perhaps the most crushing of all the experiences occurred
when the revival came to West Branch Monthly Meeting, the
home meeting of Joel and Hannah Bean. The Springdale Quarterly Meeting was one of the most conservative within the Yearly
Meeting, and when an attempt was made to introduce revivalism,
West Branch became "the main point of attack and Revival aggression."[59] David Updegraff was called to West Branch to conduct a series of evangelistic meetings as the culmination of a succession of protracted meetings. In recounting the event, Joel
Bean wrote to Rufus Jones about David Updegraff:

> His magnetic personality and attractive theory of a short and
> easy way to perfection drew a large following. It was an open
> onslaught with a declared purpose to overcome what was claim-
> ed the false teaching of the past. In three weeks a work was
> wrought in that and Springdale meetings that has never been
> repaired. D.B.U. said that he "did not need to preach conver-
> sion at West Branch, for that had been attended to." At the
> end he said "the teaching of 30 years has been revolutionized in
> three weeks." A large number claimed the new, second exper-
> ience of entire Sanctification, and were committed by rising
> vote over and over again to the new doctrine taught. They re-
> garded themselves advanced to an experience and knowledge of
> the truth to which no others had attained. Three out of eight
> ministers of our meeting joined the crusade. Our meeting was
> left in confusion. Confidence was impaired. Fellowship was
> broken. Beloved neighbors became estranged. Elders of long
> standing—nursing Fathers and Mothers in the Church—Elders
> of sound judgment and discernment, were powerless to stem

the tide, and when the time came for reappointment were dropped because they could no longer be appointed in unity. Few could know what we passed through in that, and a few subsequent years, of the desertion of friends, of charges of unsoundness, and of heresy; and of practical displacement from position or part in the organization of our loved Society.[60]

It is obvious that the struggles had deeply taken their toll. Joel Bean had done all in his power to keep his home meeting together. He had deplored separations, feeling that the church should allow for great diversity of opinion and liberality of spirit within its ranks. But the changes ushered in by revivalism were too drastic for the conservative Friends. The old spirit of unity and fellowship was now gone, and rather than stay in the meeting filled with controversy or separate himself from the organized body of Friends, Joel Bean decided to join the westward migration to California. He wrote of his decision:

The strain wore me down, and preyed upon my health. And when the way opened for it, the pointing seemed clear to remove in 1882 to California, and to retire if possible from the conflict.[61]

5

Migration of Friends to California

AS THE VAST frontiers of America began to open for settlement, Quakers joined in the westward migration. We have seen how some of the Quaker pioneers had moved in a northwesterly direction and settled in Iowa. Other families migrated in a southwesterly direction and established homes and meetings in Kansas. There were many factors that provided the impetus for eastern Quakers to move westward.

The slavery question in the south undoubtedly caused many Quakers from North Carolina to migrate. Jones reminds us that the migration into Kansas by Friends, for example, was dominated by a moral purpose as a result of the Kansas-Nebraska Bill in 1854, which left the whole question of slavery to be settled by popular vote in these particular territories.[1] The migration for others may have been an extension of the spiritual urge to reach into the unknown. Undoubtedly for most, the reasons may have been purely economic. The fertile lands of the west offered economic promise to a largely rural people. The ties to eastern settlements of Quakers were never really severed by the pioneers; rather, a spirit of expansion characterized much of the migration.

It must not be presumed that the pioneer spirit was universal among Friends. Many older meetings were reluctant to see their membership depleted by the migrations. Their reluctance was soon duplicated by many western meetings who saw their

63

members continue farther west. There came a time when "the incoming migration from the East ceased to equal the continued movement of the Quakers to the farther West and the effect . . . was disheartening."[2] From Kansas and Iowa, hundreds of families moved to the Pacific coast, following the lure of Oregon and California. Myron Goldsmith has carefully documented and traced the founding of Quakerism in the northwest,[3] and it is not in the province of this study to deal with that phase of the continued westward migration of Quakers. It is important to note, however, the movement of Friends, both Orthodox and Hicksite, into California.

California had begun with an Indian society. Superimposed upon this foundation, the Spaniards had extended the limits of their empire. Following a brief Mexican period, the territory was annexed to the United States. Pioneer settlers began to move into California in increasing numbers, using the overland trails and coming largely from the midwest. During this early period, prior to 1849, California took a back seat to Oregon in popularity, for migration records for the early forties show a preference to Oregon in the ratio of eight-to-one![4]

But this was soon to change. On January 24, 1848, James Marshall discovered gold while in the process of constructing a sawmill at Coloma on the American River. For five months the news was generally kept secret, and the furor for mining lay dormant. But by the middle of the year, California began to throb with the excitement of the gold discovery. Major towns became deserted as men rushed to take part in the diggings. The news soon spread to the eastern states and on December 5 President Polk took official notice of the discoveries in a message to Congress. This signaled the start of the now-famous stampede.

From all over the country, and abroad, the Forty-niners made their way to California by three major routes: overland by stage and wagon trains, and by sea around Cape Horn, or across the Panama isthmus. This worldwide interest in California "brought to an end the intellectual as well as physical isolation of the province. . . . Gold, without question, has influenced the state's history more than any other single factor."[5]

Quakers were not exempt from the gold fever. Many became Forty-niners and tried their hand at the diggings; few, however, were successful. But their participation in the westward migration signaled the entrance of Quakerism into California. Two distinct periods can be noted in these migrations. For the first twenty years, 1849-1869, those who traveled to California seemed to have been motivated primarily for economic reasons or by a spirit of adventure. After 1869 and following the Great Awakening in Quakerism, a new motivation appears. Deep-seated religious convictions and a renewed zeal for the mission of the church provided midwestern Quakers with the evangelical vision of extending the Society to the coast. To be sure, economic factors still played an important part, but now these factors were reinterpreted with more noble ideals.

In the course of this and the following chapter, we shall examine some of the trends and more notable examples of the Quaker migration to California. Prior to 1869, the sources of information are meager. The most important single document of this period, as we shall see, is the diary of Robert and Sarah Lindsey, English Quakers who traveled extensively among Friends in California in 1859 and 1860.[6] In addition, however, accounts are available of some of the Quaker Forty-niners and fortune seekers.

Following 1869, sources of information are more readily available. In 1873, the San Jose Monthly Meeting was formally established by Iowa Yearly Meeting, and records were kept of the growth of the Society. The arrival of Joel and Hannah Bean in San Jose in 1882 is an important phase of this second period of Quaker migration to California.

Early Migration of Friends—1849-1869

Quaker Forty-niners

Immediately following the discovery of gold, numbers of Friends from the United States and England set out for the new land of promise in California. Some headed for the gold fields, while others contented themselves with agriculture or business. Many of the Quaker miners became discouraged and soon returned to homes in the east. An English Quaker, John Candler, and his wife were traveling from Jamaica to the North American mainland in 1850 and recorded some of the accounts of their fellow passengers:

1850. 6 mo. 18ff. Had much conversation with some of our fellow passengers from California and the isthmus of Panama Several on board are returning from California with plenty of gold in their trunks, which they have acquired by hard labor and under many severe privations, at the gold mines; others with gold acquired by trading and speculation; and not a few weary, disgusted, sick, and almost destitute. "The grave yards grow faster in California than the towns," said one of the returning wanderers to me. I asked him what induced him to go there, and, having gone, why he returned so soon. He went, he said, hoping, like many others, to get money and do himself good, but he did not succeed as he expected, and seeing how badly the people conducted themselves he thought if he staid there, he should lose all moral principle and become like the rest. It was wonderful, he said, how soon the moral perceptions became deadened in such a society of adventurers. He was himself a "Friend," a member of the Hicksite persuasion; he had been brought up to hate all war and aggression, but he thought that he could now shoot a man dead without remorse, if he attempted to rob him of gold, or do him irreparable injury. "On the First Day," I use his words, "the people abandoned themselves to gambling and cockfighting."[7]

Another account was given of a young Quaker who left Lynn, Massachusetts, against the advice of his minister and traveled more than 5,000 miles overland to the diggings in California. On his return to Massachusetts, he reported to John Candler that only eight of the original party of forty-seven men remained at the gold mines, and the others "were either dead or dispersed." He confided that if "he got safe home, he would never venture on such an expedition again."[8]

Another Quaker, Richard Pancoast, has left a detailed account of his adventures in the gold mining fields of California.[9] In 1840, he left Philadelphia for St. Louis. Bad luck, however, seemed to dominate his business ventures in the midwest. An attempt at the drug business failed; a boat that he helped purchase to ply the riverways became severely damaged; debts continued to mount. In April, 1849, he resolved to join the caravans crossing the plains from St. Joseph and head for the gold mines of California. He wrote, "Here I was again, about to plunge into a Sea of Troubles, with the distant hope that Fortune lay in the path before me."[10]

Pancoast joined a party headed for California by way of the Santa Fe, Rio Grande and Gila rivers to southern California. After almost nine months of travel, he passed through the Cajon Pass of the San Bernardino Mountains and headed for Los Angeles, finding it to be a "dreamy old Spanish Town, more animated than some others on account of the presence of numerous Emigrants."[11] Although he felt it "possessed a most salubrious climate, and was surrounded by some of the most beautiful and fertile land on the Globe,"[12] he continued his journey to the gold fields, arriving at the Mariposa Mines in a snow storm on February 15, 1850.[13]

His first reaction to the diggings was one of discouragement. The lack of facilities, the high prices, and the mud made the "whole aspect so repulsive and dismal" that he returned to his camp sick at heart with the prospect of the new enterprise.[14] During the next three years, he worked at a number of mining locations, accumulating varying amounts of gold, which was then often lost on unprofitable enterprises. Finally, in 1854 he began his return trip to Philadelphia, arriving on April 28, unrecognizable by most of his friends after fourteen years of wandering.

In her **Diary**, Sarah Lindsey makes mention of a number of Quakers who were still engaged in the mining fields five years later in 1859, and concluded that "they have not been fortunate and seem only just able to keep themselves."[15] In a comment on her visit to the northern mining district, she wrote,

Few of the frds. who are at present engaged in mining in the different places where we have traveled seem to have been fortunate and several have lost instead of gained money in the end.[16]

Other Quaker Settlers

Not all of the Quakers who traveled to California during this early period, however, became gold miners. Opportunities in business and farming seemed more lucrative and promising than digging after the elusive gold. In 1849, William Sherman arrived in San Francisco from Ohio, via the Panama isthmus.

He soon established himself in business and became one of the few Quakers of prominence in the city.[17]

James and Hannah Lloyd Neal were married in Philadelphia in 1850 and then traveled to San Francisco, where they settled. James Bean, brother of Joel, wrote that the Neals gathered a few Friends together and held several meetings for worship in their home during their first winter in California. No minister was present, however, and when the Neals moved in the spring to another town, the meetings were discontinued.[18]

At about this time, several members of the Hobson family came from North Carolina to California. After working in the gold mines for a short while, David, Stephen, and Alfred settled in San Jose, where they appeared to have prospered more from real estate than gold.[19] By 1855, the Hobsons were holding meetings in a rented hall with Alfred Hobson, Sr., and another brother Jesse.[20] These meetings were informal public meetings and prepared the way for the establishment of the first regular meeting within the next decade. The Hobsons were part of the Quaker migration from Yadkin County, North Carolina. A large number of these southern Friends settled in Indiana and Ohio, but others came on to Iowa and to the Pacific coast.

Some Quakers traveled even farther to come to California. For example, John and Thomas Bevan came to San Francisco from England and established a drugstore in the city. The brothers had originally studied at Ackworth School in England and then traveled to South America to join their parents. From South America they went to California and began their business. Thomas built a brick house in the suburb of the city, providing a welcome home for Quaker visitors.[21]

The Lindsey **Diary** also makes reference to other Quaker settlers in the Bay area. Dr. and Mrs. Hardy had come from the Hawaiian Islands;[22] the Henry Gibbons family and the Norris Palmer family were Hicksite Quakers and had homes in the Oakland area;[23] Dr. McClure and his family lived in Redwood City. He had come to San Francisco "some years ago, and being successful as a tradesman, in about three years he cleared $40,000, but soon lost it again by speculation."[24]

The Lindsey Visit, 1859-1860

Reference in this chapter already to Robert and Sarah Lindsey suggests the importance of their visit to California. An accurate and detailed account of their journeys along the Pacific coast is well-preserved and supplies valuable information about the migration and settlement of Friends in California during this period.[25] Their visit not only promoted great interest in the west among eastern and English Quakers, but it provided rich inspiration and encouragement to the scattered members of the Society of Friends.

Robert and Sarah Lindsey were members of London Yearly Meeting and made a number of extensive journeys to preach the Gospel in various parts of the world. In 1857, they received a minute to visit "all the isolated families of Friends in the world,"[26] and set sail for the North American continent.

During the course of the next three years, they visited Friends in the populated eastern areas, ministered effectively in the midwest,[27] and then set sail for California in June, 1859, from New York City. The visits of these English Quakers were of profound importance to American Quakerism,[28] and characterized the evangelical concern of Friends in England for their brethren in America. A midwestern Quaker who traveled with the Lindseys on their visit to the midwest, Benajah W. Hiatt of Kansas, wrote of them: "Robert was a fine minister and Sarah was a Pro(p)hettes for her sermons have all proven true in that line. They had many Converts wherever we held meetings."[29]

The Lindseys arrived in San Francisco on July 15, 1859, traveling the 5,890 miles from New York via the Panama in twenty-five days. Sarah described the city as a

most singular looking place, its extent being about three miles by three and a half. Its population is 70,000. It is a succession of hills and valleys. Sometimes in going up the hills we are up to the ankles in sand, and then come abruptly upon a solid surface like hard rock, but it is only the hard earth upon which even the heavy rain seems to have little effect.[30]

Many of the streets in this city are laid with planks over the shallow water, and the sides of the sand hills. Many of the latter have been taken down and are still decreasing. Windmills are very numerous, and are found convenient in raising water which is in great demand in the dry season for watering the gardens.[31]

Robert and Sarah made the International Hotel their head-quarters for the next four months while visiting Friends in various parts of the interior. Their visit seemed to have been well-publicized in the press. Sarah wrote, "Our arrival in this State having been announced in the newspapers, and also by private letters, we do not seem to require much introduction."[32] In addition to the private visits they had with Friends and numbers of non-Friends, the Lindseys held public meetings wherever they traveled. On July 17, 1859, the first service to be conducted in California by Friends ministers was held in San Francisco.[33] Sarah Lindsey wrote:

> Arrangements having been made for us to sit a few hours with a few persons connected with our Society at James Neal's this morning, 20 persons assembled. The solemnizing presence of the Lord was spread over us, and I was constrained to supplicate at His holy foot stool. My dear husband had good service, particularly for the encouragement of some who had been mercifully visited with the day spring from on high in the morning of life, who were invited once more to review their covenant with Him by resigning themselves to his disposal, who could revive His own work in their hearts in the midst of the years, and enable them to put away strange gods. Thomas Bevan supplicated in a broken manner for the Lord's blessing. I believe many of our hearts were contrited, and we had cause to set upon Ebenezer to the Lord's praise. Our company seemed to be very respectable persons from various parts of the world, who were most kindly disposed to us poor wanderers having no certain dwelling place.[34]

A week later, a second meeting was held with over forty persons in attendance, including some Hicksite Friends. It was the first meeting that many of the attenders had participated in for several years, and "the privilege seemed to be duly appreciated."[35] Wherever the Lindseys traveled, they were called upon to minister. Often private and intimate meetings were held to encourage the Friends, followed by large and well-attended public meetings. These latter meetings were usually held in the town halls or frequently in local Methodist or Congregational churches. Their messages were simple and direct. They proclaimed the

Gospel of Jesus Christ and pointed the way to redemption and salvation through Him. Not all Friends, however, agreed with their message. The **Diary** makes several references to a Sarah Pearson who often visited their meetings in San Francisco. On July 31, the third meeting for worship was held in the Town Hall with about one hundred and fifty persons present. Following the message by Robert Lindsey, Sarah Pearson began to speak "in a very excited manner and with much gesture," disagreeing with what had been said.[36] Several weeks later, the **Diary** recorded an interview between the two Sarahs:

> Sarah Pearson, a Hicksite, whom I mentioned in a former letter as having been intrusive in one of our meetings, called upon us yesterday, accompanied by another woman holding similar views, and wished to know if the friends intended to keep up meetings when we were not in the City. During our conversation they expressed their belief that Jesus Christ was only a man, and that his mission was confined to the Jews, and that we received no benefit from either his sufferings or death, etc., etc. We were much shocked to hear such doctrines advanced, and expressed our entire disunity therewith. But whilst denying the only foundation upon which the Christian builds his hopes of salvation, S. P. professes to be guided by an inward light, and to hold communion with George Fox, and other spirits of just men made perfect. She is one of those called spiritualists. The friends here are just as much opposed to S. P.'s views as ourselves, and have no unity with her, but fear she may trouble them as she seems to have a great desire to preach, and propagate her unsound doctrines.[37]

While they were in the San Francisco area, a variety of public meetings were held. On August 3, the Lindseys traveled with John Bevan to a School of Industry "lately established as an asylum for destitute and vagabond boys." Twenty-three boys, ranging in age from ten to fifteen, were gathered in the dining room to meet and hear the Lindseys.[38] On another occasion they visited San Quentin prison, where over five hundred men and three women were kept under armed guard. Sarah was deeply impressed with the visit and wrote:

> We had a meeting with the prisoners in their dining room this morning. Your dear Father addressed them at some length. Great quietude prevailed, and I believe some hearts were ten-

dered, whilst the gospel message of reconciliation thro' repentance toward God, and faith in our Lord and Savior Jesus Christ was enlarged upon. My heart was affected in looking over the assembled multitude which included many who might truly be called the offscouring of the earth. There were Chinese, Indians, Africans, Mexicans, Spaniards, Italians, Englishmen, and I suppose other nations, suffering the penalty of the law, and the clanking of the chains with which some were loaded, impressed my mind with mingled feelings. . . .[39]

In addition to their preaching ministry, the Lindseys performed a lasting service by distributing books. Over 1,500 volumes had been supplied by friends in New York and Philadelphia for distribution in California, in addition to a large number of books and tracts that had been sent from London.[40] These books were stored in a fireproof building being used by Jacob Underhill, a Quaker, for a hardware store.[41] Many hours were spent in sorting and distributing the books. Volumes were placed in the Young Men's Christian Association, in local libraries, in the School of Industry, in private collections, and were distributed widely among those who indicated an interest in Christianity or in Quakerism.

From San Francisco, the Lindseys traveled to the surrounding towns and villages, seeking out every Quaker in the area. In Redwood City they met Dr. McClure, who arranged a public meeting for them.[42] In Santa Clara they met two Quakers, Robert Reave and the wife of Dr. Scott. While conducting a public meeting in the Methodist church, they experienced their first earthquake. The **Diary** records the event:

Whilst the tracts were being distributed, there was a noise not unlike thunder, and the people jumped up, opened the door, and many rushed out. At first I thought someone had fallen down in a fit but I heard a call to the people to keep their seats, there being no cause for fear. We were informed that there had been a shock of an earthquake, but we were not sensible of it.[43]

Following their meeting in Santa Clara, Robert Reave drove the Lindseys "thro' an avenue of willows planted in former times by the Spaniards to San Jose, a busy and improving little city."[44] Here they were the guests of Asa Vestal and his family and were delighted and amazed at the abundant vineyards and productive

gardens. Stephen and Portia Thorne were Quakers who also lived
in the area and befriended the Lindseys. Sarah wrote, "We have
not met with greater kindness anywhere than from persons
whom we have been with during the past week."[45]

San Jose was to become an important center for Friends,
and the first meeting conducted by the Lindseys in the city was
perhaps prophetic of the interest in Quakerism by residents of
the area. The **Diary** records this account:

> Some who have been separated from our Society for years feel
> their attachment renewed, and are much pleased to attend a
> friends' meeting held in gospel simplicity, being tired with
> forms and ceremonies of religion. In the evening attended an
> appointed meeting in the Town Hall, which was well filled,
> and proved satisfactory. At the close we were greeted by
> several persons who thought they had a claim upon us. One
> young woman was from Bristol in England. . . .[46]

Asa Vestal himself was a member of the Methodist Church,
but his father was a birthright Quaker and was disowned for
marrying outside of Friends. The impression that the Lindseys
made upon Asa Vestal was undoubtedly of importance in opening
the way for Friends in San Jose. Sarah wrote,

> Tired of the empty forms and ceremonies of religion, our
> friend seems prepared to join our Society, and expressed his
> intention to invite those around him who are connected with us
> to hold meetings in his home."[47]

On August 16, the Lindseys took leave of Asa Vestal and his
family and headed back to San Francisco. Their hearts were
burdened for the ministry of Friends in California and Sarah
Lindsey recorded her concern in these words:

> Truly the fields are white unto harvest, but the laborers are
> few. If some consistent and well concerned friends would come
> and settle in this State, I believe there are persons in various
> localities who would be prepared to join them.[48]

But it was almost twenty years before any significant migration
of Friends was to meet the challenge presented by the Lindseys.

On August 31, Robert and Sarah Lindsey left San Francisco for their first extended visit into the California interior. They
crossed the Bay by steamboat and took a stage coach seventy-
five miles to Stockton, "a neat and increasing city."[49] From here

they ventured still another day's journey to the mining districts of San Andreas and the famed Angels Camp. Their first impression was one of disappointment:

> On descending a steep hill, the gold mines opened to our view. Some Chinese were washing the gravel in a ditch, others were engaged in emptying the drains. Flumes are brought from the hills across the valleys, conveying water from the springs in the mountains. The soil looks red. As we approached the town of San Andreas, we were in no wise favorably impressed with its appearance, the hillsides being covered with small huts. . . .[50]

At Angels Camp they held a public meeting in a schoolhouse where many undoubtedly came to hear the visitors from England and to see the novelty of a woman minister. The meeting was

> well attended by all classes, every seat appearing to be filled and some outside listening at the open windows. . . . The people were remarkably quiet from beginning to end. Many were present who were not in the habit of attending any place of worship.[51]

Many individuals discussed Quakerism with the Lindseys while they were in the area, and as was their custom, a carefully selected group of books and tracts was left with the schoolmaster, who was formerly from London. A side trip to visit the Big Trees of Calaveras County brought joy and rest to them. Before returning to Stockton, meetings were held in Valecito, Columbia, Sonora, and Knights Ferry. Whenever they spoke they were warmly received. Sarah Lindsey testified, "Thus from day to day, the Lord goes before us and opens the way in the minds of the people."[52] After two weeks of traveling and ministering the Gospel, the Lindseys returned again to San Francisco.

The next extended trip was to Sacramento and the Feather River mines. On September 28, they boarded a boat for the one hundred twenty-five mile trip to the capital. A number of Friends lived in the area, most of them "connected with the Hicksites," but they were graciously received and made welcome.[53] An interesting entry in the **Diary** records Sarah Lindsey's impressions of the many Chinese who were living and working in Sacramento. She wrote:

> Some of the Chinamen make good house servants. Many of these take in washing at their own houses. They have a dis-

agreeable plan for dampening the clothes, which is performed by filling the mouth with water and squirting it upon them. When ironing they use a pan with a long handle, filled with charcoal. The bottom of the pan is of brass. . . . The dress of the sexes is much alike. They wear wide trousers, and instead of a coat, a tight fitting smock made of coarse cloth or lashing. . . . The hair is shaved off the back and front of the head, while that in the center is allowed to grow very long and is plaited. A silk tassel is added to the extremity, which reaches very nearly to the heels. This is a badge of which they seem quite proud and very few would cut their hair off on any account; when activity is engaged in, it is wound round the head. . . . It is reported that most of the Chinese who are in this country are the slaves of the merchants; their habits are dirty and disagreeable, and they generally inhabit the meanest dwellings.[54]

From Sacramento the Lindseys traveled to the Feather River mining districts, visiting Marysville, Comptonville, Downieville, Nevada City, and Grass Valley. At each town they met those who were Quakers or who had been acquainted with Quakerism and held public meetings. At Grass Valley, they had an interesting visit with Alonzo and Mary Delano, who recounted for them their pioneering experiences and gave them a book that they had published.[55] Gold mining was extensively carried on in this area and provided a great deal of interest to Robert and Sarah Lindsey. The **Diary** records this brief description of the mining process:

I can only give you a faint idea of the process: suffice it to say that water is brought here in flumes or iron pipes a distance of 20 miles, and passing thro' hose, it is poured against the hillsides, which displaces both the stones and gravel, the whole of which passes into the flumes, (which are deep wooden dishes) and so constructed that the gold is separated from the mass by means of quicksilver, and falls into the bottom of the flume, the water forcing the gravel and stones into the ravine below. On looking into one of the flumes we were informed that 3,000 dollars worth of gold had been deposited in it in nine days time. These mines are worked by companies, some of whom have to pay 100 dollars a day for the use of water. The wages for common workmen are 3 or 3½ dollars per day, and those who are engaged underground have more. Altho' surrounded by rich treasures, I did not observe one grain of gold, it being incorporated with the earth, and only separated by the process before spoken of.[56]

The Lindseys also visited Folsom, riding from Sacramento on the only railroad in the State, and conducted meetings in Placerville, Dutch Flatt, and Auburn. Upon their return to Sacramento, a significant public meeting was held on November 9, attended by a reporter from the local newspaper. Sarah Lindsey records the occasion in these words:

> On ascending a raised platform, we noticed a young man seated opposite to us, before whom a small table was placed, containing writing materials. On Father's going to him to ask why he was in such a position, he replied that he was sent by the editors of a newspaper to note down what was said, and as he seemed to think he must obey his orders, he was requested to take a more private seat, when he at once removed to one side.[57]

The **Sacramento Daily Union** printed Robert Lindsey's entire sermon on its front page two days later, and gave this account of the meeting:

> Notwithstanding the inclemency of the weather, there were probably two hundred persons in attendance at the Congregational Church last evening in response to the call of Robert Lindsey and wife, travelling ministers of the Society of Friends or Quakers. The audience was addressed at considerable length by Robert Lindsey, who subsequently offered a prayer, and, after distributing, with the assistance of others, religious tracts to all present, delivered an impressive benediction, whereupon the audience dispersed.[58]

On December 18, the Lindseys left San Francisco for an extended visit into the northwest, meeting Quakers in Oregon, Washington, and Canada. On March 24, they set sail for the Hawaiian Islands, returning to San Francisco four months later. Finally, on August 16, 1860, Robert and Sarah Lindsey boarded the **Lizzie Spalding** on their final departure from the United States and began their homeward journey to England by way of Melbourne, Australia.

The Lindseys had a unique opportunity to visit with and observe Quakers in California. Few members of the Society of Friends had not come in contact with them, and therefore they were in a position to comment on the condition of Quakerism within the State. By and large, the **Diary** indicates that they found a scattered, lonely, financially poor, and spiritually needy people. Most of the Quakers had not struck it rich in the gold strikes; indeed, many were very discouraged. A typical example was the young Quaker from Monte Christo who attended the Lindsey meeting in Downieville and reported to them that

> he came out with the prospect of remaining three years in the State, but had now been seven years. He compared the chances in mining to a lottery, but he had not succeeded in getting a prize, and said he hated to return home no better off than when he came.[59]

Fire, scarlet fever epidemics, financial reverses, all seemed to bring discouragement to those who were trying to make a living at the mines. Those who turned to farming and business, however, were more prosperous and contented with life in California.

Of deepest concern to the Lindseys was the lack of spiritual vitality among the isolated and scattered Quakers. Most did not attend any place of worship, and even where several Quaker families had settled, few had enough initiative to start a regular meeting for worship. Many had compromised their Quakerly testimonies and had become unconcerned about their witness. Note, for example, the observation of Sarah Lindsey regarding the Friends in Sacramento:

> The Friends and those connected with them in this city are of a mixed class, more than half of them having been connected with what are called Hicksite and very few of those called Orthodox have any appearance of friends, many having launched out into the fashions of the world, and laid aside the plain scripture language, yet divers retain a love and esteem for our principles, who have not courage to carry them out in the face of the world. Had it not been for this falling back, this shrinking from the cross of Christ in those whom the Lord hath called, and would also have chosen, our little church would have shone more brightly. . . .[60]

The visit of the Lindseys did revive much interest in the work of Friends, but it was not enough to stem the tide of general indifference. A lack of vital leadership and religious zeal must account for the slow growth of Quakerism in California during this early period. A significant exception was the group of Friends in San Jose, who within a few years established the first regular meeting for worship in California. Robert and

Sarah Lindsey arrived home in England in the summer of 1861. A few months later, in November, Robert suffered a stroke and was forced to curtail his work on behalf of Friends. He died near Manchester on June 20, 1863.[61] Sarah's own health became very frail and she too was forced to cease from active work. She died at Worcester on March 17, 1867.[62]

The Bean Visit, 1861

Shortly after the Robert Lindseys had left for Australia, Joel and Hannah Bean visited San Francisco and the Bay area. They were headed for the Hawaiian Islands with a minute from Indiana Yearly Meeting and were delayed in California while waiting for a boat to take them across the Pacific. In San Francisco, they were welcomed by William Sherman, Dr. Hardy, and other Friends and conducted a meeting in the home of William Sherman. The Beans also visited and ministered in San Jose, little realizing that in twenty years they would leave Iowa to make their permanent home within its pleasant surroundings. There is evidence to substantiate the later statement of James Bean that "Robert Lindsey and Joel Bean were the first ministers to hold Friends' meetings in California."[63]

Establishing the San Jose Meeting, 1861-1866

In the history of San Jose, written by McMurry and James, the following statement appears: "The Coast's first Society of Friends was formed here in 1861 by Jesse and David Hobson and met in members' homes."[64] The influence of the Lindsey and Bean visits undoubtedly prompted the establishment of a regular meeting for worship. Within a few years, a colporteur for the American Tract Society, Abel Bond, visited the Hobsons and encouraged them to build a meetinghouse.[65] Abel Bond had been acquainted with the Hobsons in North Carolina and remained with them during the winter of 1865-1866, helping to build the modest structure. The first meeting was held in the new meetinghouse in June, 1866.[66]

The meetinghouse was located on the north corner of Ninth and St. John Streets on a small lot, eighty feet by eighty feet. The records of the County Recorder of Santa Clara County show that on February 2, 1867, the property was deeded to seven Quakers, who were named "Trustees for the Society of Friends," namely: Jesse Hobson, John Barker, David Hobson, William C. Ables, David I. Hobson, Thomas Henry Knowles, and Stephen Thorne.[67] For many years they had no resident ministers, yet the meetings were well-attended, both by members and nonmembers.[68] In 1883, the property was sold to the Methodist Church.[69]

Later Migration of Friends—1869-1882

The year 1869 becomes a convenient date to note the demarcation between the periods of Quaker migration to California. On May 10, 1869, the final gold spike was driven into the rails at Promontory, Utah, and the lines of the Union Pacific and Central Pacific Railroads were joined. For the first time, a new and far more convenient way of travel was opened to the west. John Caughey says of this achievement:

> . . . the Pacific railroad remains one of the epochal developments in western history. Perhaps even more significantly than the discovery of gold, it marked the end of an old era and the beginning of a new. . . . What California was to lose in provincialism was to be more than compensated for in stimulus to new and greater attainments. The Pacific railroad heralded transformation of California and the West.[70]

Economic reasons still supplied motivation to Friends to travel westward to the "land of promise," but following the beginning of the Great Awakening in Quakerism, a new and deeper motivation for migration appears. A religious zeal and missionary vision had now challenged the thinking of midwestern Quakers, many of whom were willing to commit themselves in dedicated pioneering. In 1869, James Canney, formerly from New England, came from Minnesota to San Jose, followed in a few years by the remainder of the family, including his wife, Jane, his daughter, Elvira, and her husband, William Ward.[71]

On November 11, 1871, William Hobson left Union, Iowa, for California. William Hobson had a burden to establish a Friends settlement in the west, and headed first for a visit with his brothers in San Jose. During the three months that he spent with Friends in San Jose, he worshiped regularly with them, encouraging them with his testimony, visited with numerous fami-

lies in the area, distributed literature, and helped establish a
First-Day school.[72] However, he considered California unsuitable
for what he had in mind and ultimately established a settlement
of Friends in the Chehalem Valley of Oregon in 1875. David
Hobson loaned a substantial sum of money to his brother William
in order that he could make this journey into the northwest.
Professor Goldsmith therefore suggests that since David Hobson
had received his start in California as a gold miner during the
Gold Rush, "it can therefore be said that a link exists between the
discovery of gold in California and the founding of Quakerism in
Oregon."[73]

In 1873, the Honey Creek Quarterly Meeting of Iowa Yearly Meeting officially recognized San Jose as a monthly meeting.
Since it was the custom of many Friends, when members moved
beyond the limits of their monthly meeting, to send transfer of
membership certificates to the nearest monthly meeting to the
place where they had newly settled, San Jose Monthly Meeting
received many certificates of membership for some Friends who
did not live within hundreds of miles and never did see San Jose.
San Jose was the only monthly meeting of Friends on the Pacific
coast, and thus the nominal membership of the small group was
increased.[74] When the meeting was organized, James Canney was
named as clerk and his wife, Jane M. Canney, was named as the
first pastor of a Friends meeting in California.[75]

In 1873, the religious concern of Friends for California was
minuted by Iowa Yearly Meeting. After amending the Discipline
for those who were to make religious visits in the far west,[76] the
report of the Yearly Meeting Ministers and Elders contained
references to several individuals who were encouraged to travel
to the west. Thomas and Mary B. Pinkham were liberated to
"sojourn for a time in California, Oregon and Washington territory . . . in the service of the gospel."[77] John S. Bond was also
liberated "for religious service in the gospel in California, Oregon, Washington territory and other places in the far West,
particularly in some parts among the miners in the mountains."[78]

In his paper, James Bean records the advent of other Quaker families to San Jose. John Bell came from Indiana in 1876 with

his sister Wilhelmina.[79] Sarah P. Morrison, also of Indiana, spent two months in San Jose in 1879 and organized the first Women's Christian Temperance Union (WCTU) chapter among California Quakers.[80] Still later, Benjamin and George Jones, father and son from New England, visited the San Jose meeting and proved to be a blessing to its members.[81]

Friends were also beginning now to migrate to southern California. This aspect of the migration will be dealt with more fully in a subsequent chapter;[82] suffice it at this time to indicate the arrival in 1876 of Lawson D. Hollingsworth and his wife, Lucinda, who settled in the area of Pasadena. They operated a grocery store in which their son, H. T. Hollingsworth (later mayor of Los Angeles) kept the local post office.[83] Three years later, in 1879, Micajah D. Johnson came to the valley and subsequently served as city treasurer of Los Angeles.[84] In the same year, a group of Quakers came from Pelham, Canada, to settle in Alamitos.

Henry and Mary Ann Hansler and their children and James Swayze led this migration to southern California, followed the next year by John and Susan Beckett and their niece, and Alfred and Mercy Beckett and their three daughters.[85] These Canadian Quakers started a First-Day school in the Alamitos schoolhouse, where for several years Susan Beckett served as superintendent, with the others as teachers and helpers.[86] This work was the forerunner of an active meeting that was established fifteen years later.

This, then, is the picture of Quakerism in California in 1882, the year Joel and Hannah Bean left Iowa for San Jose. Revivalism had transformed the Society of Friends, and Joel Bean felt constrained to remove himself from the revolt of younger Friends against the older traditions and practices. Though far from the centers of Quakerism, Joel and Hannah entered with zeal into their new interests and were quickly recognized as leaders. His influence was far-reaching, and the ultimate development of the Society of Friends in California went even beyond his expectation. This is the aspect of the story to which now we turn.

6

Controversy and
Innovation in the West

THE UNITY AND FELLOWSHIP that once existed in the West
Branch Meeting in Iowa had now gone. Following the impact of
revivalism into this Quaker community and the impact of the
preaching of David Updegraff, the church had become divided
over issues both theological and practical. Those who insisted upon
the traditional ways of worship in silence soon withdrew and
began their own meeting in harmony with other Conservative
Friends in Iowa. Not only was the community divided, however;
even families were torn apart. Mildred Crew Brooke reflected
upon her childhood experiences and wrote:

> Gone were the peaceful, quiet hours of the simple services, and
> gone were the friendly feelings among old and young. . . . In
> all cases young people, that is, the unmarried ones, went with
> their parents; young married couples, supposedly having minds
> of their own, did not necessarily follow their parents, and
> strained relations in families consequently arose. The gather-
> ings on First Day afternoons were apt to end in altercations on
> religious subjects, causing the women to weep long into the
> night.[1]

The strain of the threatening division and faction weighed
heavily upon Joel and Hannah Bean, and when the opportunity
came to leave Iowa for California, they felt this would be the best
way to avoid further involvement in a distasteful situation.
Little did they realize that the controversy would even follow
them to the west coast! In 1882, the decision to relocate was made,

the family property sold, the journey to California begun. Twenty years earlier the Beans had traveled to San Francisco by steamer from New York, but now the transcontinental railroad afforded a quicker and more convenient way of travel. James Bean, the brother of Joel, had corresponded with John Bell of San Jose and purchased a home on Chapman Street.[2] This was the destination of the two brothers, their families, and their mother. Old ties were severed and final goodbyes were said as the families boarded the train to take them to their new home. The roots had grown deep in Iowa, and leaving friends, former students, fellow ministers and neighbors was no easy task. Mildred Crew Brooke recalls the event in these words:

> When the time of their departure drew near, a tourist car was held on the railroad siding and its prospective occupants were given several days in which to furnish their respective compartments. We visited the car one day, and Cathie, the younger of the Beans' two daughters, showed us how they curtained off their rooms in the end of the car and had a place to eat and a place to sleep.[3]

San Jose eagerly awaited the arrival of the Bean families. The Monthly Meeting that had been established in 1873 as a subordinate meeting to Honey Creek Monthly Meeting in Iowa had experienced difficulty in maintaining a growing and unified fellowship. It was hoped that the coming of such a distinguished family of Friends would give encouragement to the Meeting. After their arrival in San Jose, the Bean families lived together for awhile in the Chapman Street house until James Bean could make arrangements to purchase "the Saunders house on The Alameda, a short distance north of Newhall Street."[4] The Joel Bean residence was then later enlarged with new rooms on the north, providing quarters for Elizabeth Bean, called affectionately "Grandma Great."[5]

Joel and James attended the Ninth Street Meeting regularly with their families and quickly began to give much-needed encouragement and leadership to the California Quakers. But the ministry and influence of Joel Bean was far-reaching, not merely local. He continued to write and to preach and was constantly in demand as a speaker.

Instead of retiring from the national scene, Joel Bean was soon thrust again into the conflict with the revivalists. In the fall of 1882, shortly after his arrival in California, Joel Bean was urged by Isaac Sharp to visit Friends across America with him. Isaac Sharp was an English Quaker and had arrived in San Francisco from Australia with the "desire, approved by English Friends" for Joel Bean to become his traveling companion.

Joel Bean later wrote to Rufus Jones, "I felt it right to join him and was liberated by our Mo. Mtg. here [note: in San Jose], and went with him thro' portions of most of the yearly meetings in our Country."[6] Joel spoke frequently in the appointed meetings that were held in many parts of the nation, and used the opportunity to speak of his concerns for the Society of Friends.[7] In some areas, however, their reception was less than cordial. Joel Bean wrote:

> Strenuous efforts were made by Authorities in Iowa to stop me on the way, but without avail, as I was duly liberated by my own Mo. Mtg. and authorized by the choice of English Friends. The effort was decisively met by Isaac Sharp who said "Joel Bean sits at my side with a clear certificate of the unity of his mo. mtg. and the choice and entire approval of English Friends, **and you** can't stop him."[8]

By now the effects of revivalism among American Quakers was being widely publicized. Articles in **The British Friend** and in **The Friend** (London) were read and circulated. Some English Friends began to call for a disassociation with those in America who had adopted the "new doctrines" and techniques. In a letter to the editor of **The British Friend**, Charles Thompson spoke the minds of many when he wrote:

> Friends of London Yearly Meeting, with the knowledge they possess, have . . . persistently ignored the fatal schism now rending asunder the (so called) Society of Friends in many of the American States. . . . Are we to continue to hold close relationship with Iowa when we are informed on authority upon which we can rely, how well-concerned Friends, some of whom we have seen here, are being dealt with by their discipline?[9]

The reference to "some of whom we have seen here" undoubtedly referred in part to Joel Bean. The problems of division in the western yearly meetings had become personalized, and Joel Bean was seen as the leader and martyr of the cause to maintain traditional Quakerism. Indeed, immediately following the article by Charles Thompson, **The British Friend** published a letter from Joel Bean. The tone of this letter conveys the deep burden and apprehension under which Joel Bean was laboring, and indicates the breadth of his reaction to the effects of revivalism. Although Joel Bean had left Iowa to "retire if possible from the conflict," it is now obvious that there was no escape possible from a collision course, whose end seemed inevitable. Because this letter summarizes much of his feelings, and because it points to issues which brought division in San Jose, it is important to note the letter and its contents. Writing from San Jose, Joel Bean penned the following words to the editor of **The British Friend**:

> Dear Friend, Often has my heart been drawn to thee in sympathy and fellowship, when physical depression has compelled me to lay aside the pen. And as from month to month **The British Friend** has reached this distant coast, it has been read with deep interest which lives with us, in all that concerns the welfare of our people and the Church of God.
>
> I am prompted by thy last issue to express the joy I felt to see the place given in its columns for the "Voice from Iowa,"[10] presenting a different view of what Friends are passing through, from that which meets the readers of most of the published accounts—not that the exposure of evils and wrongs gives pleasure, only so far as a faithful witness to the **truth** requires, and that the oppressed, and the proscribed, and the outcast may have a hearing.
>
> As I have read, the reports of the Yearly Meetings this year, representing them as in a condition of great favor with the Lord and success in His work,[11] and knowing as I do so many places of suffering, and so many wrongs against brethren, like those in Springdale Monthly Meeting described in the moderate and candid letter of A. Crosbie, the question meets me over and over again, how is it if the Church is so alive and in sympathy with its Head, that there is not in the great bodies a heart to feel, a spirit to discern, an ear to hear, and a disposition to search out the causes of these things and to remove them?
>
> How is it that the perpetrators of these wrongs receive the right hand of fellowship, and are strengthened to press on in their course?

How is the burning desire to "save souls" and to send the glad tidings of the gospel to distant lands, to be reconciled with the indifference towards the thousands of the living members of the body who feel their services rejected, and the places they have long filled taken from them, on whose behalf we hear of no voice of appeal, or no visit of sympathy. And when it is known that so many of this class are the very salt of the earth, who have borne the burden and heat of the day, in the building up of many of the strongest meetings of the Society in our land, the sweet savour of whose Christian lives is owned with grateful love in the communities around them, their treatment at the hands of those who publish to the world a profession of "entire sanctification," and "perfect love," has brought a burden to the cause of Christ, and a strain upon the faith even of believers, which as yet have had little utterance save as a suppressed undertone of anguish amid the exultations and rejoicings of the multitudes. But they are heard on high; and the time must come when they will have a hearing in the body of our Lord on earth when His Spirit reigns. For these true mourners in Zion, in obscurity and loneliness, oftentimes have the token of the Savior's regard, the evidence of His watchful love being proportioned even in the day of trial, to the depths of proving through which they are called to go.

It is time that a trumpet voice should arouse our people to danger, when, hurried onward by a leagued leadership in many places, almost unbounded liberty is given to innovations upon the doctrines and the order of the Society, and the liberty of criticism and caution is suppressed to such a degree, that a paper like "The Issue," which appeared in **The British Friend** 2½ years ago, is not allowed to rest, until a Yearly Meeting condemnation of it (and of course of the writer of it) has been obtained.[12]

It is the sensitive repellance of inquiry and discussion regarding the **propriety** of new teaching and methods that has stilled the voice of dissent, until the harmony of meetings which have set aside the judgment of half their numbers, or made them withdraw altogether from the expression of judgment, is published as a remarkable evidence of divine favor.

What acquisition of numbers, unconvinced of our principles, can compensate for the loss of our most consistent members? What multiplicity of works can compensate for a degraded standard? And what glorying in sanctification can affect our fellow-Christians and our fellowmen like the humble leaven of holy lives and tender loving hearts?

A searching gaze is on us from those who see our walk. The flower of our youth who are finding their place and work in the generation following us are testing the value of the legacy we are leaving them.

In the midst of all the disorganization of systems, and the disheartening disclosure of human frailty, our Lord reigns over all, and carries forward His work in the world, and all that is of Him, and all that is like Him in the individual or associated lives of His children, will tell to his glory and the advancement of His Kingdom of Truth and Righteousness. —J.B.[13]

By the end of 1883, the lines of demarcation were clearly drawn. Friends in the midwest, particularly in Iowa and Kansas, were enjoying the fruits of the Great Awakening. Membership was increasing at an unhoped-for rate; the pastoral system had been established, and the voices of opposition were muffled in the flush of evangelical fervor. Revival came as a long overdue blessing to the Society of Friends, but as is often the case, with it came unwise and thoughtless acts of extremism. But what had been gained seemed to be so far superior to the former state of the church, Friends were willing to press for an extension of awakening in spite of its exigencies. On the other side stood Joel Bean, who now symbolized the opposition to the teachings and practices of the Revival. A once highly respected Friend in Iowa Yearly Meeting, his admonitions and pleas for caution were now disregarded. During the next fifteen years, the two factions clashed frequently, and the little, subordinate meeting at San Jose—once unknown and unnoticed—was thrust into the international spotlight as the scene of both controversy and innovation.

Schism in San Jose

On December 6, 1883, the San Jose Meetinghouse was sold to the Methodists. The reasons for the sale of the property are not clear; the attendance at services had fluctuated during the past decade, leadership had been scarce, ministers were few—these facts are known. But whether the sale of the property was for economic reasons, or whether the Bean controversy had already begun to take its toll, is not clear. Within three months, however, there is evidence of marked division among the membership. Joel and Hannah Bean insisted upon worship in the traditional patterns, without pastoral supervision. They consequently withdrew from the Meeting and began to hold services in Rutherford Hall, on the corner of Second and San Antonio Streets.[14] According to an entry in Joel Bean's **Diary**, the first meeting was held on Thursday, February 21, 1884.[15] The Joel Bean group, as it came to be called, met regularly on the second floor of Rutherford Hall in a room used by the local Masonic Lodge. On the first floor was located a saloon, which prompted James Bean to write later:

There are spirits above and spirits below,
There are spirits of love and spirits of woe.
The spirits above are the spirits of love,
And the spirits below are the spirits of woe.[16]

The feelings between these two groups of Quakers were deep and often bitter. The Joel Bean group was not recognized as Friends, and the San Jose Meeting, with its minister, was considered unorthodox and un-Quakerly. The very schism and separation that Joel Bean had left Iowa to avoid had followed him to San Jose!

Within a few months, the San Jose Meeting had secured new property as a meetinghouse on Stockton Avenue. On November 21, 1884, a deed was acquired by seven Quakers who served as trustees for the San Jose Society of Friends. The seven trustees named were Moses Mendenhall, Benjamin H. Jones, James Canney, William E. Ward, James Bean, George N. Jones, and David Hobson.[17] The appointment of James Bean as a trustee would seem to indicate some conciliatory attempts between the two groups.

Meanwhile, Joel Bean made plans to erect a meetinghouse for the use of his own group. Property on Morse Street was donated by James Bean, and on March 17, 1885, Joel and James purchased the lumber and began construction of the modest structure.[18] Six weeks later the building was completed, and on Sunday, April 26, 1885, the first meeting was held in the new meetinghouse.[19]

There now existed two groups of Friends in San Jose; and yet, because of the organizational procedures of Quakers, both groups were considered as members of the one San Jose Monthly Meeting, subordinate to Honey Creek Monthly Meeting of Iowa

Yearly Meeting. The obvious disintegration and division among San Jose Friends led to disciplinary action by Honey Creek Monthly Meeting. Joel Bean and his associates were committed to a nonpastoral meeting, and following the construction of a new meetinghouse, they made application to Honey Creek to be recognized as the College Park Monthly Meeting. The application was, however, denied and instead, the San Jose Monthly Meeting was dissolved on the ground that "the governing part of the monthly meeting is not sound in the doctrines of the Christian religion."[20] This action caused widespread alarm, both in America and in England, and because of its implications, must be examined carefully.

The Dissolvement of San Jose Monthly Meeting

In an article prepared for **The British Friend**, and reprinted the following month in **The Friend** (London), Joel Bean wrote, "There are two societies **within** our organization in nearly all the Yearly Meetings on this continent."[21] This was nowhere more evident than in the San Jose Monthly Meeting. And the reasons that Joel Bean gave were probably as true on the local level as on any Yearly Meeting level:

> It is not the result of occasional extravagances which could be easily remedied, nor of exceptional crudeness of teaching here and there which might be patiently treated, but of radical doctrinal differences and corresponding modes of worship and working, of greater magnitude than those which distinguish us from most other Christian denominations.[22]

The gradual process of separation that Joel Bean feared was underway throughout the Society of Friends became crystallized in San Jose. Although he deplored separation, and withdrew from Iowa in order to avoid it, yet his very presence and ministry in San Jose was enough to make the meeting suspect, and separation became the inevitable outcome.

When the San Jose Meetinghouse and property were sold to the Methodists in 1883, division arose among the membership as to the location and construction of a new place for worship. As we have noted, two meetinghouses were constructed by the faction groups: one on Stockton Avenue and one on Morse Street.

The application by the Morse Street Meeting (College Park) for recognition as a separate monthly meeting brought the matter to a head, and an investigation was begun by the Honey Creek Quarterly Meeting in Iowa. It soon became obvious, of course, that the immense distance between the parent meeting in Iowa and the subordinate meeting in San Jose precluded any personal inspection and interview by members of the committee. And so a technique, common to other denominational groups but new to Friends, was adopted—a questionnaire was sent to the members of the San Jose Meeting. The trend toward an understanding of Quakerism as having a basic standard of beliefs or declaration of faith becomes explicit in the manner in which Honey Creek Quarterly Meeting dealt with its subordinate meeting in San Jose.[23]

The appointed committee devised a set of six queries, "asking for direct and explicit answers 'yea' or 'nea' thereto, that we might judge understandingly of their condition relative to soundness of doctrine and loyalty to the Yearly Meeting."[24] The queries that were posed to San Jose Friends were as follows:

First—Are you in unity and sympathy with Iowa Yearly Meeting, of which Barclay Hinchman is Clerk?

Second—Do you unite with the Declaration of Faith recorded in the revised Book of Discipline of the said Yearly Meeting?

Third—Do you unite with the evangelistic work as directed by that Yearly Meeting?

Fourth—We ask in **particular**, Do you believe in the statement on the 22nd page of said Book of Discipline, that the Holy Spirit dwells only in the righteous?

Fifth—Do you believe in the Deity of the man Christ Jesus, whom the evangelists represent as the Son of God, born of the Virgin Mary?

Sixth—Do you believe the sacrifice of the life and of the literal blood of Jesus Christ which was shed on Calvary was and is a propitiation and atonement for sin?[25]

It must be made clear that although there was division within the San Jose Meeting and separate meetings for worship were being conducted, both the College Park and the Stockton Avenue groups were still united in any meeting for business. The leadership and influence of Joel Bean in the Meeting, however, had shaped the majority position. Consequently, the views represented in the answers to the queries reflected his thinking and guidance.

The answers that were sent by the San Jose Meeting were not satisfactory to the committee and were judged to be largely evasive. To the second query, San Jose responded that they believed "in the Declaration of Faith authorized by the universal acceptance of all the Yearly Meetings of our Society."[26] This answer was seen as both evasive and indefinite, for the committee did not know what was alluded to by "the Declaration of Faith authorized by the universal acceptance of all Yearly Meetings." To the third query, San Jose responded, "There has been no opposition to evangelistic work, and our members favor and encourage genuine revivals,"[27] which answer the committee also labeled evasive. The real problems, however, arose with the answers given to the fourth, fifth and sixth queries. To these queries, San Jose responded as follows:

Fourth—We have never heard the expression used in teaching by any of our members that the Holy Spirit "dwells" in the unrighteous. That the light and Spirit of Christ is in all men is believed and taught.

Fifth—We believe in the man Christ Jesus, whom the evangelist represents as the son of God, born of the Virgin Mary. That He is true God and perfect man, and in Him dwelleth all the fullness of the Godhead bodily. (Col. 2:9)

Sixth—We believe that the sacrifice of the life and blood of Christ, who died on the cross, was and is a propitiation or atonement for sin.[28]

The committee felt that the fourth answer was directly opposed to their declaration that "He dwelleth only in the righteous." This was an obvious reference, also, to the opposition of many Friends to Joel Bean's understanding of the "Inner Light."[29]

The fifth answer was held to be both evasive and ambiguous. "They do not say that they believe in the Deity of the man, but in the man only. . . . This savours of the Hicksite declaration that they believe in the Christ that was in the man Jesus, and that is in us."[30] The committee also felt that the sixth answer was evasive, claiming to know that at least one member of the

San Jose Meeting taught that the blood that cleanses the soul was spiritual and not literal. These answers led the committee to feel that the leaders of the San Jose Meeting were not sound in the doctrines of the Christian faith. Their recommendation to the Honey Creek Quarterly Meeting, duly considered and approved by it, was as follows:

> In view of their doctrine, disunity and practice, we are united in believing that they are disqualified for holding a Monthly Meeting profitably or reputably. We therefore propose that San Jose Monthly Meeting be discontinued, and the members attached to Honey Creek Monthly Meeting.[31]

The action of the Honey Creek Quarterly Meeting was a particular disqualification of Joel Bean's leadership. The disunity in the meeting was recognized, indicating the presence of minority views in opposition to those expressed by Joel Bean. By discontinuing the San Jose Meeting, Honey Creek Monthly Meeting now assumed the responsibilities for leadership in San Jose.

The public reaction to the discontinuation of the San Jose Meeting as a separate and independent monthly meeting was swift and widespread. The **Friends' Review** wrote that "the investigation was unwisely conducted and its result is very much regretted."[32] **The Friend** (London) reprinted the statements, as did **The Friend** (Philadelphia).[33]

In a letter to the editor of **The Friend** (London), James Backhouse of York, England, declared that the action of the Quarterly Meeting to pose a series of theological queries to one of its subordinate meetings and to discontinue the meeting on the basis of unsatisfactory answers was "a step without parallel in the history of our Society."[34]

Although the monthly meeting status of San Jose Friends was terminated, meetings for worship were held regularly. The Joel Bean group, obviously the cause of the termination, met in their Morse Street Meetinghouse, and since this property did not belong to the Monthly Meeting, it could not be confiscated by a Quarterly Meeting almost 2,000 miles away. James Bean wrote to the editor of the **Friends' Review** of the local growth of the group:

Yesterday, Eighth mo. 30th, 26 were at school and 37 at meeting, some from Santa Clara and one (Hannah Neal) from San Francisco, being present. Fifty-seven different persons were at the school and meeting, although a few (half a dozen) members, under the advice of those who laid down the Monthly Meeting, do not now meet with us, continuing to go to the hall; yet there has been a perceptible increase in attendance since meeting in the new house. Several young people and some among the best families in San Jose, who before had known but little of Friends, have become quite regular attenders on First-days. One attending non-member would have requested to be received a member last Monthly Meeting, but for the hasty action of the Quarterly Meeting.[35]

Efforts, of course, were made to appeal the action of Honey Creek Quarterly Meeting. Iowa Yearly Meeting, at its 1886 sessions, approved of San Jose Friends referring "the subject if they deem it best, through Honey Creek Quarterly Meeting in the usual course of appeals to the Yearly Meeting."[36] A copy of the proceedings of the Quarterly Meeting had been sent to Iowa Yearly Meeting with the following appeal:

The members of this Meeting having been pronounced by the Quarterly Meeting as not sound in the doctrines of the Christian religion, we appeal to the Yearly Meeting, and ask its decision upon the following questions, viz.:

1st. Are the answers of San Jose Monthly Meeting to the questions of the Committee of the Quarterly Meeting at variance with the doctrines of the Christian religion, as understood and held by Iowa Yearly Meeting?

2nd. Does the discipline give to a Quarterly Meeting the right or authority to entertain and act upon statements obtained from private sources, so as to abridge the rights of members of a subordinate meeting, without investigation, or giving such members an opportunity of knowing or disproving the charges made against them?

3rd. Have we, as members of the Society of Friends, attached without our consent to a meeting of entire strangers 2,000 miles distant from us, any right of choice as to the Monthly Meeting in the Society to which we might ask the transfer of our membership?[37]

In true Quaker fashion, the appeal was referred to a committee for its report in one year, but since the Honey Creek Quarterly Meeting was still negative toward San Jose Monthly Meeting, the appeal was not forwarded to the Yearly Meeting and no real action could be taken. One of the members of the San Jose Meeting expressed his feelings to the editor of **The Friend** (London) in these words:

Our case was laid before the Yearly Meeting in a way to give it the opportunity to remedy the wrong if it would. We did not ask the restoration, but a relief from the charge of unsoundness on the evidence of the published report on which the Quarterly Meeting based its action. We felt that the Yearly Meeting itself had something at stake in the matter, and asked redress from wrong rather than restoration of privilege.[38]

The division among Quakers at San Jose was now intensified. Joel Bean was the obvious center of the storm of controversy, and although the Monthly Meeting had been duly disciplined, further action was still to be taken by Iowa Yearly Meeting regarding the Beans. To this account we must now turn.

The Disownment of Joel Bean

Joel and Hannah Bean had settled into the community of San Jose and were soon active in its civic and cultural affairs. Joel Bean joined the Pastor's Union, frequently presenting papers to the group.[39] Hannah Bean became a member of the Monday Club, the oldest literary club in the city. She also furthered the work of such groups as the Women's Christian Temperance Union, the Young Women's Christian Association, and the Indian Association.[40]

During the summers they went to Pacific Grove and attended the Chautauqua Assembly, finding spiritual uplift and intellectual stimulation.[41] But the quiet and repose were soon disrupted as Joel Bean found himself the target of attacks by the evangelicals. The theological position of Joel Bean was now well-known. His travels across the country and abroad had afforded a public platform for the expression of his concerns. His articles in the leading Friends periodicals had identified his position on many of the major issues among Quakers. These articles eventually were used as the basis for his disownment as a minister within the Society of Friends.

Iowa was undoubtedly the source of his greatest opposition. It was here that Joel Bean had begun to raise his voice against what he considered to be dangerous tendencies among Friends. In 1887, Joel Bean felt under a "call of apprehended duty" to return to Iowa and visit the sessions of Honey Creek Quarterly Meeting. **The Friend** (London) reported of the visit:

> He did not go to ask for a certificate or to speak of any "prospect" or to ask anything; it simply appeared right to go, and he went accordingly and feeling to be in his right place, was glad to be there. He found that strange reports had been in circulation respecting his wife and himself, as that they did not believe in regeneration, etc., and some to whom they were strangers thought them very heretical. The service in the ministry to which he felt called in the Quarterly Meeting was received as a complete refutation of these charges by some and was acknowledged as such in subsequent converse. Both the meetings at West Branch were attended; a remarkable change was manifested, with great cordiality by some who were once in hostility.[42]

In spite of such attempts to create avenues of understanding between himself and his opposition, the controversy intensified and the breach was widened between the two factions. Joel Bean's strong stand against the "new doctrines" and the "new measures" of revivalism had branded him as being less than evangelical. We have already briefly alluded to his theological positions, but it is important now to identify more clearly his view of Quakerism, for it forms the basis of the action taken against him by Friends in Iowa.

Joel Bean's Understanding of Quakerism

Two major articles published by Joel Bean in **The British Friend** and the **Friends' Review** have already been cited. "The Issue" was printed in 1881 in **The British Friend**, reprinted in **The Friend** (London) and later circulated in pamphlet form by New York Yearly Meeting. The article entitled "The Light Within" appeared in the Philadelphia-published **Friends' Review** two years earlier, in 1879. These two articles give valuable insight into the thinking of Joel Bean. A third article, published in the newly-established **American Friend** in 1894 under the title, "Why I am a Friend," supplies additional information.[43] From these three articles, supplemented by shorter letters and other accounts, it is possible to determine specifically the views of Joel Bean upon those subjects of discussion and controversy.

Joel Bean felt that the rise of the Quaker movement in the seventeenth century was "the highest ground reached by Protestantism in the direction of spiritual Christianity."[44] He viewed the Church as being composed of those who are in "vital union with Christ, and actuated by His spirit."[45] It was not identical with, nor limited to, any outward organization, but was comprehensive in its scope. Joel Bean wrote:

> The Friend conceives the true church, the body of Christ, to include all in whose lives the **Spirit of Christ** is embodied and expressed. It comprehends and combines all agencies wherein He works and rules. It is confined to no nation or denomination, and none are excluded from it. In it there is no schism. All is harmonized and unified in one life. All is subject to one Head. It is because I accept this grand view of the Church that I am a Friend.[46]

In keeping with this view of the Church, he recognized Jesus Christ as the "only essential medium through whom every soul may come directly to the Father, and the Father may speak directly to every soul."[47] Christ was held to be both Savior and Teacher. He was the supplier of spiritual gifts and strength to those within the Church. The full and free exercise of these gifts demanded that meetings for worship be held in a simple manner; "no prearrangement of exercises was suffered to intrude upon the liberty to speak, or to be silent, under the presidency and power of the Holy Spirit."[48] These views of Joel Bean, however, were not controversial. They merely identified his stance within the thrust of historic Quakerism. The major theological difficulties arose when he parted company with the evangelicals in their understanding of the person and ministry of the Spirit of Christ, and of the work of Christ in salvation.

In a letter to Rufus Jones, dated September 8, 1893, Joel Bean stated that whenever the Society of Friends would lose that which was distinctive in its witness and message, the reason for its existence would be gone. This distinction, he felt, was in the concept of the Light of Christ within. He wrote:

> The fundamental declension of the Society in the Western States began in a denial of the Light of Christ within. . . .

This was the great doctrine at issue in Iowa fifteen years ago
when almost every minister denied it in private and public.
And apart from this basis, as the result has proved, there was
little to hold the Society to its characteristic ministry or mode
of worship.[49]

Joel Bean affirmed his belief of the presence of the Light or
Spirit of Christ in the soul of every man. Yielding to this Light
led to salvation. This belief, however, did not abrogate or sup-
plant his concept of the necessity of atonement. In his article,
"The Light Within," he wrote:

> Some there are who, owning the efficiency of the light mani-
> fested, the word spoken, the grace appearing **in the soul**, come
> to the conclusion that it is **sufficient**, and therefore that the
> outward coming in the flesh and the atoning sacrifice upon the
> cross of our Lord and Savior Jesus Christ, were not essential
> to our salvation. The heresy here is (I think) not in the accept-
> ance of that which is believed, but in the rejection of that
> which is denied.

> It does not follow that salvation is possible without the atone-
> ment, if it be admitted to be possible without the knowledge of
> the atonement. If the Holy Spirit saves, it does not follow that
> He saves without the Lord Jesus Christ. He is the one door,
> the one way of salvation; the one Mediator for all men, the
> one Propitiation for the sins of the whole world.[50]

This article, however, brought immediate protest and raised
much consternation among those Friends who were calling for a
conversion experience in the lives of individuals. Such a crisis
experience, they held, could not be possible without the knowledge
of Christ and His redeeming work.[51] But Joel Bean did not feel
that his view in any way diminished the importance of the Cross.
This truth, he felt, was both necessary and universal. The saving
light of Christ was as universal as His saving love.[52] This fact, he
maintained, was self-evident in a study of other religions.

> So marked and manifold, indeed, are the proofs of a Divine
> impress in the great religions of mankind, that many survey
> them and explore them as rival systems in competition with
> Christianity.[53]

Those Friends who saw in Christianity a certain uniqueness were
further disturbed by Joel Bean's statement that "Christianity is
the harmonizer, and Christ the center of all the good in all the

religions of all the nations, kindreds, tongues, and peoples of the earth."[54]

Another area of controversy was the view that Joel Bean held regarding Christian perfection. The revivalists had preached a "full and free salvation," not only from the guilt of sin, but to all the fullness of Christian perfection. Complete sanctification was claimed as a definite experience, instantaneously received, and often defined as the eradication, not merely the subjugation, of the disposition to sin. Joel Bean could not agree with these concepts, for he felt that such a condition of perfect restoration taught, "as must necessarily be inferred, that all impulses from within must be right."[55]

Conjoined with the doctrines that were being promoted by the revivalists, the new techniques of worship and church administration also came in for censure by Joel Bean. He felt that the church was not being strengthened and built up, but rather that "disorganization and disintegration are confessedly making rapid progress, and most rapid where protest is most silenced and conservatism most inert."[56]

As a result of his views, disciplinary action was taken by the Honey Creek Quarterly Meeting. It instructed the Monthly Meeting to which the Bean memberships had been transferred from San Jose, not "to liberate either the writer of 'The Issue' or his wife to travel as ministers, until they should be convinced of and acknowledge their errors in these particulars."[57] This action, however, was only preliminary to yet sterner measures.

Joel and Hannah Bean Deposed as Ministers

In 1891, Iowa Yearly Meeting revised its Discipline and introduced a set of queries that were to be answered by ministers and elders as an indication of the correctness of their beliefs.[58] Such a procedure was not new, for as early as 1876, New York Yearly Meeting had prepared a set of questions which were to be answered affirmatively by any person "under consideration for acknowledgment as a Minister."[59] Iowa Yearly Meeting sent its questions to Joel and Hannah Bean, and when the answers were returned, they were deemed unacceptable.[60] The committee appointed by Honey Creek Quarterly Meeting to act upon the results of the queries recommended to the New Providence Monthly Meeting, the meeting to which the Bean memberships had been transferred, that Joel and Hannah Bean be no longer recognized as Friends ministers. The committee judged that Joel and Hannah Bean were

> entertaining and advocating doctrines, which, according to their own statements to us in writing, are contrary to the fundamental principles held by our church, as expressed in our Declaration of Faith.[61]

The New Providence Monthly Meeting then acted upon the recommendation of the appointed committee and on July 22, 1893, deposed Joel and Hannah Bean as ministers, together with Benjamin Jones, another member of the College Park Meeting.

As might be expected, reaction from across the Society of Friends was swift and varied. **The Friend** (Philadelphia) deplored the action of the New Providence Monthly Meeting,[62] whereas **The Christian Worker** defended the action and commented:

> So soon as we deprive a Quarterly or Yearly Meeting of the right to judge who shall be sent forth as their representative in teaching the views of Friends, we threaten our very existence.[63]

The College Park Meeting in San Jose also minuted their reaction at a business meeting on November 7, 1893. The minute read:

> The Friends residing at College Park, Santa Clara Co., California, have heard with deep regret of the action of New Providence Monthly Meeting in "deposing from position of ministers" Benjamin Jones, Joel Bean, and Hannah Bean, life-long and honored members of the Society of Friends. . . . Friends united in expressing their sympathy with the three friends mentioned, and their hearty appreciation of the service their ministry has been to this meeting, and in continuing to acknowledge them as ministers of the gospel.
> > By order of the meeting,
> > Samuel J. Brun
> > Augustus T. Murray[64]

The strongest, and perhaps most organized, reaction, however, came from abroad. A series of letters, now kept in the Friends Library, London, indicates the rising feeling of support for the Beans and the College Park Meeting during this period.

A protest appears to have been organized by Thomas Hodgkin and a letter circulated to which English Friends affixed their signatures.[65] The response, generally, was indicative of the strong support and sympathy felt for the Beans.

A letter from Helen B. Harris to Thomas Hodgkin stated,

In reply to thy very interesting suggestion concerning the Y.M. and the expression of sympathy with our friends J. and H. Bean—Rendel and I feel that if there would be a chance of carrying such a manifestation of liberty, it would be a most excellent thing to do.[66]

Another correspondent wrote to Thomas Hodgkin,

Please add my name to your list of sympathizers with the Beans. . . . If this prohibition against the Beans is upheld by their Y. Meeting, it will probably become difficult for London Y.M. to maintain correspondence or receive Ministers traveling with so invidious a certificate as must come from such a body.[67]

Not all of the English Friends, however, took as strong a position against Iowa Yearly Meeting as did Thomas Hodgkin. Correspondence between Henry S. Newman, editor of **The Friend** (London), and Thomas Hodgkin indicate some basic disagreement over the source of the Bean controversy. Thomas Hodgkin had blamed the Iowa pastors, but Henry Newman writes:

I do not know whether thou wishes thy letter re Joel Bean to be inserted in **The Friend**, but if so, I think the expression about the "inquisitorial practices introduced by the Pastors"! must be expunged. I am not aware that the Pastors of Iowa Yearly Mg. have anything to do with this difficulty. . . . The truth is many of the cruel things that have been said about these Western "Pastors" are not only unjust, but **untrue**, and I only wish English Friends would go and see for themselves the way in which they are working to build up, and **are** building up, real Quaker communities, in which there is, as far as I am aware, room for every member, male or female, to take vocal part in the worship, and as a matter of fact, a **very much larger** number of Friends are taking vocal part in these Western Mgs. where there are Pastors than in our own mgs. in England. But it is **not** the pastors that have got up this trouble about Joel Bean. They are too busy with their own work to have much time for doctrinal controversy. . . .[68]

Finally, in January, 1894, a letter of sympathy to Joel and Hannah Bean was published in **The Friend** (Philadelphia) and in

The British Friend. The letter obviously took note of Henry
Newman's criticism and no mention was made of the pastors of
Iowa. A total of 410 English Friends signed the letter, which
was then reproduced in pamphlet form and widely circulated. The
letter read as follows:

> Dear Friends, Joel and Hannah Bean,
> We whose names are subscribed hereto, having read with sur-
> prise and sorrow the proceedings of Iowa Yearly Meeting of
> Ministry and Oversight in your case, desire to assure you of
> our undiminished regard for your Christian character and of
> the unbroken bond of religious fellowship which still unites us
> to you. We deeply regret the inquisitional proceedings, as they
> appear to us, which your Friends have instituted towards you,
> and feel ourselves bound to protest that they are entirely out of
> harmony with the discipline of our Religious Society as under-
> stood and practiced among us.
>
> Please convey to our honored Friend, Benjamin H. Jones, the
> expression of our love and sympathy. We are, your friends....[69]

A reply from Joel and Hannah Bean was not long in coming. Writing from College Park, San Jose, on January 23, 1894,
the Beans responded:

> To our Dear Friends, Thomas Hodgkin and Others,
> Your letter in **The Friend**, and in **The British Friend** has reach-
> ed us. We feel it due on our part to acknowledge the encour-
> agement inspired by your words of sympathy and unity, sub-
> scribed by such a list of honored and endeared names. While
> we desire neither to minimize or magnify the importance of
> the official act of "Deposition," it is an exceeding great relief
> and help to us to know that there are many who neither by ex-
> pressed or silent acquiescence concur in this recorded disfellow-
> ship of the Church. Above all personal considerations, we are
> thankful for the effect of such messages as yours, upon dear
> and earnest young Friends around us, in restoring and
> strengthening a loyal attachment to our Society, which was in
> danger of being lost.
>
> And now, whatever may be permitted us still to suffer, of dis-
> trust and rejection on the part of many whom we love, our con-
> cern and prayer is, that it may not be suffered in any degree to
> be a means of extending schism in the body of Christ, that
> "that which is lame may not be turned out of the way, but
> rather that it may be healed." May largeness of heart and
> pureness of love avail to the healing of divisions, and the re-
> storing of dissevered brethren, and to the growth of upbuilding

of all in the truth and Spirit of the Lord Jesus, "till **we all come**
in the unity of the Faith, and in the knowledge of the Son of
God, to the perfect man, to the measure of the stature of the
fulness of Christ." Affectionately your friends. . . .[70]

The English Friends were undoubtedly motivated in their
action by their love and respect for Joel Bean and the knowledge
of his liberal spirit. The frontier spirit in America was still an
enigma to them and they must have considered western Quakers
as being provincial in their attitudes. Henry Newman, however,
provided a much-needed corrective when he wrote later to
Thomas Hodgkin:

I think the poetry and articles signed by Joel Bean . . . have
conclusively proved that the English Friends were hasty in
speaking of the action of Iowa Friends as "inquisitorial" when
it is now quite clear that it was not by secret search or query
that his views were made known, and the fact is clearly established that Iowa Friends knew his views and therefore the
elders or Committee had a perfect right to enquire of him, and
that they were **not** views which Joel Bean kept to himself but
which were well known in San Jose and in Iowa. The system of
having a series of questions put to ministers which is so contrary to our custom and mode of thought in England, did not
originate with Iowa Friends, but with our conservative Friends
in New York Yearly Meeting, and was afterwards adopted by
some of the Western Y.M.s. American Friends have suffered
so much from their ministers introducing points of doctrinal
divergence that it was perhaps natural that the conservative
element in America should have felt that some safe-guard for
the church was needed on points on which they are very sensitive . . . the more cautious Friends in America feel that we
ought to be very careful in censuring the Western Yearly
Meetings in their endeavor to maintain the truth. I think that
it is possible that our love and esteem for Joel Bean and for
his ministry have carried us too far in our attitude towards
Iowa Friends.[71]

Joel and Hannah Bean Disowned as Members

In January, 1898, the New Providence Monthly Meeting appointed a Correspondence Committee to contact inactive and non-
resident members and to drop from membership those who showed no interest in retaining their membership in the Monthly
Meeting.[72] This action was in accord with the Discipline of Iowa
Yearly Meeting, which indicated "if no information has been or

can be received from a member for two years, his Monthly Meeting may, at its discretion, remove his name from the list of members."[73] Through this action, the committee removed ninety-one names from the membership lists of New Providence Monthly Meeting, or about twenty-one percent of their membership.[74] Thirteen of these individuals were members of the College Park Meeting, and included Joel and Hannah Bean, Joel's aged mother, his daughters, and two of his grandchildren.[75] The clerk of the committee explained that the burden of church dues was so heavy, because the Meeting's share was based on the total membership, "many of whom, really, we are of no benefit to, or they to us, spiritually or otherwise."[76]

This action had become common practice in the American yearly meetings,[77] especially among western Quakers. The extensive revivals brought an increase of members. In order to pay the salary of the pastors who were subsequently engaged, dues were apportioned to the membership. Joel and Hannah Bean could not conscientiously support a stipendiary pastorate, and so they were dropped from membership in New Providence Monthly Meeting, and thus from the Society of Friends. No appeal was made to the Quarterly Meeting, for they felt that such action would receive no more consideration than their former appeal.[78] Others, however, protested the action of disownment. **The British Friend** protested

> the action of the "Friends Church," which first deposes from the ministry, and then, through one of its branches, disassociates from membership, Friends who are highly esteemed and valued on both sides of the sea for their devout Christian character, and their service as ministers of the Gospel as understood by the Religious Society of Friends.[79]

The editor concluded:

> We hope there are still some thoughtful Friends in Iowa who regard with dissatisfaction such unconstitutional procedure,—procedure which could not exist in the weakest or most remote Monthly Meeting in this country. To say that it is a common practice in the Western States only emphasizes the fact, that in discipline as well as in principle, we are rapidly becoming two distinct bodies, with diverse interpretations of Quakerism. We see no parallel in the new methods of the West with the distin-

guishing features of the Quakerism of more than two hundred years. The "family likeness" is imperceptible.[80]

The Formation of the College Park Association of Friends

Joel and Hannah Bean showed no bitterness toward the action of Iowa Friends; instead, they doubled their efforts in the building of fellowship among like-minded Quakers of College Park and the surrounding areas. We have already noted the building of the College Park Meetinghouse on Morse Street in 1885. Four years later, the group was named the College Park Association of Friends and was incorporated in December, 1889, under the laws of the State of California.[81] This Association was a unique Friends organization and an innovation in itself. Members of the Association retained their memberships in their home meetings, and thus a wide variety of Friends from a number of different yearly meetings were grouped together.[82] As we shall later see, this group followed the leadership of Joel Bean and his traditional views of Quakerism, but became the forerunner of innovation in Quaker organization.[83] Paradoxically, Joel Bean, who took such a strong stand against the innovations introduced by revivalism and the Great Awakening, himself introduced innovations as a result of his reaction against revivalism.

Controversy and innovation were thus part of the picture of Friends in the west. But while Joel Bean was having his difficulties in the Bay area, midwestern Quakers were streaming into southern California, leading Iowa and Kansas Yearly Meetings to foster monthly meetings and eventually to form the California Yearly Meeting of Friends. While Friends in the Bay area were struggling against the changes brought by revivalism, Friends in the southern part of the State were extending the nature and concerns of the revival into California and beyond. California, therefore, becomes the setting of two very distinct groups of Quakers. The establishment and growth of these two groups, the California Yearly Meeting of Friends and the Pacific Yearly Meeting of Friends, is the study of the following two chapters.

7

The California Yearly Meeting
of Friends Church

AS AN AFTERMATH to the discovery of gold in California, thousands of travelers began to make their way to the west. The transcontinental railroad opened a more convenient way of transportation, and the lure of a promising future brought visitors from near and far. Those who visited California would often write in glowing terms of the climate and landscape, encouraging still others to come. By the time the 1880s arrived, large crowds were participating in southern California's fantastic development. In his book, **The Boom of the Eighties**, Glenn S. Dumke describes the era:

> Men stood excitedly in line for days at a time in order to get first choice of lots in a new subdivision. Flag-draped trains hauled flatcars jammed with enthusiastic prospects to underdeveloped tracts far from centers of settlement. Exuberant auction sales, accompanied by brass bands and free lunches, helped sell $100,000,000 of southern California realestate during the boom's peak year. . . . More than two thousand real estate agents paced the streets of Los Angeles, seizing lapels and filling the balmy air with windy verbiage. Business blocks sprang like toadstools, and residences sprawled far beyond earlier city limits. . . . It is impossible to tell exactly how many people came to southern California during these exciting months, but more than 130,000 remained as permanent settlers, and the city of Los Angeles increased in size 500 per cent.[1]

The immediate cause of the great land boom was the rate war between the Southern Pacific and the Santa Fe railroads, beginning in March, 1887. The drastic reduction of fares stimulated the migration of great numbers of people from the midwest and east. For several years the transcontinental prices had been gradually lowered, but on March 6 the two railroads drastically cut the normal fares from Kansas City to Los Angeles to eight dollars, and then the Southern Pacific offered tickets at one dollar! These ridiculously low fares did not last long, however, but for over a year the price of a ticket from the Missouri River to Los Angeles remained under twenty-five dollars. Many inducements were offered to the travelers: "emigrant cars," such as the Bean family had earlier used; temporary employment services; the privilege of buying railroad-owned land, with reduced rates for colonists traveling and settling together; and railroad-planned excursion trips.

By capitalizing on the attractions of southern California, the railroads initiated and helped maintain the great boom of the Eighties.[2] Just as the railroad opened the way for Quakers like Joel Bean to migrate to northern California, the railroad was also greatly responsible for the migration of Quakers to southern California.

A major basis for the intensity of the boom was the growing strength of the agricultural economy. The land boom was promoted in literature through the emphasis upon the beauty of the landscape, the exploitation of its mineral wealth, and the praise of its agricultural products. Of the three, agricultural production ranked first in contemporary consideration.[3] It is no surprise, therefore, to see a major influx of Quakers into California during this period. Generally, Quakers have been a rural people. The promise of rich, new soil waiting to be cultivated and planted, coupled with an evangelical urge to extend the church through the witness of the Gospel, was an irresistible combination of powerful forces. Whereas in the earlier days, especially in northern California, migration to California was generally an individual affair, during the Eighties, Quakers migrated to southern California in carloads and settled in colonies. It is this aspect of the westward migration to which we now turn, and observe the establishment and growth of Quakerism in southern California through the California Yearly Meeting of Friends.

Extending the Great Awakening to California

The revival movement had gained remarkable headway in Iowa, and by 1880, two years prior to Joel Bean's departure, a recommendation was made in the sessions of Iowa Yearly Meeting that recognition be given to the right of local meetings to call qualified ministers with "suitable provisions being made for their partial, or entire support."[4] The suggestion was premature and was not adopted, but the first step toward a break with the past had been taken. Within a few years, the conservative opposition yielded, and in 1886, the pastoral system was officially introduced into the Yearly Meeting. It was deemed advisable for "each particular meeting to have a regular ministry and that meetings be encouraged to call and support ministers."[5] It was further established that "the Evangelistic Committee of Iowa Yearly Meeting be authorized to provide as far as possible for the supply of ministers and workers in meetings desiring such help. . . ."[6] In order that the new system be supervised, coordinated, and extended, Iowa Yearly Meeting established in the same year the office of "General Superintendent of Evangelistic, Pastoral and Church Extension Work." A dynamic evangelist, John Henry Douglas, was the first to be appointed to this office.[7]

John Henry Douglas left a profound impression upon the church and was influential in the extension of the results of the revival movement to the far west. Douglas was born in Fairfield, Maine, in 1832, attended the Friends School in Providence, Rhode Island, and then moved to Ohio in 1853 following a dramatic conversion during a storm at sea. In 1858, he was recorded as a minister by Ohio Yearly Meeting and then migrated to Iowa, indicating that he was ready "to throw himself heart and soul into a movement to revive and transform the Society."[8] For a brief period, he traveled throughout England and the Continent, preaching and witnessing to the need of renewal. When he arrived back in Iowa in 1867, the evangelistic movement was just getting underway, and he entered enthusiastically into the work, giving the movement a great impetus. When he was appointed as general superintendent almost two decades later, he was in the prime of life and at the height of his influence.

Douglas was "keen of mind, eloquent in speech, magnetic, and tireless" and firmly rooted the pastoral system in Iowa Yearly Meeting.[9] The year following the adoption of the system, three meetings were fully supporting a pastor, six meetings were sharing the services of pastors, and fourteen were partially supporting a pastor.[10] Within three years, there were fifty-one pastors in Iowa Yearly Meeting, fifteen of whom were fully supported, while thirty-two received partial support.[11] The emphasis upon evangelism, the increasing membership, the functioning pastoral system, and the leadership of John Henry Douglas all combined to give impetus to the extension of the revival concerns of Friends to California.

Establishing Friends Meetings in Southern California

We have already noted the beginning of a noticeable migration of Quakers to southern California in 1876. Lawson Hollingsworth and his family were a few of the Quakers who came from West Branch, Iowa, to settle in the newly formed Indiana Colony of San Gabriel Valley.[12] The colony was later renamed "Pasadena," a word coined from the Chippewa language and first suggested by Dr. T. B. Elliott, in whose home in Indiana was held the first meeting of prospective colonists prior to their migration to California.[13]

Within a few years a substantial number of Quaker families had migrated to the area and on July 23, 1882, the first appointed Meeting for Worship was held in the home of William Sharpless.[14] Those present at this first meeting included "Emmor and Tracy Rood, Wm. Sharpless and family, Adonijah Gregory and wife, Samuel and Leon Bundy, Lawson Hollingsworth, Mrs. Frank Ball, and Frank Heald and wife."[15]

Throughout the following year, the Quakers of the area met regularly in various homes until July 15, 1883, when the first meeting was held in a house rented from Edith Painter, located on Marengo Avenue and renovated for a place of worship.[16] Many of the families had come from Springdale Quarterly Meeting in Iowa, and request was made by the Pasadena Friends for the establishment of a monthly meeting. The request was granted by

Iowa Friends and on March 1, 1884, the first monthly meeting was held, appointing Thomas K. Bufkin and Edith Painter as clerks.[17] The Minutes of Iowa Yearly Meeting presented the following report of Springdale Quarterly Meeting:

> . . . A meeting for worship at Pasadena, Los Angeles County, California, held on First days at 10 o'clock and a monthly meeting, at the same place, held the first Seventh-day in each month. . . .[18]

Within a year, the meeting outgrew the small place of worship, and in 1885 property was purchased from John Painter for $135 for the erection of a new meetinghouse. The structure was completed in 1887 and comfortably accommodated 300 people.[19]

While Friends were organizing in Pasadena, another group of Quakers was migrating to an area still further south. In 1883, Abel, Cyrus, and William Frazier came from Lawrence, Kansas, and settled in the area now known as El Modena, in Orange County.[20] After the arrival of additional families, a Sabbath School was organized and held in private homes. In 1885, a small house was rented for use as a place of worship and was later purchased for $100. Impetus for the establishment of the meeting came from a series of evangelistic meetings held by Samuel Loyd and Mahlon Stubbs.[21] The following year request was made to Hesper Quarterly Meeting for recognition as a monthly meeting. That same year, 1886, Kansas Yearly Meeting reported:

> Hesper Quarterly Meeting has authorized the establishment of a meeting for worship and a monthly meeting by the name of Modena, to be held at Modena in Los Angeles County, California, on Fifth-day following the First Seventh-day in each month at 10 o'clock A.M.[22]

The Meeting was originally named Earlham Monthly Meeting and held its first meeting on November 11, 1886, with official representatives present from Kansas Yearly Meeting.[23] Within a month, plans were made for the erection of a new meetinghouse. Residents of the area, many of them non-Friends, contributed to the building of the new structure. By the fall of 1887, the building was completed and dedication services were held. But the joy of these Friends was short-lived. In December, severe wind storms caused the structure, with its proud and heavy bell, to collapse. The pioneers, however, were undaunted and rebuilt the structure, which stands to the present day.[24]

Formation of Pasadena Quarterly Meeting

With the establishment of two monthly meetings in southern California, the formation of a quarterly meeting appeared to be the next logical step. Although Pasadena and Modena (Earlham) Monthly Meetings were organized by two different yearly meetings, they shared a common background of revivalism and evangelical concern.[25] Requests were forwarded to Hesper and Springdale Quarterly Meetings, suggesting the formation of a new quarterly meeting as a constituent of Iowa Yearly Meeting, to be called Pacific Quarterly Meeting.[26] A committee appointed by Iowa Yearly Meeting recommended the following action, which was approved:

> We are united in recommending the Yearly Meeting to grant the request, but propose that the name be Pasadena Quarterly Meeting instead of Pacific; and we suggest that Hiram Hammon, Cyrus Beede, R. H. Hartley, Sarah J. Pickrell, Esther A. Hiatt, Joseph Arnold, Alfred H. Lindley, and Eliza J. Lindley be appointed to attend the opening thereof. This meeting unites with the report and directs that the Meeting be opened at Pasadena, California in the 11th mo. next; to be held alternately at Pasadena and Modena on the third 7th day in the 2nd, 5th, 8th and 11th mos. The Quarterly Meeting of Ministry and Oversight to be held on the 6th day preceding at 2 o'clock.[27]

The following year, 1888, the committee reported to the Iowa Yearly Meeting that the Quarterly Meeting "was opened as directed, to good satisfaction."[28] In the meantime, Friends in California had continued to grow and new meetings were being established at Whittier, Wildomar, and Alamitos. The first statistical report from the new Pasadena Quarterly Meeting indicated five meetings under its care, with twenty-two recorded ministers (seventeen male and five female) and a total membership of 722.[29] This ranked Pasadena Quarterly Meeting as the seventh largest of the fifteen quarterly meetings in Iowa Yearly Meeting. The migration of families to California is reflected in the further statistic indicating the largest membership increase during the year in the Yearly Meeting. There were 275 new members added to the rolls of Pasadena Quarterly Meeting; 13 by birth, 43 by request, and 219 by transfer of membership certificates.[30]

The Whittier Colony

The organizer of the most successful of the Quaker colonies in southern California was a Friend from Chicago by the name of Aquilla H. Pickering. In 1886, he conceived the idea of establishing a Quaker colony in the west, and in the following year, 1887, he set out for California with his wife, Hannah. He had been earlier impressed with "the need of Christian work, and saw an open door for Friends to work on the lines of Temperance, Sabbath observance, and other reforms."[31]

Aquilla and Hannah Pickering traveled over seven hundred miles in a carriage from Sacramento in the north to San Diego in the south. Conversations were held with Friends throughout the state and possible sites were discussed and explored. The search, however, was one of discouragement. It was not until a visit to the Los Angeles area that they began to be hopeful of the enterprise. After consultation with Friends in the area, he organized a land company and purchased the John M. Thomas ranch on May 3, 1887.[32] Aquilla Pickering wrote of the site:

From the first we were favorably impressed with this beautiful situation; the high ground sloping away from the Puente Hills from which we could see the whole valley reaching toward the south and west, until our eyes rested upon the ocean, some eighteen miles away.[33]

A council of local Friends was called and held a meeting in early May in an old barn located on the ranch. Enthusiasm for the project was evident as officers were elected to serve on the board of the land company. Because of his age and business interests in Chicago, Aquilla Pickering declined to serve as president of the company. In his stead, Jonathan Bailey was elected president, and Hervey Lindley as secretary of the Pickering Land and Water Company.[34]

The company platted a town and held the first lot sale within the month. Town lots were sold for one hundred and two hundred dollars each, while five-acre plots in the suburbs were sold for a thousand dollars.[35] The town itself was given the name "Whittier," in honor of Quakerism's most famous poet.[36] In July, a trainload of Quaker colonists arrived from Iowa and were transported to Whittier in the wagons belonging to Jonathan and Rebecca Bailey, the first residents of the city. Throughout the year, other groups arrived to establish residence in Whittier, and before the year was over, the Pickering Land and Water Company had recorded seventeen plats.[37]

Glenn Dumke has called the Whittier Colony "unique." The basis for such a statement may have been the fact that the company did not enter into speculative activity, but was wholly concerned in providing the economic advantages and privileges of colonization to Friends of like mind and spirit. Aquilla Pickering's concern for a Quaker center of influence was widely shared, and honesty and integrity marked the business dealings and transactions. The deep religious convictions of these Friends served as a basis for extending the Society by establishing and promoting various Friends churches.

When Jonathan and Rebecca Bailey took up residence in the old ranch house on May 11, 1887, they resolved to hold a meeting for worship regularly in their new home, even if no others were present but themselves. Within a few months, a meeting-house was erected by the Pickering Land and Water Company and donated to the group of Quakers worshiping regularly in Whittier. On August 14, 1887, the building was formally opened for worship.[38] A Sabbath School was established and by January, 1888, it had an enrollment of 103 students and eight teachers.[39]

On December 10, 1887, Whittier Monthly Meeting was established by Pasadena Quarterly Meeting.[40] Cyrus Lindley was named the temporary clerk, and the first individual to be received into membership after the meeting was organized was Dr. Elias Jessup, who later became the first pastor of Whittier Monthly Meeting. It is interesting to note that two years later, in 1890, the meeting secured the pastoral services of Thomas Armstrong of New Providence Monthly Meeting in Iowa, the same meeting that deposed and disowned Joel Bean![41]

The Growth of Pasadena Quarterly Meeting

Quaker families soon began to arrive in other localities in southern California. In 1883, Dr. Q. A. R. Holton and his family migrated to the Santa Maria valley and the little town of Ramona. Four years later, in 1887, a Quaker minister from Kansas, W. E. Mills, and his family moved to Ramona, together with J. H. Thomas, James Williams and their families. Plans were formulated for a Friends Meeting, but it was not until 1891 that Modena Monthly Meeting granted a status of Preparative Meeting.[42] A number of evangelistic campaigns were conducted by visiting Friends ministers, adding to the membership of the Meeting. Ramona was finally established as a monthly meeting in 1892.

Further north, in the small community of Wildomar, a number of Quaker families organized a Sabbath School in the local schoolhouse. The earliest families had arrived in 1885, but were joined by a substantial number of Friends during the next two years. In 1887, the Wildomar Town Company donated two lots to the Friends and a fine meetinghouse was erected. In November, 1897, Wildomar Monthly Meeting was established by Pasadena Quarterly Meeting.[43] Revival services again were the means used to strengthen the church and add to its membership.

Reference has already been made to the migration of Canadian Quakers to Alamitos.[44] The success of the Sabbath School conducted by Susan Beckett encouraged several Friends ministers to visit the area and conduct occasional services at the schoolhouse. Perhaps the most prominent of the visiting ministers was John Henry Douglas, general superintendent of Iowa Yearly Meeting, who saw the possibilities of a strong meeting being established at Alamitos.

In 1890, a large tent was secured from the Whittier Monthly Meeting and erected on a corner of John Beckett's ranch, about three miles west of Garden Grove. For two weeks, an intensive evangelistic crusade was conducted by several Friends ministers with the result that "so many converts had been won to Christ, a meeting for worship was organized, with Ella C. Veeder as pastor in charge."[45] Seven months later, a simple frame meetinghouse was erected on the same site. On September 9, 1891, the Monthly

Meeting was established by Pasadena Quarterly Meeting with thirty-nine charter members.[46]

One of the more substantial Friends monthly meetings was organized in Long Beach on June 15, 1892. A number of Quaker families had settled in the pleasant little town bordering the Pacific Ocean. The first meeting for worship was conducted by Mary M. Brown on February 11, 1888, in the Cerritos Hall of the Congregational Church.[47] During the next four years, interest in the meeting grew steadily, evangelistic meetings were conducted and new converts were made. A church building was constructed in 1889, making the congregation the fourth to be established in the city, following the Methodists, the Presbyterians, and the Congregationalists.[48]

On May 21, 1892, Whittier Monthly Meeting proposed to Pasadena Quarterly Meeting that a monthly meeting be established at Long Beach. On June 15, 1892, the committee appointed by the Quarterly Meeting met in Long Beach with "the members of the Society of Friends residing at this place . . . to take into consideration the organization of a Monthly Meeting."[49] A permanent organization was effected, clerks appointed and the following action minuted: "This meeting shall be known by the name of Long Beach Monthly Meeting of Friends, to be held on Fourth day following the second Seventh day in each month at two o'clock P.M."[50] Three months later, a statistical report to the Quarterly Meeting indicated a total membership of eighty individuals from twenty-two different families.[51]

Southern California, however, was not the only part of the state that came under the evangelistic concerns of Friends. The Stockton Avenue Meeting of Friends in San Jose attempted to keep an evangelistic witness, although greatly weakened by the earlier division with Joel Bean and the College Park Meeting. Addison and Rebecca Naylor and their family moved to the San Jose area after a fruitful ministry among Friends in southern California. Following a period of ministry among San Jose Friends, the Naylors went to Berkeley, where a Friends meeting had been started in the home of Joseph Johnson. Following a series of evangelistic meetings, a public hall was rented for regular meetings for worship and Rebecca Naylor was named as pastor.[52] The meeting continued to grow and was finally recognized as a monthly meeting in 1894 by Pasadena Quarterly Meeting.[53]

Meanwhile the Friends in the San Jose area had been meeting regularly in the Stockton Avenue Meetinghouse, and had come under the jurisdiction of the Pasadena Quarterly Meeting. On April 10, 1889, request was made to the Quarterly Meeting through Pasadena Monthly Meeting to be recognized as a monthly meeting. The request was approved as follows:

Dear Friends: We the undersigned members of San Jose Preparative Meeting and other Friends who reside within its limits believe the time has come when the prosperity and growth of the church would be advanced by having a Monthly Meeting, therefore we request a Monthly Meeting to be held in San Jose on the second Seventh day in each month and to be called San Jose Monthly Meeting of Friends.[54]

The pattern of the growth of the church in Pasadena Quarterly Meeting can be seen now in bold relief. The evangelistic thrust of the Great Awakening, coupled with the successful pastoral system of Iowa Yearly Meeting, was used to great advantage in California. From the beginning it appeared that Friends in Pasadena Quarterly Meeting attempted to take the best of the old, traditional Quaker practices and mold them to the new methods employed by revivalism in an effort to meet the needs of a mushrooming society. Evangelists and ministers who were successful in the midwest came to California to share in the challenge of the work. In 1890, John Henry Douglas made one of his many trips to California. In his last report to Iowa Yearly Meeting as general superintendent, he wrote:

After making a tour of inspection to Tacoma, Seattle, and so on, we went to San Jose, California, where we received a warm welcome and we enjoyed a good tabernacle revival which was greatly blessed in the conversion of souls, and the building up and strengthening of the church. . . . Our next work was in southern California, where we held a ten days meeting which was owned by the presence and power of God. . . . Whittier also received us with open arms and nearly all were built up in our most holy faith. . . . Long Beach was visited. Garden Grove and El Modena, all of which are places of interest; we preached in each place. . . . We left California much encouraged about the church and are sure if Friends there keep under the power of God through the baptism of the Holy Ghost, a good future is before them. . . . Our church in that land will be made strong and useful.[55]

The report from Pasadena Quarterly Meeting was even more specific. Dr. C. R. Dixon reported a total of

eight meetings and occasional meetings at other places; there are six houses and twenty-five recorded ministers: six engaged as pastors, one is engaged in W.C.T.U. work as county president and organizer, the others engaged in different lines of industry and doing such gospel work as comes to their hand.[56]

The pastoral system had been extended to California by Iowa Yearly Meeting as an enlargement of its revival concerns, and "the good fruit of it was apparent on every hand."[57]

There was, however, one exception to the establishment of pastoral meetings in southern California. On December 5, 1886, a meeting of Conservative Friends was held at the home of William Penn Evans in Pasadena.[58] Meetings were conducted regularly in the homes of various members until a meetinghouse was erected on Villa Street in 1894. The following year, the Villa Street Meeting was recognized as a Monthly Meeting by Hickory Grove Quarterly Meeting of Iowa (Conservative) Yearly Meeting.[59] The traditional customs of speech are still maintained, and meetings for worship are based upon silence without the use of a pastor.

The Establishment of California Yearly Meeting

As Quakerism began to grow in California, it soon became evident that further organization would be necessary, and the meetings of Pasadena Quarterly Meeting were asked to consider "a proposition to divide Pasadena Quarterly Meeting and create a new Quarterly Meeting."[60] Upon the concurrence of Friends, a request was made to Iowa Yearly Meeting in 1892 for the establishment of a new quarterly meeting to be called Whittier Quarterly Meeting.[61] The matter was referred to a committee and after two years, in 1894, the request was granted and Whittier, Modena (Earlham), Alamitos, and Ramona (Nuevo) Meetings were organized into a quarterly meeting.[62] Whittier Quarterly

Meeting held its first sessions on February 16, 1895, with a total membership of 643, including twelve ministers.[63]

Together with its request for a new quarterly meeting, a request was made to Iowa Yearly Meeting to establish a new yearly meeting. The request originally cited Long Beach as the location for the Yearly Meeting, but this was subsequently amended and Whittier was named as the chosen site.[64] The request was granted "without a dissenting voice, and with the approval of the other Yearly Meetings, California Yearly Meeting will be opened at the time specified. . . ."[65] Seven leading Quakers of Iowa Yearly Meeting were instructed to be present at Whittier in March, 1895, in order to effect the new organization.

On March 26, 1895, eighteen delegates from the two Quarterly Meetings met together with appointed delegates of ten Yearly Meetings, including Iowa, New England, North Carolina, Western, Wilmington, Indiana, New York, Ohio, Kansas, and Oregon.[66] In addition, several hundred Quakers gathered with them in the new auditorium built for the use of Whittier College. One reporter indicated that it was a "rare meeting":

Some of the older ministers stated that there were not a half dozen unfamiliar faces in the audience. The meeting seemed to be composed largely of old-time friends who had been absent from each other for ten or twenty years. A sweet spirit of Christian fellowship prevailed.[67]

The following day, March 27, Dr. William F. Coffin was appointed as presiding clerk, and various committee members were named. The Articles of Incorporation were adopted and eight departments of concern were organized, each with a superintendent. These included: Evangelistic, Pastoral and Church Extension; Bible Schools; Christian Endeavor; Missionary; Book and Tract; Education; Temperance; and Peace.[68] The statistical report indicated a total membership in the Yearly Meeting of 1,248 individuals from nine monthly meetings.[69]

The proceedings of the sessions were widely reported in Quaker journals both in America and in England, with the exception of **The Friend** (Philadelphia), which took no notice of the Yearly Meeting's formation.[70] **The American Friend** noted that "inquiry discovered thirty-four persons who were present at the opening of Iowa Yearly Meeting thirty-one years ago!"[71]

A great spirit of zeal and earnestness pervaded the sessions. A distinctive feature was the large number of young people in attendance, causing Allen Jay, of Indiana Yearly Meeting, to predict "a bright future for Quakerism in this State."[72] In their glowing report to Iowa Yearly Meeting, the delegates said:

> We attended all the various sessions thereof, which we think embraced nearly half of their entire membership. The love of God was manifest in all their deliberations, a full Gospel was preached as we verily believe by men and women of God, and the Holy Spirit manifested His Living Presence from day to day.[73]

The revival movement had now extended organizationally from Iowa and Kansas to California. The Yearly Meeting was officially denominated as the "Friends Church" and not as "The Religious Society of Friends." The pastoral system was inherent from the beginning, and the "new doctrines" and "new techniques" that Joel Bean had strongly opposed were now the basis for the new Yearly Meeting.

A new openness to the needs of the hour and the spirit of the times appeared to characterize the early years of California Yearly Meeting. This attitude is reflected in an article written by Nannie Arnold in 1895, entitled, "The Church of the New Era":

> That we are in a state of transition, upon the threshold of a new era as to the scope of our work as churches, no one conversant with the spirit of the times can for a moment doubt. We may retain our distinctive titles as Methodist, Presbyterian, Baptist, Friends, etc., until the end of time and doubtless will. No dogma, tenet or creed may be erased from our separate church books, but our methods will be improved and enlarged, and our forces better drilled and more wisely utilized if we retain our places as the salt of the earth and the light of the world. . . .
> The church of the new era will seek to **save** men. It is true it has always been the aim of the church to some extent to save those without, and to keep those saved within its fold. And the church that has done most for those without has best kept its own. . . .
> The church of the new era then will not only redouble its efforts to bring personal salvation first to all men, but will feel

its equal responsibility in giving them the best possible social
and moral conditions. This would soon settle many an important question for the highest good of society. The church of the
new era will be altruistic in spirit. It will inconvenience itself
for the good of others. Moral reformers will not be the exception, but the rule of the church.[74]

This spirit of evangelism and compassionate outreach became the trademark of California Yearly Meeting, together
with those social concerns that were the natural concomitant of
the interest in transforming man and his society.

The Growth of California Yearly Meeting

It is not the purpose of this study to give a denominational
history; nevertheless, it is important to note the growth of the
California Yearly Meeting of Friends Church following its organization. Within a few years, new congregations had been
formed and established as monthly meetings: Los Angeles Monthly Meeting in 1896; San Francisco and San Diego Monthly Meetings in 1901; Bell Monthly Meeting in 1904; and Bethel Monthly
Meeting in Long Beach in 1906. Preparatory meetings were also
begun in Puente in 1895; in Stony Ford in Colusa County in 1894;
in La Habra and in Los Nietos in 1896.[75] But these latter meetings
did not succeed. The collapse of the economy following the land
boom also led to the closing of the Monthly Meeting at Wildomar.
Owenyo, a meeting which had begun in 1902, lasted only three
years for the same reason.[76] The Modena Monthly Meeting, which
had such a promising beginning, also suffered because of the
economy and many of its members left the community.

In 1901, a quarterly meeting was established in northern
California and was called Berkeley Quarterly Meeting.[77] Still
later, quarterly meetings were established in San Diego[78] and in
Long Beach.[79] By 1969, California Yearly Meeting had grown to
thirty-five monthly meetings, including two in Arizona.[80] Current statistical reports indicate a total membership of 7,574, making California Yearly Meeting one of the largest American yearly meetings in terms of average membership per monthly meeting.

Since 1902, California Yearly Meeting has been fraternally
associated with other Yearly Meetings in this country and abroad.

At a General Conference of Yearly Meetings held at Indianapolis, Indiana, the Five Years Meeting of Friends in America was organized with a common Constitution and Discipline.[81] California Yearly Meeting was a charter member of the Five Years Meeting and has generally cooperated since then with the other Yearly Meetings. In 1966, the name of the Five Years Meeting of Friends was changed to Friends United Meeting.[82]

Although the numerical growth of California Yearly Meeting is directly related to the evangelistic concerns of the Great Awakening, a more important index of the relationship can be seen in the various concerns that were held by California Yearly Meeting in its formative years and continue to be held, at least in measure, to the present. We now turn to this aspect of our study.

The Concerns of California Yearly Meeting

A close correlation exists between the basic principles and essential truths that are held by California Yearly Meeting and the doctrines that were taught and promoted by the revival movement in Quakerism during the second half of the nineteenth century. An examination of the "concerns" of California Yearly Meeting will further indicate the extension of the Great Awakening to the Pacific Coast. For the sake of clarity, these concerns will be considered under the following general topic areas: The Nature of the Church, The Message of the Church, and The Mission of the Church.

The Nature of the Church

California Yearly Meeting understands itself as being an essential part of the Quaker movement begun by George Fox in 1647. As such, it identifies itself with the Church of Jesus Christ and stands upon the great traditions of the Protestant Reformation. The Church is understood to be a visible, gathered community in Christ. The Authorized Declaration of Faith states:

> The Church of Christ is composed of those persons who, through repentance of their sins and faith in the Lord Jesus Christ as their Savior, have been born into His kingdom by the Holy Spirit. By the revelation of the Holy Spirit they look to Christ, as their Prophet, Priest and King, and by the Spirit's baptism and power are enabled to resist temptation and to live in obedience to God's holy will.[83]

A Christian denomination is understood to be an organization composed of those

who hold similar views of the teachings of the Holy Scriptures, and maintain certain practices based upon these teachings, and who voluntarily associate themselves for joint participation in worship, for fellowship and mutual help, and for united effort in the promotion of truth and righteousness.[84]

California Yearly Meeting considers itself to be such a Christian body.

The Church, then, is considered to be a gospel-ordered community, holding certain truths as being essential, and subsequently witnessing to these truths. The Church is thus both a worshiping and redemptive community, a community of those people of God who hear and obey the will of God.

It is interesting to note that in the **Faith and Practice** of California Yearly Meeting, with the exception of a brief historical statement, nowhere does the term "Religious Society of Friends" appear. The Yearly Meeting consciously denominates itself as a "church," and has done so since its inception. This attitude grew out of the revival movement when many Quakers called themselves a "church" in order to distinguish the movement from the Conservative or Hicksite Friends. This designation stands in sharp contrast to the attitude of the Pacific Yearly Meeting of the Religious Society of Friends, as we shall see in the next chapter.

The Message of the Church

The California Yearly Meeting of Friends Church is orthodox and evangelical in its position on all the great doctrines of the Church. While it is in agreement with the historic beliefs of the Church, it insists that these beliefs should never be static, as merely articles of faith to be subscribed to, but should be dynamic in the lives of God's people, lived out before the world.

In identifying the "essential truths," the Authorized Declaration of faith states, "the vital principle of the Christian faith is the truth that man's salvation and higher life are personal matters between the individual soul and God."[85] Salvation is understood to be deliverance from sin, and the possession of spiritual life through faith in Jesus Christ. The spiritual life grows out of the "soul's relation to God and its cooperation with Him, not from any outward or traditional observances."[86]

The Declaration of Faith that was issued by the Richmond, Indiana, Conference of 1887 is included as a section of the **Faith and Practice** of California Yearly Meeting.[87] God is believed to be one God, yet Triune, making himself known to man as Father, Son, and Holy Spirit. Jesus Christ is identified as the divine Son of God, worthy of honor and worship. The Holy Spirit is believed to be in unity with the eternal Godhead, and, indwelling the hearts of believers,[88] he opens their minds that they may understand the Scriptures and becomes to the surrendered person, his Guide, Comforter, Teacher, and Sanctifier. In general accord with such earlier revivalists as David Updegraff and Dougan Clark, California Yearly Meeting views Christian perfection as "a condition resulting from both a crisis and a continuing experience of sanctification,"[89] and endorses the Richmond Declaration of Faith, which states:

> Thus, in its full experience, Sanctification is deliverance from the pollution, nature and love of sin. To this we are every one called, that we may serve the Lord without fear, in holiness and righteousness before Him, all the days of our life.[90]

The Scriptures are held to have been inspired of God and are thus the only divinely authorized record of the doctrines which the Church is bound to accept and of the moral principles which are to regulate actions. There can be no appeal from them to any other authority; thus,

> no one can be required to believe as an article of faith, any doctrine which is not contained in them; and whatsoever any one says or does contrary to the Scriptures, though under profession of the immediate guidance of the Holy Spirit, must be reckoned and accounted a mere delusion.[91]

In still further accord with the theology of the Great Awakening, the **Faith and Practice** declares:

> We believe, according to the Scriptures, that there shall be a resurrection from the dead, both the just and of the unjust . . . not only in a resurrection in Christ from the fallen and sinful state here . . . but that all the wicked, who live in rebellion against the light of grace, and die finally impenitent, shall

come forth to the resurrection of condemnation. . . . We believe that the punishment of the wicked and the blessedness of
the righteous shall be everlasting.[92]

In contrast, however, to the position finally taken by David
Updegraff and some of the revivalists, California Yearly Meeting
continues the traditional view of Quakerism and finds no scriptural evidence or authority for any form or degree of sacerdotal-
ism in the Church, or for the practice of any outward ordinance
or ceremonial rite. The experience of Christ's presence "in the
believer's heart, virtually destroys every ceremonial system and
points the soul to the only satisfying source of spiritual life and
power."[93]

In this brief summary of the theological position of California Yearly Meeting, mention must also be made of the practice
of worship, an issue which was crucial for Joel Bean and those
opposed to the "new techniques" ushered in by the Great Awakening. The pastoral system has been a part of the Yearly Meeting
since its inception; nevertheless, true worship is felt to occur only
as it is in response to the influence of the Spirit of God. The
Authorized Declaration of Faith states:

Worship stands neither in forms nor in the formal disuse of
forms; it may be without words as well as with them. Both
silence and vocal exercise are recognized and valued not as
ends, but as means toward the attainment of an end, which is
the divine blessing upon the individual and the congregation.[94]

Although the Yearly Meeting is committed to the pastoral system, it is clear that the issue is not whether worship can only
occur in a programmed meeting under the direction of a pastor
or in an unprogrammed meeting, for both can be held under the
inspiration of the Holy Spirit. It is not the pastor nor the absence
of a pastor that makes the difference; rather, it is the recognition
of and obedience to the presence of God.[95]

The Mission of the Church

Inherent in California Yearly Meeting has been a deep spiritual insight and concern for the work of the Church. As part of
society, a responsibility was acknowledged from the beginning to
undertake the historic Quaker testimonies of social concern as

part of the evangelical mission of the Church. To the extent that the Yearly Meeting has fulfilled its responsibility, it has succeeded at its task. The thrust and influence of the Great Awakening can be noted also in this area as we briefly observe the concerns for man and his society, both at home and abroad.

The Church at home. The concerns of California Yearly Meeting for social conditions within the state can be identified in the following major areas: education, temperance, welfare, minority groups. Our discussion will center on these areas.

EDUCATION. From the beginning, Friends in California have sensed their responsibility in providing suitable education for their children. In the Minutes of the first sessions of Pasadena Quarterly Meeting held November 19, 1887, it is noted that a committee was appointed

> to work with the superintendent on the subject [of education] and report to the next meeting if they think that the time has come for a graded school in our midst, or whatever they may conclude in the matter.[96]

Three months later, the committee "urged that academies be established in each locality."[97] It was at this same meeting on February 18, 1888, that a report was made to the Quarterly Meeting regarding the building of a college in Whittier. The report stated:

> After holding several preliminary meetings and writing Friends of other neighborhoods to assist by their counsel and advice, we decided that the time had come for taking definite steps toward erecting suitable college buildings at Whittier.[98]

The report further indicated that a total of $113,000 had been received and pledged, in addition to a site for the school donated by the Pickering Land and Water Company at an estimated value of $25,000. Although the committee making the report was not an authorized committee of the Quarterly Meeting, it expressed its desire to be closely affiliated with the church by indicating its willingness to allow two-thirds of the board to be Quakers, two of whom would be appointed by the Quarterly Meeting to serve as liaison between the church and the proposed college. The report won the enthusiastic endorsement of the Quarterly Meeting and plans were made to begin a college.

From the earliest announcement of the plans for a Quaker colony, a prospectus emphasized the support for an educational institution in the following words:

> It is the proper location for a "Yearly Meeting," a "Quarterly Meeting," and a "Friends College," all of which we will encourage with land and money. As to the college, we are making and will continue to make strenuous efforts to have the construction of a suitable building commenced at once. Our company offers ten acres of choice land and $1000 in money, and this will be supplemented by some thousands from stockholders who are much in earnest to make this an entire success.[99]

In May, 1888, contracts were let for the construction of a three-story Gothic building, and in June the pastor of Pasadena Monthly Meeting, Reuben Hartley, was elected temporary president and sent east to secure further financial support.[100] Before the summer was over, however, the plans and dreams for a college were aborted as the great land boom collapsed.[101]

Whittier, however, was not the first attempt to build a Quaker educational institution in southern California. Minutes of Kansas Yearly Meeting indicate that preliminary plans had been made for an institution at Modena,[102] plans which also were not carried out. But there was a difference between the two settlements—Whittier would not relinquish its dream. Attempts were made in 1888 to conduct an academy in a building owned by the Pickering Land and Water Company, and in 1889 in the public school building, but it was not until the Pasadena Quarterly Meeting endorsed the establishment of an independent Whittier Educational Association in 1891 that the Academy took root and developed into Whittier College ten years later.[103]

On August 23, 1893, construction was started on the first college building.[104] Aid for its completion came from the Pasadena Quarterly Meeting in a plan to complete and furnish a second floor auditorium to be used for the sessions of the proposed California Yearly Meeting. In appreciation for this help, the Whittier Educational Association deeded one-fourth interest in the building and land to the California Yearly Meeting.[105] This was the closest that the Yearly Meeting would come to owning a college of its own!

A proposal to turn the assets and control of the college to the Yearly Meeting in 1900[106] was never completed because of certain legalities.[107] On January 7, 1902, Articles of Incorporation were filed and Whittier College began its career as an independent college.[108] Today, Whittier College is an outstanding liberal arts college, giving important service to southern California.[109]

The most illustrious alumnus of Whittier College is, without doubt, Richard Milhous Nixon, the thirty-seventh President of the United States. President Nixon was born into a Quaker home in Yorba Linda and was raised in Whittier. His parents were active members of the East Whittier Friends Church, the same church in which the President has retained his own church membership.

Another effort by California Quakers to establish a school must also be noted. In 1899, a concern was felt to start a Bible school. Within a few years, the Huntington Park Training School for Christian Workers was established, and young people began training for service in the church. Many of its young people found their way to the foreign mission fields. A strong emphasis was placed upon doctrinal standards, including the plenary inspiration of the Scriptures, the necessity of the Atonement, and the experience of Entire Sanctification as a second definite work of grace.[110] These emphases are indicative of the extension of the doctrinal concerns of the Great Awakening into California.

The first report of its work to California Yearly Meeting was made on June 21, 1902 by Irvin Cammack as superintendent of missions.[111] He indicated the school had begun classes in Whittier, February 1900, under the direction of Mary A. Hill, a recorded minister of Ohio Yearly Meeting. At the time of the report, the school was situated in Los Angeles. Within two years, over one hundred students had received some training and twenty-six were involved in missionary work in the Philippines, Guatemala, India, Venezuela, Cuba, Alaska. Eleven students and the first principal of the school were serving as missionaries in China.[112]

Although the Training School was largely supported by California Quakers and gave training to a goodly number of their missionaries, the school was never recognized as an official project of the Yearly Meeting. The name of the school was later changed to Pacific Bible College, and upon relocation to Azusa, it was renamed Azusa College. Its present name of Azusa Pacific College is the result of a merger in 1965 with Los Angeles Pacific College.

TEMPERANCE. Reference has already been made to the first WCTU chapter formed among California Quakers by Sarah P. Morrison at San Jose in 1879.[113] The concerns fostered by Iowa and Kansas Yearly Meetings against the sale and consumption of liquor were continued among Quakers in southern California as well. In 1883, Frances E. Willard, the national and world president of the Women's Christian Temperance Union, visited California and organized a number of chapters.[114] The first chapter among Quakers in southern California was organized in Whittier with Ella C. Veeder as its first president.[115] Membership began with sixteen women, but grew rapidly until over sixty were involved in the struggle to keep liquor out of Whittier.

The first attempt to establish a saloon in a tent was defeated by the aggressiveness of the Chapter. Subsequent attempts also failed for when the

W.C.T.U. tried the crusade method of prayer and visitation in the saloon, and after many harrowing experiences, the saloon was banished, never to return, and one saloon keeper was converted.[116]

At the first Yearly Meeting sessions in 1895, considerable time was given to the discussion of temperance, indicating the importance of the work. Local WCTU chapters had been organized for some time in the various monthly meetings, and a report presented to the Yearly Meeting indicated an active interest in temperance work.[117] Before the sessions had concluded, the following resolution was adopted:

We will accept no compromise, but demand the destruction of this nefarious business. We declare to all the world that the Church of God ought always and everywhere to be known as the relentless foe of this ungodly business, and it is the duty of every Christian to wage ceaseless war against it.[118]

Throughout the years, California Yearly Meeting has maintained its emphasis upon Temperance.

WELFARE. The hospitality of Friends is well-known, and through the individual monthly meetings, concerns in the area of social welfare were practically demonstrated. At the time of the First World War in 1917, however, the American Friends Service Committee was formed as a relief agency to gather funds and clothing for work in France and to provide areas of service that conscientious objectors might undertake during the period of conflict.

The American Friends Service Committee was then asked by Herbert Hoover in 1919 to undertake a large German child-feeding operation. Relief work was also undertaken in Austria, Poland, and Russia. Although the American Friends Service Committee was not organized by the church, it did provide an avenue of service to many members of California Yearly Meeting. At the Yearly Meeting sessions of 1918, a report was made by Allen Tomlinson indicating that the delegates to the Five Years Meeting had been approached by the Central Committee of the AFSC and urged to form a cooperative program in California. A committee was formed and a campaign was launched to raise funds from the monthly meetings for the work of reconstruction. Upon request for official endorsement, the California Yearly Meeting approved the action taken and named the members of the committee as the official Yearly Meeting Committee.[119]

Since that time, several members of the Yearly Meeting have given valuable leadership to the American Friends Service Committee, helping to establish and maintain a regional office in Pasadena. However, because of its controversial peace education program in recent years, the Yearly Meeting has not supported its work to the extent that Pacific Yearly Meeting has done, as we shall see in the succeeding chapter.

Individual Quakers, however, have given leadership in several areas of social concern within the state. A key example is the work of Jesse R. Townsend and his wife, Elizabeth, who began the well-known Children's Home Society of California in 1891. The Townsends had been sent as missionaries to Jamaica in

1883, but upon the death of their son returned to the midwest. Later they joined the migration to California and out of their grief and bereavement began the Children's Home Society. Today this nonprofit organization is supported by the work of one hundred eighty auxiliaries and is the largest adoption agency of its kind in the state.[120]

MINORITY GROUPS. At one of the early meetings of the first session of California Yearly Meeting, concern was expressed for minority groups within the state. A paper was read by Mary Jenkins of El Modena to the Christian Endeavor Society, indicating the need for work among the Chinese and Spanish speaking people.[121] Three years later, in March 1898, a decision was made to unite with the Interdenominational Spanish Society, and Quakers serving on its board took an active part in fostering and directing the work. In September, 1909, a Spanish Mission and Industrial Home was opened in the Whittier home of Philena B. Hadley. From this beginning, the work grew in the Whittier area until a home for Mexican girls was established, Bible schools begun, and finally, in 1922, a Mexican church was built and dedicated. A community room, kitchen, and medical dispensary rooms served to alleviate the social, physical, and spiritual needs of the Spanish speaking people in the area.[122]

In addition to the work within the Mexican-American community, California Yearly Meeting fostered work among the Japanese-Americans. In May, 1903, an initial meeting was held with some Japanese in the Oakland home of a member of Berkeley Monthly Meeting. For the next two years, meetings were held every two weeks in the home of Mr. and Mrs. Takahashi, developing into an evening school for the Japanese in the parlors of the Berkeley church. By 1908, work was being conducted in Long Beach, Pasadena, Fresno, and El Modena. The following year, a school was started in Whittier, coming under the care of Whittier Monthly Meeting in 1913.[123] The work continued until the Second World War. In 1949, however, report was made to the Yearly Meeting indicating the reestablishment of work in Norwalk as well as substantial relocation aid being given to those returning to southern California following internment.

QUAKERS IN CALIFORNIA

132

The plight of the American Indian has been a concern of American Quakerism ever since George Fox met with some Indians on his first visit to America in 1672. This concern is reflected in the work of the Associated Committees on Indian Affairs of several yearly meetings. Iowa and Kansas Yearly Meetings had long undertaken work among the midwestern and southwestern Indians, and a number of Quakers were appointed as Indian agents by President Grant in 1869.[124] Two men who were closely associated with Indian Affairs migrated to California and continued to share their insights with the new Yearly Meeting. William G. Coffin had served for a time as manager of the Southern Indian Superintendency, and Dr. William Nicholsen had served in 1876 as the superintendent of the Central Superintendency in Indian Affairs.[125] For a number of years, California Friends have been active in the Indian Center of Los Angeles as a consequence of this continuing interest.

We have briefly discussed thus far the work of the California Yearly Meeting of Friends Church within the state in the areas of education, temperance, welfare, and minority groups. We now consider the work of the church abroad.

The Church abroad. One of the clearest examples of the extension of the Great Awakening is seen in the foreign missionary enterprise undertaken by California Yearly Meeting. The fact that such work was entered upon at the first Yearly Meeting sessions in 1895 is a further indication of California Yearly Meeting's close tie to the vision and motivations of the revival movement. California Yearly Meeting conducts missionary work on two major fields, Alaska and Central America. A brief account of the beginnings of this work follows.

ALASKA. During the Christian Endeavor meeting on the closing Sunday of the 1895 Yearly Meeting sessions, Anna Hunnicutt offered herself for missionary work in Alaska. Accompanied by Lizzie Morris of Whittier and supported by the young people of California Yearly Meeting, she went to work in southeastern Alaska. In 1897, work was begun among the Eskimos of Kotzebue Sound by Robert and Carrie Sams, together with Anna Hunnicutt.

At the Yearly Meeting sessions that year, a resolution was presented by the Women's Foreign Missionary Society:

Resolved, that we ask the Yearly Meeting to adopt Kotzebue Sound Mission as its mission field and that all money received for that work pass through the hands of the Yearly Meeting Missionary Board.[126]

The Yearly Meeting was united in adopting its first mission field. Through the years the work in Alaska has grown: there are eleven churches with a total membership of 1,500, a Bible Training School, and, until recently, the only high school in Alaska north of the Arctic Circle.

CENTRAL AMERICA. California Yearly Meeting's work in Central America began when two young men from the Huntington Park Training School for Christian Workers took it upon themselves to do colportage work in Guatemala in 1902. These two men were Thomas J. Kelley and Clark Buckley.[127] After a period of service, Thomas Kelley returned to the United States to recruit help. While he was gone, Buckley was found dead beside the road with his pack of Bibles and tracts. When the news reached California Friends, its appeal was electric! A small band of five adults visited most of the monthly meetings in southern California, raised their support, and went to Guatemala. For the next few years, the work challenged the vision of the young people, and in 1905 the Christian Endeavor Union sent the following communication to the Board of Missions and the Women's Foreign Missionary Society:

Dear Friends, Greeting:
For the past few years some of our young people of California Yearly Meeting have been looking for a field in which the Endeavorers could work as a Union. As we followed the Master's leadings the open door presented was Guatemala, with our two Spirit-filled workers, Esther A. Bond and Alice C. Zimmer. At the Christian Endeavor session at our last Yearly Meeting our Missionary Superintendent was instructed to take pledges for Guatemala and when the amount reached $250 to ask the Yearly Meeting Board of Foreign Missions to adopt the field and let us be responsible for raising the required amount. The Lord has now answered our prayers and has given us more than we asked. We have pledges of $276.40 and two societies to hear from. Yours for the million and a half in dark Guatemala. . . .[128]

In 1906, R. Esther Smith and Cora Wildman went to Guatemala to work as missionaries. In succeeding years, they were joined by many others who gave unselfishly of their love and devotion. Especially noteworthy was the work of W. Lester Stanton and Matilda Haworth. Today the work in Central America encompasses the countries of El Salvador and Honduras, in addition to Guatemala. There now exist seventy-two churches and sixty-five preparatory meetings, with a total membership of 10,750, an agricultural mission, a Bible School, high schools, grade schools, and medical dispensaries.[129]

This examination of the concerns of California Yearly Meeting has shown clearly the high correlation that exists between revival movement in the midwest during the nineteenth century and the establishment and growth of California Yearly Meeting. One further task remains: the identification of the leadership of California Yearly Meeting during its early years, for it was primarily through these men and women that the Great Awakening was extended to California.

The Leadership of California Yearly Meeting

The preface to the Minutes of the California Yearly Meeting in 1895 contains the following biographical entry:

> Without mentioning the names of the many ministers and others who have labored earnestly in the building up of these meetings, and most of them are still spared to us, the name of Jeremiah A. Grinnell, now gone to his reward, is so closely connected with the early history of all of them that it would be unjust not to speak of him in this connection. He was the pioneer minister in nearly all of these meetings, and it is largely due to his faithful ministry and fatherly counsel that they were brought into existence.[130]

Jeremiah Grinnell is characteristic of the leadership that came to California. In 1859, he ministered with Allen Jay near Lafayette, Indiana, in a meeting that was attended by revival kindlings.[131] The following year, he was at the sessions of Indiana Yearly Meeting when the first indication of the Great Awakening occurred among Friends. Jeremiah Grinnell was one of the leaders of the revival movement, and his work in California was built upon his past experiences.

One of the most dynamic of the young evangelists was John Henry Douglas. A persuasive speaker and fervent soul winner, he spearheaded the revival movement in the midwest, served as the first general superintendent of Iowa Yearly Meeting, and then moved to California. In the new Yearly Meeting, he assumed the post of superintendent of the Evangelistic, Pastoral, and Church Extension Board. He also served for a time as pastor of the Long Beach Monthly Meeting. His dynamic leadership had a profound effect upon California Yearly Meeting, molding it in the pattern of the Great Awakening.

Allen Jay, one of the earliest leaders of the Great Awakening, was present at the opening sessions of California Yearly Meeting.[132] Leaders of the revival movement in Iowa who migrated to California and gave leadership to the new Yearly Meeting included Thomas Armstrong, Charles and Ella Veeder, and Levi Gregory. W. E. Mills and William Nicholsen had come from Kansas Yearly Meeting, and Mary M. Brown from Indiana Yearly Meeting. Others who shared in the leadership of the Great Awakening and extended it to California include Luther Gordon, Elwood Scott, John Y. Hoover, Amos Kenworthy, and William G. Hubbard.[133]

An institution has been described as the lengthening shadow of a man. California Yearly Meeting is undoubtedly the lengthening shadow of a host of men and women who were challenged and inspired by the Great Awakening in Quakerism.

8

The Pacific Yearly Meeting of the Religious Society of Friends

IN THE PRECEDING chapters, we have noted the westward movement of Quakerism, and have seen the profound changes that nineteenth century revivalism introduced. When the movement arrived and developed in the State of California, two distinct forms of Quakerism became evident. The one, California Yearly Meeting of Friends Church, was a direct result and extension of the Great Awakening. It remains now for us to observe more clearly the second form of Quakerism within California.

Joel Bean's reaction against the revival movement has been identified. His concern for a Friends meeting, worshiping in the traditions of Friends as he understood them, led to the formation of the unique organization called the College Park Association of Friends. This Association brought together a number of Quakers belonging to a variety of yearly meetings and was the forerunner of the Pacific Yearly Meeting of the Religious Society of Friends.

Pacific Yearly Meeting is an independent, unaffiliated yearly meeting, the first of its kind among Friends.[1] It stands in sharp contrast to the California Yearly Meeting and is the result of the original concerns expressed by Joel Bean. If California Yearly Meeting is indeed the extension of the Great Awakening into the far west, Pacific Yearly Meeting is the result of the reaction against the Great Awakening, fathered by Joel Bean

137

and fostered by like-minded Friends. It is to this study that we now turn.

The Establishment of Pacific Yearly Meeting

The Pacific Yearly Meeting of the Religious Society of Friends was founded in 1947 as the result of the development and growth of a number of unaffiliated Friends groups on the west coast.[2] The College Park Meeting was the first of these groups and its success soon prompted other groups to form. When these groups felt the need to organize for greater permanence, mutual strengthening and more effective action, regional associations were formed. It was then a simple step to move beyond the regional associations and form an entirely new Yearly Meeting. This development can be clearly traced in California.

The Growth of the College Park Association

When the College Park Association was formed and incorporated in December, 1889, it gave the following purposes for its organization:

> To promote the interest of Christianity and morality and to disseminate religious and moral principles.
> To acquire and hold property for religious and church purposes, and for a burial ground.
> To maintain a meeting for worship of the Society of Friends at the meeting house of the said Corporation.[3]

This Association was not considered to be a religious denomination, but a fellowship of Friends who gathered to worship. From the beginning, its membership was composed of concerned members of the Society of Friends from various parts of America, from England, and from the meetings of Friends in southern France. Some of its members were affiliated with other religious denominations; others had no church ties whatsoever.[4] In this fellowship, the members met for two reasons: to "realize the Kingdom of God within the soul through the act of worship" and "to realize the Kingdom outwardly in the world."[5]

In its meetings for worship, Friends gathered without the benefit of a programmed service. The Divine Presence was sought in a "living silence" with no individual having any special function or authority. There was no distinction between clergy or laity, male or female, learned or unlearned. Each worshiper waited in silence until messages or insight would come that were to be spoken for the profit of the whole meeting. Thus, each meeting for worship was "a new experiment in religion."[6]

In pursuit of its ideal to realize the Kingdom of God outwardly in the world, it endeavored to act upon the conviction

> that all men are brothers and children of a common Father; that accordingly love should be substituted for violence as far as possible in human relations; that war should be abolished as a means for settling disputes between nations; and that all national, racial, and class antagonisms should give way to sympathy, helpfulness and understanding.[7]

The College Park Association thus held to a type of outward conduct which recognized and appealed to what it believed was the Light of God within every man.

As late as 1910, the Association was often called "Joel Bean's Meeting."[8] His influence continued to mold and shape the content and direction of the Association.[9] His gentle spirit pervaded the whole and, in general, characterized the attitude of the meeting toward others. One visitor commented in an article to **The Friend** (Philadelphia) of the lasting impression the Association had made on him. He wrote:

> I have frequently observed amongst conservative Friends, at home as abroad, a loving tenderness either to withhold information as to the actual facts, and to condone the situation, when speaking about modern methods in the "Friends' Churches," or, on the other hand, to exhibit a human tinge of bitterness at the remembrance of past wrongs, and waste of goodly heritage. But these College Park Friends did neither. On the contrary, they fully and freely discussed the remarkable separation from Friends principles that they had been obliged to withstand in past years, and did it in a spirit of good humor and love for dear brethren who, they felt, had made a mistake.[10]

The enlargement of the Association. On May 4, 1918, the bylaws of the Association were changed to allow the establishment of other meetings under the direction of the College Park Association. The new article declared:

> The Association may at its discretion constitute and establish meetings for worship and the transaction of local business;

such meetings being known as monthly meetings. These shall be co-ordinated with each other under this Association.[11] During the next few years, three meetings were established at Berkeley, Palo Alto, and Los Gatos. Twice a year, on the first Saturday in May and the first Saturday in November, the Association met as a whole for a Semi-Annual Meeting.[12] These gatherings brought together members and attenders of the four meetings, as well as visitors from a distance and other interested individuals. A meeting for worship was convened in the morning, followed by a business session, a common meal, and an afternoon session.

The concerns of the Association. The very first action taken by the College Park Association in its initial meeting in 1889 was prophetic of the type of concern that would occupy the attention of the Association during the ensuing years. The minutes record the nomination of one of its members to the Board of the Young Men's Christian Association of San Jose.[13] This concern for society characterized one of the major unifying principles of the Association.

Various reports of the Semi-Annual Meetings indicate that considerable attention was given to the problems of society. The plight of the Negro was discussed, as well as the situation of the Chinese-American. Of particular interest in earlier days of the Association was the welfare of a Chinese student, Tong Sing Kow, who became a Quaker while attending the services of the College Park Meeting.[14] Many years later, in 1930, the Association took an active part in the celebrated Mooney Case. Fourteen years earlier, two labor organizers, Tom Mooney and Warren Billings, had been sentenced to life imprisonment for a bomb explosion that had occurred in San Francisco. Few events in the State had so sharply divided the people. When Mooney was later offered a parole, he rejected the offer, declaring his innocency.

On March 9, 1930, six representatives of the College Park Association met with Governor C. C. Young at the Palace Hotel in San Francisco. They reported to him that Friends had met in prison with Mooney, were convinced of his innocence, and had raised money for a new suit to be given him. They urged the

Governor to release him, saying, "He is a man of manly bearing, sweet natured, with a very intelligent sense of his own situation."[15]

In sharp contrast to the many social concerns that can be identified through the years, stands the absence of any concern for theology or declarations of faith. The Discipline of the College Park Association is characterized by brevity and is noteworthy more for what is omitted than for what it contains. It states simply:

1. Doctrine: Friends believe in the continuing reality of the living Christ, available to all seeking souls.
2. Worship: The worship of God is in spirit and in truth, and shall be held on a basis of the leadership of the Holy Spirit.
3. Ministry: All members and all attenders are free to participate vocally in meetings, under a sense of God's presence.
4. Manner of Living: Friends are advised to conduct their private lives with simplicity and directness, ever sensitive to the world's needs and eager to engage in service.
5. Relation to State: Friends are urged to feel their responsibility to the nation, and at the same time to recognize their oneness with humanity everywhere, regardless of race or nation, abstaining from all hatred.[16]

In contrast to California Yearly Meeting, there was little concern for developing theological statements or articles of faith. Joel Bean had long insisted upon a Friends Meeting that would be liberal in its hospitality, allowing for divergence of theological views. His own deposition as a minister of Iowa Yearly Meeting had occurred because of theological disagreement, and so the College Park Association eliminated all theological requirements as the basis for receiving or maintaining membership. An example of this liberal spirit is the statement of Otha Thomas of San Jose about the Scriptures:

While Friends believe that the Spirit of God still leads men to speak and write, they believe that full and ample testimony has been given, and would distinguish between a new revelation of the good old gospel, and the revelation of a new gospel. As to the canon being full, they would see no reason why the "Prophecy of Enoch," the "Book of Nathan" or of "Joshua," should they be unearthed by the archeologists, should not be added thereto.[17]

The leaders of the Association. In addition to Joel Bean, a number of outstanding individuals gave leadership to the Association. Such a person was Charles Cox, a graduate of Haverford College, who met Lydia Bean while he was principal of the Academy at Le Grande. The year following the migration of the Bean family to San Jose, he came to California and married Lydia. For fourteen years he served as president of the College Park Association, working closely with Joel Bean, his father-in-law, in establishing an effective organization.[18]

One of the most influential leaders of the Association was Augustus T. Murray. For forty-eight years he was connected with Stanford University and gained worldwide recognition as a classical scholar and was known everywhere among scholars for his translation of Homer for the Loeb Library. Augustus Murray also served as president of the Association, giving valuable guidance to the organization. Rufus Jones called him "a Friend of the deeply convinced, thoroughly seasoned, elder type of Quaker."[19] His emphasis upon worship was rich and significant. When Herbert Hoover was elected President of the United States, Augustus Murray left California for Washington, D.C., and served as a spiritual counselor and "pastor" to the President. In a letter to Philadelphia Yearly Meeting just prior to his death, he wrote, "Communion with God is the one true source from which a group can gain clarity of vision and unity of purpose."[20]

Others who gave valuable leadership included Andrew and Hannah Erskine, William James, Arthur Heeb, and Herbert C. Jones.[21] Outstanding Quakers from the east and from London Yearly Meeting often visited the meetings of the Association. The **Friends Bulletin** wrote of one such visitor, Frederick B. Sainty, "This London Friend is a veritable Saint Paul come over into Macedonia to unite the isolated and lonely Friends Meetings in America."[22] Of particular importance also was the leadership of Howard and Anna Brinton, as we shall later see.

The death of Joel and Hannah Bean. On January 31, 1909, Hannah Bean passed away in San Jose, in her seventy-ninth year. For many years, she had been a close companion to Joel and had exerted a wide influence for good. Her spirit of kindness and warm, affectionate nature endeared her to the hearts of many. "A subtle influence for good, the reflected radiance of Christ was felt in her presence."[23]

Later that year, Joel set sail for a short visit to Hawaii, but before long his strength began to fail. Throat surgery demanded a stay in a San Francisco hospital in 1912,[24] and then he returned again to Hawaii. On January 11, 1914, Joel Bean died in Honolulu, the place of his first missionary labors more than a half century before.[25] Joel deeply loved Hawaii and its people. In these islands, he loved to linger and reflect; perhaps in these wanderings his mind would recall the days when he and Hannah made their first missionary journey, when life was still uncomplicated with criticism and controversy.

On February 15, 1914, a memorial service was held in the College Park Meetinghouse in San Jose. Many spoke with thankfulness for the life that had been so generously lived in their midst. An English Friend said:

> Joel Bean stood always for freedom and for progress—for the freedom of the spirit as against the bondage of the letter. Firmly rooted in the foundation truths of Christianity, he could fearlessly welcome truth from whatever quarter it might come.[26]

A Friend from Iowa later wrote in high tribute:

> In the death of Joel Bean the Society has lost one of its most useful members. A deep religious feeling possessed him always, and a life consecrated to service was his aim. In spite of deep sorrow, of grief and many obstacles, he labored on, with only one aim, that was to be useful to his fellow-men. He also had an exultant faith that in the end good would triumph over evil, no matter how deeply tried he was or how dark it seemed. . . .
> He lived close to the heart of humanity, and still at the same time in a different manner from most of the people, so far removed when it came to the purely spiritual things.
> His personal views on some matters may not have coincided with those held by many members of the Society, but it may have been that his vision was larger and his experiences different. His religion was a life rather than a system of belief. The elements most strongly expressed in his life were those of worship, love and devotion to duty. With him the true test was whether or not a person was willing to offer himself for service. . . . Many will long remember the kind friend, the help-

ful teacher, the devoted neighbor and tender minister who at
all times was willing to make the world better for having lived
in it.[27]

The influence of Howard and Anna Brinton. In 1921, Howard H. Brinton married Anna S. Cox, the granddaughter of Joel
Bean. The Quaker marriage was witnessed by a host of Friends
in the College Park Meetinghouse. After teaching at Earlham
College in Indiana, they returned to California where both were
members of the faculty at Mills College. Their home was often
the gathering place of Friends and they lent their influence to
the strengthening of the College Park Association.

In 1928, the Brintons made the first of several suggestions
that were directly responsible for the formation of the Pacific
Yearly Meeting. At the December meeting of the Association,
Anna Brinton had the "happy idea" that a summary of the proceedings be prepared and printed each quarter. This idea was the
birth of the **Friends Bulletin.**[28] In the spirit of her grandfather,
Joel Bean, Anna was later to call for a closer organic unity
among like-minded Friends on the Pacific coast. It is to this
aspect of the background of Pacific Yearly Meeting that we now
turn.

The Pacific Coast Association of Friends

The College Park Association of Friends was the pioneer
in the movement to form independent and unofficial meetings for
worship in various parts of the United States. By 1929, there
were over thirty such groups in existence.[29] These groups were
generally small, relatively new, and all were unprogrammed.
Most of these meetings were composed largely of "convinced
Friends," individuals who were not birthright Quakers or who
had not been raised as Quakers, but became Friends because of
choice and convincement. Many of these meetings were located
close to a university campus or near educational centers, draw-
ing their membership from the faculty and students. One writer
suggests that such meetings were geared to the needs of the
"modern, educated, sincere seekers."[30] Unconfined by ready-made
forms and undeterred by theological exercises, these groups were

generally action-oriented and sought ways to make a living testimony of their understanding of Quakerism.

At the Semi-Annual Meeting of the College Park Association of Friends held at San Jose on November 1, 1930, Howard and Anna Brinton proposed that a conference of representatives of these groups be held at Mills College in Oakland with the purpose of forming a more inclusive association. At this time, there were nine independent meetings on the Pacific coast meeting regularly for worship on the basis of silence. Six others were meeting irregularly.[31] It was the hope of the Brinton's that a more effective organization might bind these meetings together in a closer fellowship.

An April 25, 1931, the conference was convened on the campus of Mills College. Since the dormitories were in use, the home of Howard and Anna Brinton was used as the site of the conference. William and Anna James, Andrew and Hannah Erskine, were some of those Friends who assisted the Brintons. Invitations were printed and mailed to all interested Friends, including the alumni lists of Quaker colleges.[32] The suggestion of a more inclusive association met with enthusiastic approval and the Pacific Coast Association of Friends was formed.

William Lawrence, of Corvallis, Oregon, described the Association in these words:

It is not a movement, a new denomination, nor another Yearly Meeting. It is not an official spokesman for the Society of Friends nor any branch of the society on the Pacific Coast. It is a banding together through mutual interest and concern of all Friends and others in sympathy with Friends' principles. Each person may become a member upon his own affirmation, and each meeting or group may affiliate with the association or not as they may elect. The association does not seek to commit its members nor the affiliated groups to any set of stated principles or creeds. Each member is free to make his or her own testimony, and, without the stigma of vacillation, to grow in grace according to his own inner light.[33]

The Association met annually, bringing together a variety of Friends from the Pacific coast. Independent Friends meetings in Riverside,[34] Berkeley,[35] Palo Alto, San Jose, and Los Gatos were represented, in addition to those from the Villa Street Meeting in

Pasadena, and the Orange Grove Meeting in Pasadena. The latter meeting was composed of Hicksite Friends and was a part of Philadelphia Yearly Meeting, General Conference.[36] But the Association was not restricted to the State of California. Friends meetings at Corvallis, Oregon; Seattle, Washington; and at Victoria and Vancouver, Canada, also became part of the Association. By the time of the 1940s, the annual meetings of the Association were being held the third week of August, alternating the sites between the northwest, southern California, and the San Francisco Bay area.[37]

Cooperative projects were undertaken in areas of social concern. Conferences were held on the plight of the Japanese-American,[38] Institutes of International Relations were held, and peace between classes and races was discussed. From the beginning, the work of the American Friends Service Committee was promoted and its projects were undertaken. There was little or no concern, however, for theological consensus. It did not "commit its members to any set of stated principles or creeds," but each individual was free to "make his or her testimony."[39]

Howard Brinton served as the first clerk of the Association and, together with Anna Brinton, gave valuable leadership during the formative years. He wrote of the first session:

> It was an interesting experience to preside as Clerk over the first session of the Pacific Coast Association, as no one knew who were the weighty Friends and who ought to serve on committees, but in a few days unity arose out of chaos.[40]

In addition to his duties as clerk, Howard Brinton also served for several years as editor of the **Friends Bulletin**, the official organ of the Pacific Coast Association. The Association met regularly until it further enlarged the scope of its organization and formed the Pacific Yearly Meeting in 1947.

The Founding of Pacific Yearly Meeting

As early as 1931, Howard and Anna Brinton had raised the question of a yearly meeting that would "aim to include all Friends of all branches (as well as other persons) who cherish ideals of worship similar to those of historic Quakerism."[41] Although there was little desire for forming a traditional yearly meeting, the need of greater unity was acknowledged among those Friends groups on the west coast that were not in sympathy with the pastoral system and the programmed meetings for worship within California Yearly Meeting. The immediate result of the suggestion of the Brintons was, as we have seen, the loosely organized Pacific Coast Association. For sixteen years, this Association provided a means of fellowship, but it soon became apparent that a more structured and efficient organization was needed. The Pacific Coast Association had repeatedly rejected individual membership and all centralized authority, but gradually "the more outwardly directed organizational Friends prevailed over the more inwardly directed anarchistic attenders."[42]

In 1941, Howard Brinton specifically called for the formation of a new yearly meeting. In a letter to the members of the College Park Association, now a division of the Pacific Coast Association, he wrote:

In regard to the formation of a Yearly Meeting, I can see no real difficulty in the way. It would simply amount to a change of name—or perhaps not even that. With a Discipline and a well defined membership you would in no way differ from other Yearly Meetings, no matter by what name you might call yourselves. . . . I think the best set-up for the Pacific Coast would be for the Pacific Coast Association of Friends to become Pacific Coast Yearly Meeting, with three Quarterly Meetings—one centering at Pasadena, one in the center (The College Park Association of Friends), and one in the north (Willamette Valley Friends Association and others). This, I think, is bound to come sooner or later, and the possibility of it ought to be discussed at the next meeting of the Pacific Coast Association of Friends. . . . Such a Yearly Meeting should include the new independent Meetings in New Mexico, Arizona, and Hawaii. . . . If the Society of Friends is to be saved today it will be by such groups and not by the old stock which is so often decaying at the root.[43]

By 1946, other influential leaders within the Association had begun to press for the formation of a yearly meeting. Editorials in the **Friends Bulletin** emphasized the need for closer association with nonpastoral meetings and suggested that a new yearly meeting was the next logical step to be taken.[44] Howard

and Anna Brinton had assumed new responsibilities at Pendle
Hill in Wallingford, Pennsylvania, but kept in close touch with
the Association by writing articles and through occasional visits.
In 1946, the Brintons undertook a lecture tour throughout the
Pacific Coast Association in preparation for the formation of a
yearly meeting.[45]

Meetings as far north as Victoria and Vancouver were visited, and as far south as Pasadena. Many Friends were wary of
the idea; others were opposed. But Howard Brinton proposed
that the Pacific Coast Association had already been recognized
as a yearly meeting to all intents and purposes through correspondence with other yearly meetings and through the appointment of its members to various inter-yearly meeting committees.[46] He further proposed that dual memberships would over-
come loyalty problems for some monthly meetings, e.g., the
Orange Grove Meeting of Pasadena could belong simultaneously
to Philadelphia Yearly Meeting and to Pacific Yearly Meeting. In
recalling his travels in 1946, he wrote:

> I was able to assure doubting Friends that this could be legally
> done and that there was precedent for it. The Association had
> already been recognized by an exchange of epistles and certifi-
> cates of memberships. In these circumstances I found myself
> constantly appealed to as an authority on Quaker "canon law,"
> not because I am an expert in this subject but because in the
> kingdom of the blind the one-eyed man is king. Here, as in
> early Quakerism, there was some tension between those who
> wanted organization and the extreme individualists who did not
> want any arrangement that might appear to tell the Spirit what
> ought to be done. Some Pacific Coast Friends were, with good
> reason, fearful of the multiplication of committees and the
> creation of a bureaucracy if a Yearly Meeting was formed.
> Some Friends were ready to join with the reservation that "the
> Yearly Meeting be a consultative and service body, but not an
> authoritative, legislative, or taxing body.[47]

On April 26, 1946, the University Monthly Meeting of
Seattle, Washington, formally proposed the establishment of a
new yearly meeting.[48] When the Pacific Coast Association met in
Pasadena for its annual meeting, August 16-18, the report of an
Organization Committee was eagerly awaited. After much dis-
cussion and deliberation, and under guidance of Howard and

Anna Brinton, who were present, the report of the Committee
was approved, favoring the establishment of a Pacific Coast
Yearly Meeting. The report stated:

The Pacific Coast Yearly Meeting shall be a free association of
Monthly Meetings for mutual support and consultation and for
furthering such concerns as its members have in common. Its
relation to a Monthly Meeting is consultative and not authori-
tative.[49]

Some meetings, such as San Francisco, were fearful of a
larger budget and wanted no change in the Pacific Coast Association. The affirmative voices, however, prevailed, and a new yearly meeting was approved, to be called the Pacific Yearly Meeting
of the Religious Society of Friends.[50] Monthly meetings that
were interested in forming the Yearly Meeting were asked to
send official delegates to the 1947 sessions.

In order to accommodate those Friends who did not want to
sever ties or loyalties to other yearly meetings, a unique plan was
approved. The Pacific Coast Association was to function concurrently with the Pacific .Yearly Meeting, with the officers of
the one serving as the officers of the other. This organizational
device satisfied those who were reluctant to make the change in
spite of the obvious advantages.[51] A closer fellowship could be
maintained, relationships among younger Friends could be developed, and cooperative projects could be consolidated and reinforced. One Quaker leader wrote:

Not for a moment do I feel that a new Yearly Meeting will be
a magic wand that will bring perfection to all our meetings
and endeavors. It will merely be a very human tool—but it will
be a **tool**! And if we see it as such and are willing and able to
use it, it can help us to build the kind of strong, clear, unified
testimony we so earnestly desire to make not only in our own
Coast communities, but to the world.[52]

On August 21, 1947, the first session of the new Pacific
Yearly Meeting was convened in Palo Alto. Twelve monthly meetings accepted membership in the Yearly Meeting, which was unique in its international character. Independent meetings in countries bordering the Pacific ocean applied and were granted membership status. These charter monthly meetings were: Vancouver, Canada; Seattle, Washington; Berkeley, San Francisco,

Palo Alto, San Jose, Tracy, Pasadena (Orange Grove), Los Angeles, and Riverside, California; Mexico City, Mexico, and Honolulu, Hawaii.[53]

The Growth of Pacific Yearly Meeting

Howard Brinton has commented that the rapid growth of Pacific Yearly Meeting is one of the most hopeful signs of the Religious Society of Friends[54] and that the emergence of new independent meetings "is the most important event in modern Quaker history in America."[55] Many Friends will sharply disagree with Howard Brinton on these statements; nevertheless the growth of Pacific Yearly Meeting is remarkable. It has increased its membership at a faster rate than has California Yearly Meeting during the same period. By 1950, a total membership of 756 was listed and six additional groups had become formally affiliated: Eugene, Oregon; Victoria, Canada; Santa Fe, New Mexico; Albuquerque, New Mexico; and Shanghai, China.[56]

A steady rise in membership continued. In 1951, there were 825 members in eighteen monthly meetings; in 1952, there were 961 members in seventeen monthly meetings and seventeen other preparatory meetings.[57] In 1953, there was a total of 1,015 members in twenty-three monthly meetings, and in 1954, the statistics list 1,108 members. Three years later, in 1957, twenty-eight monthly meetings were listed, which increased to thirty in 1959 and thirty-four in 1960, representing eight states and three foreign countries.[58] The total membership in 1961 exceeded 1,300 adults, plus 1,258 children.[59] Membership has continued to grow until, in 1966, there were 1,635 adult members in forty-one monthly meetings, plus 1,272 children, 801 of whom were Junior members.[60]

The Concerns of Pacific Yearly Meeting

We have noted the close relationship that the formation of Pacific Yearly Meeting had with Joel Bean, through his granddaughter, Anna Cox Brinton. The influence of Joel Bean can be also noted by observing those concerns and principles that Pacific Yearly Meeting has held to be primary, for the Yearly Meeting clearly stands in the heritage of the founder of the College Park Association. We will consider, therefore, the Yearly Meeting's understanding of the nature, the message, and the mission of the Society of Friends.

The Nature of the Society

Howard Brinton has suggested that some members of the Pacific Yearly Meeting would not consider themselves as Protestants,[61] but as participants in a third form of Christianity, neither Protestant nor Catholic. Nevertheless, the **Discipline** clearly identifies the Yearly Meeting as part of the Quaker interpretation of Christianity, keeping in "creative tension its particular and universal character, its Christ-centered and God-centered orientation, its mystical and practical demands."[62]

A Friends meeting was a part of the church to the extent that encounter took place with God. The **Discipline** further states, "A true meeting in the Quaker sense is a meeting of men which is also a meeting with God. So far as this divine-human meeting takes place, there is order, unity, and power."[63] All of the monthly meetings are unprogrammed and meet for worship on the basis of silence. There is no pastoral system, and, since each member is considered a living part of the Meeting for Worship, there is no provision for the recognition or the recording of those who have a gift of ministry. A Committee on Worship and Ministry fosters and strengthens the spiritual life of the meeting.

Soon after the Yearly Meeting was formed in 1947, questions were raised as to standards of membership. The Pacific Coast Association did not accept members into the Society of Friends, but now as a Yearly Meeting certain standards were felt to be necessary. Statements in the **Discipline** regarding membership were then approved, indicating that adherence to specific statements of belief or agreement with certain theological formulations was not the basis of membership. Membership, however, implied a "readiness and desire to join in the common effort of the Society to search for and follow the inner Light."[64]

All persons were admitted into membership who found that the faith and practice of the Yearly Meeting met their religious needs. Instead of the attainment of some particular religious experience, "an open mind and heart and an earnest desire for ever-increasing Light"[65] were held to be of chief concern. This position parallels the concern of Joel Bean for a meeting in which a wide variety of theologies could be expressed and maintained without fear of censure.

The Message of the Society

It is very clear that, with some individual exceptions, Pacific Yearly Meeting has little concern for theology, at least as a basis for agreement in a formal creed.[66] It is this fact which sharply distinguishes it from California Yearly Meeting. In an article on the subject of Friends and Theology, Madge Seaver indicated four reasons why Pacific Yearly Meeting objected to theological inquiry. First, there was an expressed impatience with "notions." Second, since the essential of a good life was held to be good relationships, it was felt that the possession of an orderly body of knowledge might make warm relationships more difficult of attainment. Third, the Quaker vocation in the Christian Church was considered to be that of mysticism rather than theology. Fourth, theology was felt to be divisive.[67] Nevertheless, the article called for "a more cordial attitude toward those for whom it is a vocation or interest."[68] Joel Bean, it will be remembered, was deposed as a minister of Iowa Yearly Meeting because of theological disagreement and misunderstanding.

The message of the church, therefore, is not thought to be that which is couched in theological terminology or doctrinal formulations, but rather in terms of social concern. The very existence of Friends meetings in Shanghai and Hong Kong under the care of the Yearly Meeting indicates a willingness to conduct a dialogue with those of some of the major Oriental religions. The concept of a yearly meeting on the "Pacific Rim" implied not only a willingness to cooperate across international boundaries, but also a willingness to make contact with non-Christian faiths. One monthly meeting reported in 1960 that contacts had been made with Sikhs, Buddhists, and Hindus. In a cooperative worship—in discussion encounter—this meeting reported, "The worship was a moving experience and we felt no reservations or divisions."[69]

The Mission of the Society

The **Discipline** of Pacific Yearly Meeting states:

Men everywhere, of whatever race, nation, creed, or condition, are children of God and brothers to ourselves. We should have regard for the worth of each person we meet or think of, whether far away or near to us. We cannot be easy in our own lives when others suffer indignity, injustice, or want. In the Spirit of Christ we must be ready to put ourselves at our brother's side and share his burden. As we are true to the divine within us, we can answer to the divine in others.[70]

This concern for man and his society has involved the Yearly Meeting in two major areas of social concern: race relations and peace. In the effort to solve these pressing issues, it has supported and promoted the work of the American Friends Service Committee. Pacific Yearly Meeting has cooperated formally with the American Friends Service Committee, especially since the time of the opening of regional offices in California.

The Friends Committee on National Legislation is also given substantial support. In addition to the concerns of peace and race relations, other social concerns have also engaged many members of the Yearly Meeting: abolition of capital punishment, fair housing, prison reform, civil rights, migrants, and work with foreign students. Education has also been a major concern. The Yearly Meeting operates the John Woolman School at Nevada City, California, and its members maintain the Pacific Ackworth elementary school in Temple City, California.[71]

The Past Is Prologue

REVIVALISM HAS PROFOUNDLY affected and shaped the American church. But, whereas the period of religious awakening in the eighteenth and early nineteenth centuries brought renewal to large segments of the American society, it was not until after the beginning of the Third Awakening in 1858 that Quakerism experienced its own Great Awakening.

Years of controversy and separation had produced a concern among Friends to recapture the sense of unity, strength, and purpose that was so clearly exhibited by the first generation Quakers. The influence of the Evangelical movement in England, imported largely by Joseph John Gurney to American Friends, had prepared the way for the Great Awakening by promoting Bible study groups and missionary enterprises. Old and traditional barriers began to crumble. Quaker youth caught a vision of a revitalized Society of Friends. Visits from itinerating English Quakers spread the revival concern. Finally, the smoldering kindling burst into flame in 1867 and revival blazed across most of American Quakerism.

The results of the Great Awakening in Quakerism were profound. Many of the old Quaker customs were abandoned as new techniques and ideas were fostered by revivalism. Fervent evangelism brought many new converts into the yearly meetings, many of whom had no training in the unprogrammed way of worship and no background or tradition in Quakerism to support them. Recognizing the dilemma, monthly meetings began to hire the visiting evangelists to stay on, or to contract with other individuals to serve as part-time or full-time pastors, in order that coordination and direction might be given to the meetings. Within the space of a generation, most of the yearly meetings in the midwest had adopted the pastoral system.

Concurrently with this religious awakening, Quakers were moving westward. Iowa and Kansas Yearly Meetings were established, and revivalism ushered in a period of dramatic growth. Although many of the changes were necessary and welcome, revival in Quakerism also brought unnecessary difficulties, created division and made even deeper separations. In some cases, the wedge between the old and the new was driven beyond repair. The younger Quakers were enthusiastic about the Great Awakening, while many of the older Quakers were slow to recognize the reality of new spiritual life if it did not conform to the traditional and conventional patterns. This reaction against revivalism led to two alternatives: some Quakers separated themselves from the yearly meeting and established their own fellowship; other Quakers felt that they could not be separatists and remained within the yearly meeting, speaking to the issues of the day and often suffering for their convictions. Such a man was Joel Bean of Iowa.

Joel Bean and his wife, Hannah, had traveled widely among Friends, both in America and abroad. He was held in high regard and when he began to speak out against the "new techniques" and the "new doctrines" of revivalism, a great number of English Friends rallied to his support. In Iowa, however, he found himself in the minority, alienated from much of what he counted as essential in the traditional beliefs and practices of Friends. Worn down by the strain, he resolved to retire from the conflict and joined the westward migration to California.

For several decades, a considerable number of Quakers had migrated to California. Some had been Forty-niners, others settled as merchants and farmers. In the little community of San Jose, Joel and Hannah Bean found a Monthly Meeting established by Iowa Yearly Meeting. When, however, the meeting began to reflect the revivalistic tendencies and measures, the Beans withdrew and formed the College Park Association of Friends. But controversy continued. Joel and Hannah Bean were deposed as ministers of Iowa Yearly Meeting and were then disowned as members of the Society of Friends. Out of these experiences came the standards and principles that were later reflected in the Pacific Coast Association of Friends and, ultimately, in the Pacific Yearly Meeting of the Religious Society of Friends.

In southern California, meanwhile, the great land booms of the 1880s brought many Quakers who established colonies and various meetings for worship. The vast majority of these Quakers were sympathetic with revivalism and further extended the Great Awakening to the west coast. Many of the outstanding evangelists and leaders of the revival migrated to California and were instrumental in forming the California Yearly Meeting of Friends Church.

Today, these two groups of Friends exist in California as a result of revivalism and the Great Awakening. The one, Pacific Yearly Meeting, maintains the unprogrammed meetings for worship and disdains theological exercises. Thus it continues in the heritage of Joel Bean's reaction against the "new measures" and "new techniques" of revivalism. The other, California Yearly Meeting, continues to foster the spirit and vision of the Great Awakening in its emphasis upon church extension, missions, evangelism, and theological concerns.

In summary, this has been our thesis. These two Yearly Meetings reflect wide and divergent views on ecclesiology, theology, and social concerns in contradistinction to the unity of spirit and purpose exhibited when Quakers first landed on American soil and began their westward movement. The cause of this division in Quakerism was the Great Awakening, that period of revivalism during the latter third of the nineteenth century that radically transformed the Society of Friends.

There are several conclusions that can be drawn from this study. First, the merely casual observance of the variety and polarity of views among California's Quakers cannot adequately portray the reasons for the existence of these two groups. The historical perspective is needed to provide an understanding of the problem. It is to this endeavor that the author has addressed himself.

One cannot ignore the past and that which has occurred in the history of these two Yearly Meetings. In order to understand the present situation of Friends in California, one must not overlook the historical developments which gave rise to the present. If any effective dialogue is to be conducted between the two Yearly Meetings in an effort for mutual understanding, the basic reasons for the founding of the two separate organizations must at least be noted and understood.

Second, the original zeal and momentum that led to the establishment of California Yearly Meeting has generally been lost. The revival movement largely ceased with the advent of institutionalism.[1] The organization of the Yearly Meeting was so formalized that responsibilities were delegated more and more to a few individuals. A groping uncertainty as to the specific task of the Yearly Meeting in society became evident. In many areas, Quakers maintained much of the inherited conservatism of the past and failed to adjust to the new environment. Weakness and lack of growth, therefore, has characterized California Yearly Meeting for a number of years. The absence of official action upon some of the pressing social issues within the State during the first half of this century reflects the theological stance of the Yearly Meeting, often narrow and misguided. Social action was generally confined to the evangelistic and missionary endeavors. There are now, however, some welcomed changes. Studied introspection and reevaluation have led recently to the rethinking of goals and to the restructuring of the Yearly Meeting to enable it to meet more adequately the urgent tasks that are confronting the church in modern society. A reorganization of committees has given, for example, more responsibility to a new Board on Christian Social Concerns. Representatives at the sessions of the Yearly Meeting are now appointed by monthly meetings in proportion to local membership, thus allowing for a fairer representation of local concerns and insuring better communication among the meetings.

Third, Pacific Yearly Meeting has become the first of several new, independent yearly meetings in America. While professing to maintain traditional Quaker views and practices, it has actually been an innovator, e.g., in the methodology of its establishment. There are several basic reasons for its uniqueness. A large proportion of Pacific Yearly Meeting's members are "convinced Friends"; they are first-generation Quakers. Many of these individuals had been concerned with an intellectual and often humanistic approach to religion. Many were disenchanted and discouraged with the denominated church as they knew it.

Pacific Yearly Meeting provided a haven, a place of acceptance and opportunity. Fellowship within the Yearly Meeting was structured, not on the basis of theological consensus, but upon social and humanitarian concern. The social testimonies continue to play an important part in the life of Pacific Yearly Meeting.[2] For a number of its members, the American Friends Service Committee programs provided the first contact with the Religious Society of Friends.[3]

Two strands can be seen, then, in the development of Pacific Yearly Meeting: first, the desire to foster the mode of worship so important to many Friends, and, secondly, the desire of many convinced Friends, for whom the Quaker witness for peace and social justice is an important evidence for Christian integrity, to be able to gather and worship in what was understood as the traditional Quaker manner. Without doubt, the hunger for religious reality and an effective social witness sought by these convinced Friends has aided the growth of Pacific Yearly Meeting.

Fourth, it is possible to identify some of the trends within these Yearly Meetings.[4] California Yearly Meeting, for example, is one of the most evangelically cosmopolitan of the yearly meetings in America. The same forces that broke down the barriers of isolationism durings the Great Awakening continue to lead many of its members to make more of the wider fellowship of New Testament Christianity than of the singular distinctives of Quakerism. Emphasis is generally placed by them on the whole church rather than on any denominated part. The reverse appears to be true of Pacific Yearly Meeting.

Finally, although some members in both Yearly Meetings have wishfully talked about a closer union between the two, the differences seem to be irreconcilable at this point. For the first time, however, unofficial and casual discussions have recently been held between representatives of the two Yearly Meetings.[5] A report stated:

> We are becoming more and more sensitive to one another's aspirations and hopes, and increasingly appreciative of the other's earnest desire for mutual understanding. We are aware of the differences—of belief, of opinion, of method—but, knowing each other and coming to love one another, we have become less and less prone to make quick judgments concerning acts and deeds. We have come to see we have common problems and needs; we all fall far short of our pronouncements; none of us measure up to the claims of human brotherhood and good race relations. We share a common need to call on all Friends to a life and practice consistent with our professions.[6]

But what of the future? Quakers in California are now completing their first century of service and witness. The past could merely be a prologue to the future effectiveness of Quakerism in the west.

These chapters have attempted to tell something of the story of an important phase of modern church history, but they have also endeavored to point to the possibility of a renewed spirit in Quakerism. If an understanding of the past will open the doors to a renewal of spirit and vitality, if Friends will become more earnestly obedient to the Holy Spirit, if the fresh winds of revival will lead to thoughtfulness in the midst of a disheveled and revolutionary world, if a new sense of urgency arises in our churches and meetings to meet the emptiness and frustration of life, and above all, if there comes a new recognition of the centrality of Jesus Christ and our experience of Him, then this small task has been worthwhile.

Notes

Chapter I—The Background of American Quakerism

1. Williston Walker, *A History of the Christian Church* (New York: Charles Scribner's Sons, 1959), p. 420.
2. Hugh Barbour, *The Quakers in Puritan England* (New Haven: Yale University Press, 1964), p. 1.
3. Rufus Jones (ed.), *George Fox: An Autobiography* (Philadelphia: Ferris and Leach, 1904), p. 65. Cf. William C. Braithwaite, *The Beginnings of Quakerism*, 2nd edition revised by Henry J. Cadbury (Cambridge: University Press, 1955), p. 28. See also John Sykes, *The Quakers* (London: Allan Wingate, 1958), pp. 89-117.
4. "Preface" of William Penn to *The Journal of George Fox*, Vol. I-II, Bi-Centenary Edition (London: Friends Tract Association, 1891), p. xxxix.
5. *Ibid.*, p. 13.
6. *The Journal of George Fox*. Revised edition by John L. Nickalls (Cambridge: University Press, 1952), p. 3. [Hereafter referred to as *Journal.*]
7. *Ibid.*, p. 4.
8. *Ibid.*, p. 11.
9. *Ibid.*, p. 12.
10. Sidney Lucas, *The Quaker Story* (New York: Harper and Brothers, 1949), p. 23.
11. Rufus Jones, *op. cit.*, p. 31. A much needed corrective to an overemphasis of this view has been given by such contemporary scholars as Hugh Barbour in *The Quakers in Puritan England;* Arthur O. Roberts in *Through Flaming Sword* (Newberg, Oregon: The Barclay Press, 1959), and in the writings of T. Canby Jones.
12. Rachel Knight, *The Founder of Quakerism. A Psychological Study of the Mysticism of George Fox* (London: The Swarthmore Press, 1922).
13. A. Neave Brayshaw, *The Personality of George Fox* (London: Allenson and Co., 1933).
14. William Penn, "Preface," *The Journal of George Fox, op. cit.*, pp. xlii-xliv.
15. For further discussion of the political setting of early Quakerism, see Walker, *op. cit.*, pp. 402-421. Also Braithwaite, *op. cit.*, pp. 1-27; and Barbour, *op. cit.*, pp. 1-32.
16. Barbour, *op. cit.*, p. 2.
17. *Ibid.*
18. *Ibid.*
19. *Ibid.*, p. 3.
20. *Ibid.*
21. *Ibid.*, p. 32.

22. John Richard Green, *A Short History of the English People*, revised and enlarged with an epilogue by Alice Stopford Green (New York: American Book Co., 1916), p. 351.
23. Louis T. Jones, *The Quakers of Iowa* (Iowa City, Iowa: The State Historical Society, 1914), p. 21.
24. Braithwaite wrote: "It is not too much to say that over the part of England where Quakerism planted itself most readily the communities of Seekers had already prepared the way." Braithwaite, *op. cit.*, p. 27.
25. Edward Grubb, *What is Quakerism?* (2d ed.; London: The Swarthmore Press, 1919), p. 27.
26. Walker, *op. cit.*, p. 420.
27. Howard Brinton would appear to differ with this view when he identifies Quakerism as "an explicit and developed manifestation of one of the three main forms of Christianity; the other two being Catholicism and Protestantism." See a further discussion of this view in *Friends for 300 Years* (New York: Harper and Brothers, 1952), p. x. See also his essay, *The Society of Friends*, Pendle Hill Pamphlet No. 48 (Wallingford, Pennsylvania: Pendle Hill, 1948), p. 1.
28. Elbert Russell, *The History of Quakerism* (New York: The Macmillan Co., 1942), p. xix.
29. William Penn, *Primitive Christianity Revived in the Faith and Practice of the People Called Quakers* (Philadelphia: Henry Longstreth, 1877).
30. *Ibid.*, p. 9.
31. Lucas, *op. cit.*, p. 48.
32. *Ibid.*, p. 49.
33. *Ibid.*
34. *Ibid.*, p. 64.
35. For a variety of presentations on this topic, see L. Violet Hodgkin, *Silent Worship* (London: The Swarthmore Press, 1919); William C. Braithwaite, *Spiritual Guidance* (London: Headley Brothers, 1909); Edward Grubb, *op. cit.*, pp. 48-65; Howard H. Brinton, *Creative Worship* (Wallingford, Pennsylvania: Pendle Hill Publications, 1963), pp. 1-54; D. Elton Trueblood, *The People Called Quakers* (New York: Harper and Row, 1966), pp. 85-106. This book may well be the most important book on Quakerism written in this generation.
36. Trueblood, *op. cit.*, p. 90.
37. *Ibid.*, p. 88.
38. Robert Barclay, *An Apology for the True Christian Divinity* (Philadelphia: Friends Book Store, 1908), p. 332. [Hereafter referred to as the *Apology*.]
39. *Ibid.*, p. 335.
40. Lucas, *op. cit.*, p. 50.
41. Barclay, *op. cit.*, p. 343.
42. See Chapter III.
43. See Thomas Kelly, *A Testament of Devotion*, chapter on "Holy Obedience" (New York: Harper and Row, 1942).
44. For a further discussion on this topic, see Edward Grubb, *op. cit.*, pp. 105-118; Lucas, *op. cit.*, pp. 52-54.
45. Lucas, *op. cit.*, p. 53.
46. See also the following for a further discussion: Edward Grubb, *op. cit.*, pp. 105-118; Lucas, *op. cit.*, pp. 54-59.
47. See also Walter R. Williams, *The Rich Heritage of Quakerism* (Grand Rapids: Wm. B. Eerdmans Co., 1962), pp. 77-87; Edward Grubb, *op. cit.*, pp. 156-172.
48. *Journal*, p. 27.
49. Braithwaite, *op. cit.*, p. 42.
50. Barbour, *op. cit.*, p. 42.
51. Edward Grubb, *op. cit.*, p. 90.
52. Russell, *op. cit.*, p. 76.
53. *Ibid.*, p. 133.
54. *Ibid.*
55. William C. Braithwaite, "First Period, 1668-1725," *London Yearly Meeting During 250 Years* (London: Society of Friends, 1919), p. 21.
56. William C. Braithwaite, *The Second Period of Quakerism*, 2d ed. by Henry J. Cadbury (Cambridge: University Press, 1961), p. 252.

57. For a further discussion of Penington, see Trueblood, *op. cit.*, pp. 41-46; Williams, *op. cit.*, pp. 100-102; Braithwaite, *The Second Period of Quakerism*, pp. 380-383; also Maria Webb, *The Penns and Peningtons of the 17th Century* (London: F. B. Kitto, 1867).
58. For a discussion of Elwood, see Williams, *op. cit.*, pp. 102-104; and especially, Thomas Elwood, *The History of the Life of Thomas Elwood*, 3d ed. (London: Luke Hinde, 1765); also Webb, *op. cit.*, pp. 61-148.
59. Williams, *op. cit.*, p. 105.
60. For information on Barclay, see Trueblood, *op. cit.*, pp. 59-62; Braithwaite, *The Second Period of Quakerism*, pp. 385-391. The best work on Barclay is the excellent book, also written by D. Elton Trueblood, *Robert Barclay* (New York: Harper and Row, 1969). A great amount of valuable information and insight into this Quaker leader is presented. See especially pp. 236-249. Dr. Trueblood writes of the relevance of Robert Barclay for today and describes him as one of the "least dated of men."
61. Information on the life of Penn is given by Webb, *op. cit.*, and by Catherine Owens Peare, *William Penn* (Philadelphia: J. B. Lippincott, 1957). See also Braithwaite, *The Second Period of Quakerism*, pp. 55-74; Trueblood, *The People Called Quakers*, pp. 49-58; William Hull, *William Penn, A Topical Biography* (Oxford: University Press, 1937).
62. See Williams, *op. cit.*, pp. 39-57.
63. *Journal*, p. 104.
64. *The Journal of George Fox*, Bi-Centenary Edition, *op. cit.*, p. 190.
65. Elizabeth B. Emmott, *A Short History of Quakerism* (New York: George H. Doran Co., 1923), p. 136.
66. *Ibid.*
67. See Ernest E. Taylor, *The Valiant Sixty* (London: The Bannisdale Press, 1947).
68. Lucas, *op. cit.*, p. 71.
69. Emmott, *op. cit.*, pp. 148-154. See also T. Mardy Rees, *A History of the Quakers in Wales* (Carmarthen: W. Spurrell and Son, 1925); and Thomas Wight, *A History of the Rise and Progress of the People Called Quakers in Ireland, 1653-1700*, 2d ed. by John Putty (London: W. Phillips, 1800); also Braithwaite, *The Beginnings of Quakerism*, pp. 206-240.
70. See especially William Hull, *The Rise of Quakerism in Amsterdam, 1655-1665*, Swarthmore College Monographs on Quaker History, series No. 4 (Philadelphia: Patterson and White Co., 1938).
71. Lucas, *op. cit.*, p. 77.
72. See a discussion of the "Puritan Intolerants" in Charles F. Holder, *The Quakers in Great Britain and America* (New York: the Neuner Co., 1913), pp. 341-351.
73. Holder, *op. cit.*, pp. 352-355.
74. For a discussion of the Massachusetts Bay Colony, see Edmund S. Morgan, *The Puritan Dilemma* (Boston: Little, Brown & Co., 1958) and especially Perry Miller, *Orthodoxy in Massachusetts* (Cambridge: Harvard University Press, 1933).
75. George E. Ellis, *The Puritan Age and Rule in the Colony of Massachusetts Bay, 1629-1685*, 3d ed. (Boston: Houghton, Mifflin and Co., 1891), p. 439. Note also the chapter on "The Intrusion of Quakers," pp. 408-491.
76. See the chapter, "The Martyrs," Rufus M. Jones, *The Quakers in the American Colonies* (London: Macmillan & Co., 1911), pp. 63-69.
77. Russell, *op. cit.*, p. 109.
78. Jones, *The Quakers in the American Colonies*, p. 51.
79. *Ibid.*, p. 63.
80. Russell, *op. cit.*, pp. 113, 114. For a discussion of the transatlantic Quaker community and organization, see Frederick B. Tolles, *Quakers and the Atlantic Culture* (New York: The Macmillan Co., 1960), pp. 21-35.
81. Russell, *op. cit.*, p. 115.
82. *Ibid.*, pp. 116, 117.
83. Edwin B. Bronner, *William Penn's "Holy Experiment": The Founding of Pennsylvania, 1681-1701* (New York: Temple University Publications, 1962), p. 6.
84. See the chapter on "The Culture of Early Pennsylvania," Tolles, *op. cit.*, pp. 114-131.

85. For a discussion of Quakers and business in this period, see Isabel Grubb, *Quakerism and Industry Before 1800* (London: Williams and Norgate, Ltd., 1930).
86. Allen C. Thomas and Richard Henry Thomas, *A History of the Friends in America*, 6th ed. (Philadelphia: John C. Winston Co., 1930), p. 103.
87. Russell, *op. cit.*, p. 202.
88. *Ibid.*, pp. 211, 247-250. For a wider treatment of the slavery question and the leadership of John Woolman, see Auguste Jorns, *The Quakers as Pioneers in Social Work*, trans. by Thomas Brown (New York: The Macmillan Co., 1931), pp. 197-233; Earl L. Griggs, *Thomas Clarkson, the Friend of Slaves* (Ann Arbor: University of Michigan Press, 1938); Amelia Mott Gummere, ed., *The Journals and Essays of John Woolman* (Philadelphia: Friends Book Store, 1922).
89. Russell, *op. cit.*, p. 207.
90. Clifton E. Olmstead, *History of Religion in the United States* (Englewood Cliffs: Prentice-Hall, Inc., 1960), p. 117.
91. Rufus M. Jones, *The Later Periods of Quakerism*, Vol. I (New York: The Macmillan Co., 1921), p. 33.
92. Williams, *op. cit.*, p. 119.
93. Russell, *op. cit.*, pp. 251-268.

Chapter II—Separations within American Quakerism

1. Edward Grubb, *Separations, Their Causes and Effects* (London: Headley Brothers, 1914), p. 9.
2. *Ibid.*
3. Samuel Janney, *History of the Religious Society of Friends*, Vol. IV (Philadelphia: T. Ellwood Zell, 1867), p. 178.
4. For a discussion on Stephen Grellet, see *Memoirs of the Life and Gospel Labors of Stephen Grellet* (Philadelphia: Friends Book Store, n.d.), and William W. Comfort, *Stephen Grellet, 1773-1855* (New York: The Macmillan Co., 1942). Rufus Jones writes that "no other influence was as great as that of the ministry of this French convert to Quakerism in carrying the Society of Friends in America to an out and out evangelical interpretation of Christianity," *The Later Periods of Quakerism*, Vol. II, p. 875.
5. Thomas and Thomas, *op. cit.*, p. 130.
6. Edward Grubb, *Separations, Their Causes and Effects*, p. 23.
7. For an important discussion on the life and ministry of Elias Hicks, see especially Bliss Forbush, *Elias Hicks: Quaker Liberal* (New York: Columbia University Press, 1956).
8. Thomas and Thomas, *op. cit.*, p. 130.
9. Edward Grubb, *Separations, Their Causes and Effects*, p. 35. See also the chapter on "The Great Separation," Jones, *The Later Periods of Quakerism*, Vol. I, pp. 435-487.
10. *Ibid.*, p. 38.
11. Russell, *op. cit.*, p. 338.
12. *Ibid.*, p. 339.
13. Edward Grubb, *Separations, Their Causes and Effects*, p. 84. See also Thomas and Thomas, *op. cit.*, pp. 193-199.
14. Edward Grubb, *Separations, Their Causes and Effects*, p. 95.
15. Thomas and Thomas, *op. cit.*, p. 154. See discussion of the years 1835-1855 in Jones, *The Later Periods of Quakerism*, Vol. I, pp. 488-540. Rufus Jones calls this twenty-year period "the darkest and saddest in the history of Quakerism," p. 488.

Chapter III—The Great Awakening within American Quakerism

1. Timothy L. Smith, *Revivalism and Social Reform in Mid-Nineteenth-Century America* (New York: Abingdon Press, 1957), p. 45.
2. A major exception, though not dealing primarily with Quakers, is H. Richard Niebuhr's *The Kingdom of God in America* (Chicago: Willett, Clark, 1937).
3. Jones, *The Later Periods of Quakerism*, Vol. II, p. 868.
4. Olmstead, *op. cit.*, p. 156.
5. *Ibid.*, p. 158.

6. See Edwin S. Gaustad, *The Great Awakening in New England* (New York: Harper and Brothers, 1957). For further discussion of the role and theology of Jonathan Edwards, see also Perry Miller, *Jonathan Edwards* (Boston: William Sloane Associates, 1949); O. E. Winslow, *Jonathan Edwards, 1703-1758* (New York: The Macmillan Co., 1940).
7. William Warren Sweet names three major tasks that confronted American churches following independence: organization, reviving vital religion, and following the population westward. Those churches that were successful on the frontiers became the numerical giants in American Protestantism; see *Religion in the Development of American Culture, 1765-1840* (New York: Charles Scribner's Sons, 1952), p. 97.
8. Peter G. Mode, *The Frontier Spirit in American Christianity* (New York: The Macmillan Co., 1923), p. 8, 11, 14. Cf. Frederick Jackson Turner, *The Significance of the Frontier in American History* (New York: Henry Holt and Co., 1921) and George R. Taylor, (ed.), *The Turner Thesis Concerning the Role of the Frontier in American History*, Problems in American Civilization Series (Boston: D. C. Heath and Co., 1956). See also Frederick L. Paxon, *History of the American Frontier: 1763-1893* (Boston: Houghton Mifflin Co., 1924).
9. Olmstead, *op. cit.*, p. 257. See also Bernard A. Weisberger, *They Gathered at the River* (Boston: Little, Brown and Co., 1958), p. 5.
10. Olmstead, *op. cit.*, p. 258.
11. Charles A. Johnson, *The Frontier Camp Meeting: Religion's Harvest Time* (Dallas: Southern Methodist University Press, 1955), p. 25.
12. Olmstead, *op. cit.*, p. 259.
13. Sweet, *op. cit.*, pp. 149, 150.
14. Olmstead, *op. cit.*, p. 261.
15. *Ibid.*, p. 348.
16. For studies of the life and ministry of Charles Finney, see Weisberger, *op. cit.*; William Warren Sweet, *Revivalism in America: Its Origin, Growth and Decline* (New York: Charles Scribner's Sons, 1944); William G. McLaughlin, Jr., *Modern Revivalism: Charles Grandison Finney to Billy Graham* (New York: The Ronald Press Co., 1959).
17. Smith, *op. cit.*, pp. 45-62.
18. Olmstead, *op. cit.*, p. 351.
19. For a study of the life and ministry of Moody, see Olmstead, *op. cit.*, pp. 453-455; McLaughlin, *op. cit.*
20. Jones, *The Later Periods of Quakerism*, Vol. II, p. 892. Frederick Tolles has also written on the reaction of Philadelphia Quakers to such revivalists as George Whitfield and concluded that "the typical Quaker attitude toward the revival at its outset was compounded of an aloof but tolerant amusement at the antics of the preachers and a somewhat grudging admiration for their success in mending the morals of the Philadelphians. . . . as the revival progressed, the attitude of most Friends . . . tended to become one of ill-concealed disapproval and quiet hostility." *op. cit.*, pp. 97-99.
21. "Editorial," *The Friend* (Philadelphia), Vol. XXXI, No. 38 (May 29, 1858), p. 303. See also the comment by Samuel Rhoads in the *Friends' Review*, Vol. XI, No. 30 (April 3, 1858), p. 472, and the conclusion of another Quaker in the same journal that "a careful examination of the history of the present most remarkable awakening of public attention and feeling to the subject of religion, has led me to the undoubting conclusion that it is a genuine work of divine grace, and that if our Society would open the door for it, we also should be blessed in these times of refreshing," *Friends' Review*, Vol. XI, No. 34 (May 1, 1858), p. 532.
22. Tolles, *op. cit.*, pp. 104-113.
23. Allen Jay, *Autobiography of Allen Jay* (Philadelphia: The John C. Winston Co., 1910), p. 81.
24. Jones, *The Later Periods of Quakerism*, Vol. II, p. 896. For a more complete discussion of Eli and Sibyl Jones, see Rufus M. Jones, *Eli and Sibyl Jones: Their Life and Work* (Philadelphia: Porter and Coates, 1889).
25. An excellent and descriptive account of this meeting is given by Rhoda Coffin in *Reminiscences of Rhoda M. Coffin* (New York: The Grafton Press, 1910), pp. 80-83.

26. Jones, *The Later Periods of Quakerism*, Vol. II, p. 900. See also the account given by Nathan and Esther Frame in their *Reminiscenses* (Cleveland: The Britton Printing Co., 1907), pp. 60-63. Elbert Russell suggests that the first use of the "mourner's bench" among Quakers was here at Walnut Ridge. Russell, *op. cit.*, p. 427.
27. Russell, *op. cit.*, p. 331; Jones, *The Later Periods of Quakerism*, Vol. II, pp. 886-888. See also *Extracts from the Journal and Letters of Hannah Chapman Backhouse* (London: Richard Barrett, 1858).
28. Henry Richard, (ed.), *The Memoirs of Joseph Sturge* (London: S. W. Partridge, 1864), p. 224.
29. Russell, *op. cit.*, p. 400.
30. *Ibid.*, p. 401.
31. Jones, *The Later Periods of Quakerism*, Vol. II, pp. 871-885.
32. *Ibid.*, p. 890.
33. *Ibid.*, p. 891.
34. *Ibid.*, p. 897.
35. *Ibid.*, p. 899. See also the biography written by Dougan Clark and Joseph H. Smith, *David B. Updegraff and His Work* (Cincinnati: Armstrong and Fillmore, 1895).
36. See especially his *Autobiography, op. cit.*
37. Jones, *The Later Periods of Quakerism*, Vol. II, p. 901.
38. *Ibid.*
39. Russell, *op. cit.*, p. 424.
40. Clark and Smith, *op. cit.*, p. 43.
41. Russell, *op. cit.*, p. 427.
42. Personal interview with Mrs. Lois Ellis, Long Beach, California, who tells this account of her grandmother, Mrs. Hulda Enlow, and her mother, Mrs. Lauretta Hollingsworth, November 8, 1966.
43. J. Wilhelm Rowntree, "A Plea for a Quaker Settlement," *John Wilhelm Rowntree: Essays and Addresses*, Joshua Rowntree (ed.) (London: Headley Brothers, 1905), p. 142.
44. Quoted by Edward Grubb, *Separations, Their Causes and Effects*, p. 103.
45. Luke Woodard writes in an article entitled "Church Extension in Connection with the Society of Friends," *Christian Worker*, Vol. XVI, No. 36 (September 9, 1886), p. 421, "It has been found in the experience of every Yearly Meeting that has been engaged in this revival work, that to make it properly effective in building up and increasing the number of our meetings, it must be followed by pastoral work."
46. Edward Grubb, *Separations, Their Causes and Effects*, p. 109. There is evidence to support the view that Luke Woodard of Indiana Yearly Meeting was one of the first, if not the first, Quaker pastor. Alexander H. Hay suggests the date of 1873, or at the earliest possible date, 1872. See his unpublished Master's thesis, "The Rise of the Pastoral System in the Society of Friends, 1850-1900," Haverford College, 1938. See also Luke Woodard, *Sketches of a Life of 75* (Richmond, Indiana: Nicholsen Printing and Mfg. Co., 1907).
47. J. Wilhelm Rowntree estimated that 82,000 Quakers, or 62 percent of all Friends, were members of pastoral meetings in Canada and the United States. Quakers numbering 51,000, or 38 percent, were members of nonpastoral meetings in London, Dublin, Philadelphia, Baltimore, Hicksite and Conservative Yearly Meetings. Quoted by Edward Grubb, *op. cit.*, p. 110.
48. Jones, *The Later Periods of Quakerism*, Vol. II, p. 912.
49. Iowa Yearly Meeting was founded in 1863, while the first Yearly Meeting sessions in Kansas were held in 1872. For a discussion of the westward migration of Quakers see Chapter V.
50. Edward Grubb, *Separations, Their Causes and Effects*, p. 104.
51. Louis T. Jones, *op. cit.*, p. 164.
52. *Ibid.*, p. 165.
53. Zimri Horner, "An Action of a Conference of Friends," *The Friend*, (Philadelphia) Vol. 50, No. 46 (June 30, 1877), p. 365.
54. *Ibid.*
55. *Ibid.*, p. 366.

56. Louis T. Jones, *op. cit.*, pp. 171-174.
57. An editorial entitled "The Unrecognized Yearly Meetings" indicates that the separation in Kansas had first numbered from two to three hundred, but was increasing;
The Friend (London), Vol. XXVI, No. 313 (November 1, 1886), p. 276. Cf. also
with Sheldon Jackson, *A Short History of Kansas Yearly Meeting of Friends*
(Wichita: Day's Print Shop, 1946), pp. 56-59.
58. Walter Robson, an English Quaker, gives an eyewitness account of the separation
in Western Yearly Meeting, Plainfield, Indiana, in September 1877, as reported in
The British Friend, New Series, Vol. XXII, No. 10 (October 1913), p. 288. He
wrote of the event, "Ninety Friends, or thereabouts, put on their hats and left the
Meeting; as they went out, an American minister, with certificates from another
Yearly Meeting, sang at the top of his voice, 'See the mighty host advancing, Satan
leading on!' When he had finished, he turned to me and said, 'I thought they
should hear one more hymn before they went out.'"
59. Undated letter from Joel Bean to Rufus Jones, edited by Howard H. Brinton in
"The Revival Movement in Iowa," *The Bulletin of Friends Historical Association*,
Vol. 50, No. 2 (Autumn, 1961), pp. 102-110.

Chapter IV—Joel and Hannah Bean

1. Rufus Jones, *Later Periods of Quakerism*, Vol. II, p. 931.
2. Joel Bean, "The Issue," *The British Friend*, Vol. XXXIX, No. III (March 1, 1881),
p. 50.
3. See the "vita" of Joel Bean by William Bacon Evans, *Dictionary of Quaker Biography*, Typescript, Quaker Collection, Haverford College, 1964.
4. Quoted by Catherine E. B. Cox, "Joel and Hannah Bean," *Quaker Biographies*,
Series II, No. 3 (Philadelphia: Friends Book Store, n.d.), p. 211.
5. *Ibid.*, p. 212.
6. *Ibid.*, p. 214.
7. *Ibid.*, p. 211.
8. *Ibid.*, p. 215.
9. Louis T. Jones, *op. cit.*, p. 44.
10. Quoted by B. L. Weeks, "Joel Bean and His Life of Service in Iowa," *The Friend*
(Philadelphia), Vol. 88, No. 12 (September 17, 1914), p. 136.
11. *Ibid.*
12. Cox, *op. cit.*, p. 218.
13. *Ibid.*, p. 216.
14. Brinton, "The Revival Movement in Iowa," *op. cit.*, p. 104.
15. Mildred Crew Brooke writes of her impressions of the Beans and the West Branch
Meeting in a collection of articles edited and published posthumously by her
husband; Theodore Hoover, *Mildred Crew Brooke, An Unfinished Manuscript of
Reminiscences* (Casa del Oso: privately printed, 1940).
16. Catherine M. Shipley writes in a "Letter to the Editor" of *The Friend*, "He was,
when seventeen years of age, impressed with the religious duty to visit in Gospel
love the Hawaiian Islands . . ." *The Friend* (Philadelphia), Vol. 87, No. 29
(January 22, 1914), p. 356.
17. Christina H. Jones, *American Friends in World Missions* (Richmond, Indiana:
American Friends Board of Missions), p. 27.
18. Weeks, *op. cit.*, p. 137. Cf. Wayne Allman (ed.), *Spiritual Trails of a People
Called Friends: 1863-1963* (Oskaloosa, Iowa: Iowa Yearly Meeting of Friends
Church, 1963), p. 9. See also Louis T. Jones, *op. cit.*, pp. 74-79.
19. Weeks, *op. cit.*, p. 137.
20. Maud Stratton, *Herbert Hoover's Home Town: The Story of West Branch* (Privately printed, 1948), p. 19.
21. *Ibid.*, p. 20.
22. Cox, *op. cit.*, p. 228. A minute from the Yearly Meeting of Ministers and Elders
read: "We have at this time with full unity and Christian sympathy, liberated our
beloved friends Joel and Hannah E. Bean, his wife, to attend London and Dublin
Yearly Meetings, and for other religious services in Great Britain and Ireland."
Minutes of Iowa Yearly Meeting of Friends (Oskaloosa, Iowa: Herald Book and
Job Printing, 1872), p. 19.

23. Cox, *op. cit.*, p. 229.
24. *Ibid.*
25. *Ibid.*, p. 232.
26. *Minutes of Iowa Yearly Meeting of Friends* (Oskaloosa, Iowa: Herald Book and Job Printing, 1877), p. 4.
27. Louis T. Jones, *op. cit.*, p. 15. The first Sunday school was established at Pleasant Plain in June, 1844, as a result of an earlier investigation by Salem Monthly Meeting in 1841 to discover how many of its families were "destitute of the scriptures," p. 97.
28. *Ibid.*, p. 98.
29. Jay, *op. cit.*, p. 110.
30. Louis T. Jones, *op. cit.*, p. 98.
31. Brinton, "The Revival Movement in Iowa," *op. cit.*, p. 106.
32. *Ibid.*, p. 107; see also Joel Bean, "The Issue," *op. cit.*, p. 49.
33. Brinton, "The Revival Movement in Iowa," *op. cit.*, p. 106.
34. *Ibid.*
35. Joel Bean, "The Issue," *op. cit.*, p. 49.
36. Brinton, "The Revival Movement in Iowa," *op. cit.*, p. 107.
37. See Timothy Smith's chapter, "The Holiness Revival at Oberlin," *op. cit.*, pp. 103-113. See also Charles G. Finney's lecture, "Be Filled with the Spirit," *Lectures on Revivals of Religion*, edited by William G. McLaughlin (Cambridge: Belknap Press of Harvard University Press, 1960), pp. 107-123.
38. Smith, *op. cit.*, pp. 114-134. John Wesley was the foremost advocate of Christian perfection in modern times. Cf. R. Newton Flew, *The Idea of Perfection in Christian Theology: an Historical Study of the Christian Ideal for the Present Life* (London: Oxford University Press, 1934).
39. Brinton, "The Revival Movement in Iowa," *op. cit.*, p. 107. For a further discussion of the concepts of holiness and perfection among Quakers, see Arthur O. Roberts, "The Concepts of Perfection in the History of the Quaker Movement," an unpublished Bachelor of Divinity thesis, Nazarene Theological Seminary, 1951.
40. Dougan Clark and Joseph Smith, *op. cit.*, p. 200.
41. *Ibid.*, p. 203.
42. *Ibid.*
43. *Ibid.*, p. 29.
44. Dougan Clark, *The Offices of the Holy Spirit* (Philadelphia: Henry Longstreth, 1880).
45. Hannah Whitall Smith, *The Christian's Secret of a Happy Life* (Chicago: F. H. Revel, 1883).
46. Jones, *The Later Periods of Quakerism*, Vol. II, p. 927.
47. "Editorial," *The Friend* (Philadelphia), Vol. LII, No. 36 (April 19, 1879), p. 286.
48. *Ibid.*
49. "Editorial," *The Friend* (Philadelphia), Vol. LII, No. 41 (May 24, 1879), p. 327.
50. Joel Bean, "The Light Within," *Friends' Review*, Vol. XXXII, No. 29 (March 1, 1879), pp. 449-451.
51. *Ibid.*, p. 450.
52. Joel Bean, "The Issue," *op. cit.*, p. 50.
53. *Ibid.*
54. *Ibid.*, p. 51.
55. See Chapter VI.
56. *Minutes of Iowa Yearly Meeting of Friends* (Oskaloosa: Herald Printing Co., 1882), p. 7.
57. Cf. the table showing numerical growth from 1863 ff. in Appendix A, Louis T. Jones, *op. cit.*, p. 285. Beginning in 1883, Iowa Yearly Meeting coordinated its evangelistic efforts with over 5,600 individuals being added to church rolls in the following decade, *op. cit.*, p. 286.
58. Brinton, "The Revival Movement in Iowa," *op. cit.*, p. 107.
59. *Ibid.*, p. 108.
60. *Ibid.*
61. *Ibid.*, p. 109.

Chapter V—Migration of Friends to California

1. Jones, *The Later Periods of Quakerism*, Vol. II, p. 842.
2. Louis T. Jones, *op. cit.*, p. 85. See also the new book by Errol Elliott, *Quakers on the American Frontier* (Richmond, Indiana: Friends United Press), 1969. Errol Elliott presents an excellent study of the migration of Friends and the establishing of Quaker Meetings and institutions on the expanding American frontier.
3. Myron Dee Goldsmith, "William Hobson and the Founding of Quakerism in the Pacific Northwest" (an unpublished Doctoral dissertation in Religion, Boston University Graduate School, 1962).
4. John W. Caughey, *California*, 2d ed. (Englwood Cliffs: Prentice-Hall, Inc., 1953), p. 208. Professor Caughey's book is a standard text in the study of the history of California.
5. *Ibid.*, p. 255.
6. Sarah Lindsey, *Diary*. A five volume journal kept by Sarah Lindsey of her visit with Robert, her husband, to the North American continent in 1859-1860. The original manuscript is in the Devonshire House collection in London. A hand-written copy of the journal was made from the original by Elizabeth Lindsey Galleway of Yorkshire, England, the daughter of Robert and Sarah Lindsey. This manuscript was prepared for the late Professor Rayner W. Kelsey of Haverford College and is now a part of its Quaker Collection. The writer has had a microfilm made of this manuscript and it is now located in the library of Whittier College. A comparison of this copy with a microfilm of the original in London shows it to be an accurate and true reproduction. Cf. also with Elizabeth L. Galleway (ed.), *Travels of Robert and Sarah Lindsey* (London: Samuel Harris and Co., 1886). Also note the recent reprint of the diary, introduced and edited by Sheldon G. Jackson, "An English Quaker Tours California, The Journal of Sarah Lindsey, 1859-1860," *Southern California Quarterly*, Vol. LI, No. 1 (March, 1969).
7. "Some Forty-Niners," edited by Norman Penney, *The Journal of the Friends Historical Society*, Vol. XXVII (1930), p. 55.
8. *Ibid.*, p. 56.
9. Charles Pancoast, *A Quaker Forty-Niner*, edited by Anna P. Hannum (Philadelphia: University of Pennsylvania Press, 1930). Charles Pancoast wrote of the adventures of Richard Pancoast.
10. *Ibid.*, p. 171.
11. *Ibid.*, p. 270.
12. *Ibid.*, p. 272.
13. *Ibid.*, p. 286.
14. *Ibid.*, p. 287.
15. Lindsey, *Diary*, III, p. 154 (September 1, 1859).
16. *Ibid.*, IV, p. 10 (October 2, 1859).
17. C. W. Haskins, *The Argonauts of California* (New York: Fords, Howard and Hulbert, 1890), p. 391. The Shermans also owned a profitable ranch near Oakland; cf. Lindsey, *Diary*, III, p. 118 (July 25, 1859).
18. Emma T. Charles, "Friends in California," *The Pacific Friend*, XXI, No. 10 (December, 1914), p. 6. Emma Charles quotes from a paper written by James Bean entitled "The Beginnings of Quakerism in California."
19. Goldsmith, *op. cit.*, p. 220.
20. Herbert C. Jones, "The Quakers in San Jose," Supplement to the *Friends Bulletin* (March, 1950), p. 1. This article was also reprinted in a book on San Jose edited by Bertha M. Rice, *Builders of the Valley* (San Jose: privately printed, 1957).
21. Lindsey, *Diary*, III, p. 112 (July 16, 1859).
22. *Ibid.*, p. 117 (July 24, 1859).
23. *Ibid.*, p. 120 (July 26, 1859).
24. *Ibid.*, p. 131 (August 8, 1859).
25. The Lindsey *Diary* is undoubtedly the most important Quaker document from this period relating to Friends in California.
26. Galleway, *op. cit.*, p. 3.
27. For an account of the Lindsey visit to Kansas, see Sheldon Jackson's chapter, "English Quakers Visit Kansas," *op. cit.*, pp. 29-34, and especially his article, "English Quakers Tour Kansas in 1858," *Kansas Historical Quarterly*, Vol. 13, No. 1

(February 1944), pp. 36-52. The Lindseys also visited Iowa in 1858 and had the unusual experience of being present at the establishment of two quarterly meetings; Louis T. Jones, *op. cit.*, p. 72.

28. Rufus Jones commented on the Lindseys in these words: "Robert Lindsey was thoroughly evangelical in his ministry, a preacher of the gospel, an interpreter of the Bible, a teacher rather than a prophet, a Friend for whom evangelical theology counted more than did the traditions of the Society or even the principle of the Inner Light. He was earnest, wideawake, forward-looking, courageous, brave, full of endurance, at home in pioneer conditions, ready to welcome new ways for new situations, and a man of strong personal influence. *He must be regarded as an important factor in the transformation of American Quakerism* [Italics mine]; *Later Periods of Quakerism*, Vol. II, p. 891.

29. Undated letter of Benajah W. Hiatt to Herman Newman. Part of the *Newman Collection on Kansas Friends*, now preserved in the Kansas State Library. Bound Xerox copy in Quaker Library, Whittier College.

30. Lindsey, *Diary*, III, p. 112 (July 16, 1859).

31. *Ibid.*, p. 116 (July 21, 1859).

32. *Ibid.*, p. 136 (August 8, 1859).

33. Cf. Rayner W. Kelsey, "Pacific Coast Quakerism," *Bulletin of Friends Historical Society*, IV (March, 1911), p. 98.

34. Lindsey, *Diary*, III, p. 114 (July 17, 1859).

35. *Ibid.*, p. 117 (July 24, 1859).

36. *Ibid.*, p. 126 (July 31, 1859).

37. *Ibid.*, p. 146 (August 23, 1859).

38. *Ibid.*, p. 127 (August 3, 1859).

39. *Ibid.*, p. 149 (August 28, 1859).

40. *Ibid.*, p. 129 (August 5, 1859).

41. *Ibid.*, p. 116 (July 23, 1859).

42. *Ibid.*, p. 132 (August 8, 1859).

43. *Ibid.*, p. 134 (August 10, 1859).

44. *Ibid.*, p. 135 (August 11, 1859).

45. *Ibid.*, p. 138 (August 12, 1859).

46. *Ibid.*

47. *Ibid.*, p. 140 (August 15, 1859).

48. *Ibid.*, p. 141 (August 15, 1859).

49. *Ibid.*, p. 151 (August 31, 1859).

50. *Ibid.*, p. 153 (September 1, 1859).

51. *Ibid.*, p. 154 (September 3, 1859).

52. *Ibid.*, p. 164 (September 9, 1859).

53. Lindsey, *Diary*, IV, p. 2 (September 28, 1859).

54. *Ibid.*, p. 5 (September 29, 1859).

55. *Ibid.*, pp. 17-20 (October 9, 1859). An account of Alonza Delano's experiences is available today and is published under the title, *Across the Plains and Among the Diggings* (New York: Wilson-Erickson, Inc., 1936). This is a reprint of the original chronicle. An interesting comparison can be made with the accounts of T. S. Kenderdine, who called himself a "California tramp" and left Philadelphia in 1858 for a trip of "7,000 miles by steam, 1,300 on foot, and 800 riding and walking" over a period of a year; *A California Tramp* (Newtown, Pennsylvania: Globe Printing, 1888), p. 310.

56. *Ibid.*, p. 22 (October 11, 1859).

57. *Ibid.*, p. 48 (November 9, 1859).

58. *Sacramento Daily Union*, November 10, 1859, p. 1.

59. Lindsey, *Diary*, IV, p. 15 (October 11, 1859).

60. *Ibid.*, p. 49 (November 9, 1859).

61. Lindsey, *Diary*, I, p. 6.

62. *Ibid.*, p. 4.

63. Charles, *op. cit.*, p. 6.

64. Quoted by Herbert C. Jones, *op. cit.*, p. 1.

65. Charles, *op. cit.*, p. 6. For an account of the travels of Abel Bond and his visit to San Jose, see *Foot Travels from the Atlantic to the Pacific* (Carthage, Missouri: Press Book and Job Printing House, 1889).

66. Cited by Herbert C. Jones, *op. cit.*, p. 1.
67. *Ibid.*
68. Charles, *op. cit.*, p. 6.
69. Herbert C. Jones, *op. cit.*, p. 1.
70. Caughey, *op. cit.*, p. 376.
71. Charles, *op. cit.*, p. 6.
72. Goldsmith, *op. cit.*, p. 233. Cf. with the William Hobson *Diaries, 1859-1865.* In possession of Laura Blair, Newberg, Oregon. Microfilm copy in files of the library, University of Oregon, Eugene, Oregon. Another copy located in library, George Fox College, Newberg, Oregon.
73. Goldsmith, *op. cit.*, p. 269.
74. Charles, *op. cit.*, p. 7.
75. "Minutes of the San Jose Monthly Meeting, 1873." The records are preserved in the vault of the First Friends Church, Whittier, together with other documents of the California Yearly Meeting of Friends Church. Cf. with the *Christian Workman*, Vol. 5, No. 7-8 (August, 1897), p. 5.
76. *Minutes of Iowa Yearly Meeting, 1873* (Oskaloosa: Herald Book and Job Rooms, 1873), p. 9. The minute read, "In consideration of the extension of our limits by the establishment of a meeting at San Jose, California . . . ministers shall not be required to obtain the approbation of the Yearly Meeting of M. and E., in order to make a religious visit west of the Rocky Mountains. . . ."
77. *Ibid.*, p. 14.
78. *Ibid.*
79. Charles, *op. cit.*, p. 6.
80. *Ibid.*
81. *Ibid.*, p. 7.
82. See Chapter VII.
83. Harris Newmark, *Sixty Years in Southern California* (New York: Houghton Mifflin Co., 1932), p. 449.
84. *Ibid.*, p. 488.
85. *The Christian Workman*, Vol. 5, Nos. 7-8 (August, 1897), p. 10.
86. *Ibid.*

Chapter VI—Controversy and Innovation in the West

1. Hoover, *op. cit.*, p. 13. Mildred Crew Brooke's foster parents purchased the Joel Bean home when the Beans left for California, and she has vivid recollections of the occasion.
2. Herbert C. Jones, *op. cit.*, p. 2.
3. Hoover, *op. cit.*, p. 14.
4. Herbert C. Jones, *op. cit.*, p. 2.
5. *Ibid.*
6. Brinton, "The Revival Movement in Iowa," p. 109.
7. Many references are made to this trip in the biography by Frances Anne Budge, *Isaac Sharp, An Apostle of the Nineteenth Century* (London: Headley Bros., 1898).
8. Brinton, "The Revival Movement in Iowa," p. 109.
9. Charles Thompson, "Letter to the Editor," *The British Friend*, Vol. XLI, No. XI (November 1, 1883), p. 281.
10. Joel Bean refers to a letter by Archibald Crosbie, published in *The British Friend*, August, 1883, which told of separation and dissension in Iowa Yearly Meeting.
11. The pastoral system was now in wide use in Iowa and there was evident a marked increase in membership. See Appendix A, Louis T. Jones, *op. cit.*, pp. 285, 286.
12. The article by Joel Bean entitled "The Issue" first appeared in *The British Friend* on March 1, 1881, *op. cit.* It was later circulated by certain American Friends in pamphlet form. In lending emphasis to this letter by Joel Bean, the editor appended "The Issue" to the letter so that the readers might be reminded of Bean's earlier statements.
13. Joel Bean, "Letter to the Editor," *The British Friend*, Vol. XLI, No. XI (November 1, 1883), p. 282.
14. Herbert C. Jones, *op. cit.*, p. 3.
15. Cited by Herbert C. Jones, *ibid.*

16. *Ibid.*
17. *Ibid.*, p. 2.
18. *Ibid.*, p. 3.
19. *Ibid.*
20. Russell, *op. cit.*, p. 507.
21. Joel Bean's letter is reprinted in an editorial, *The Friend* (Philadelphia), Vol. 58, No. 15 (April 11, 1885), pp. 286, 287.
22. *Ibid.*
23. This trend ultimately led to the conference held in Richmond, Indiana, in 1887 and attended by representatives from all yearly meetings in correspondence with London Yearly Meeting. The conference issued a Declaration of Faith as an attempt to define clearly the attitude of Friends toward a number of theological issues and to restate the historic Christian beliefs held by Quakers. For a discussion of the Richmond Conference, see Russell, *op. cit.*, pp. 488-491. See also Arthur J. Mekeel, *Quakerism and a Creed* (Philadelphia: Friends Book Store, 1936), for a discussion of background and trends in the Society toward what he deems a "creedal" position. The proceedings of the Conference itself are published.
24. The full committee report was reprinted in *The Friend* (London), Vol. XXV, No. 300 (October 1, 1885), p. 253.
25. *Ibid.*
26. *Ibid.*
27. *Ibid.*
28. *Ibid.*
29. See Joel Bean's article, "The Inner Light," *op. cit.*, and his statement to *The Friend* regarding the preaching and practice of this "new school." He wrote, "At the foundation of this religious system, there lies the absolute denial of a doctrine which we hold sacred, that in every man there is the light and spirit of Christ which would, if yielded to, lead to salvation," *The Friend* (Philadelphia), Vol. 58, No. 15 (April 11, 1885), p. 287.
30. *The Friend* (London), Vol. XXV, No. 300 (October 1, 1885), p. 253.
31. *Ibid.*
32. "Editorial," *Friends' Review*, Vol. XXXIX, No. 94 (September 12, 1885), p. 94.
33. *The Friend* (Philadelphia), Vol. LIX (September 5, 1885), p. 35.
34. James Backhouse, "Letter to the Editor," *The Friend* (London), Vol. XXV, No. 301 (November 2, 1885), p. 277.
35. James Bean, "Friends Meeting at San Jose, California," *Friends' Review*, Vol. XXXIX, No. 8 (September 22, 1885), p. 123.
36. See report of this action in the *Friends' Review*, Vol. XL, No. 8 (September 23, 1886), p. 123.
37. "Iowa Yearly Meeting and San Jose Monthly Meeting," *The Friend* (London), Vol. XXVII, No. 316 (February 1, 1887), p. 27.
38. *Ibid.*, p. 28.
39. Cox, *op. cit.*, p. 234.
40. *Ibid.*, p. 235.
41. *Ibid.*, p. 241.
42. "Joel and Hannah Bean," *The Friend* (London), Vol. XXVII, No. 323 (September 1, 1887), p. 247.
43. Rufus Jones, the editor of the new *American Friend*, conducted an essay contest upon the subject, "Why I am a Friend." Joel Bean was the first place winner of the contest and his essay was reprinted in *The American Friend*, Vol. I, No. 23 (December 20, 1894), p. 534-536. See also the letter of Joel Bean to Rufus Jones, dated January 4, 1894, correcting typographical errors in the printed article. The original letter is in the Rufus Jones Collection, Haverford College Library, Haverford, Pennsylvania.
44. Joel Bean, "Why I am a Friend," *op. cit.*, p. 534.
45. *Ibid.*
46. *Ibid.*
47. *Ibid.*, p. 535. Other Quakers protested the fact, however, that Joel Bean made no mention of such doctrines as repentance, regeneration, and the atonement. See, for example, Newton A. Trueblood, "Kind Opinions on Those Essays," *The American Friend*, Vol. II, No. 1 (January 3, 1895), pp. 6, 7.

48. Joel Bean, "Why I Am A Friend," *op. cit.*, p. 535.
49. Letter of Joel Bean to Rufus M. Jones, September 28, 1893. Original is in the Rufus Jones Collection, Haverford College Library, Haverford, Pennsylvania.
50. Joel Bean, "The Light Within," *op. cit.*, p. 450.
51. Note, for example, the statement of David Updegraff, who said, "Justification by faith, then, means God's forgiveness of the sinner that repents, confesses, and *accepts the atonement of Christ*" [Italics mine]; Clark, *op. cit.*, p. 201.
52. Joel Bean, "The Light Within," *op. cit.*, p. 450.
53. *Ibid.*
54. *Ibid.*
55. Joel Bean, "The Issue," *op. cit.*, p. 50. He further states in an article, "A deep revolt in many minds has been produced by the almost universal and persistent inculcation of this doctrine, in connection with the extreme dogmatism upon such themes as the 'literal' or 'material blood of Christ,' 'the finished work of salvation,' 'substitution,' 'imputation,' etc." *The Friend* (Philadelphia), Vol. LVIII, No. 35 (April 11, 1885), p. 287.
56. Joel Bean, "The Issue," *op. cit.*, p. 50.
57. "Iowa Yearly Meeting and San Jose Monthly Meeting," *op. cit.*, p. 27.
58. *Minutes of Iowa Yearly Meeting of Friends* (Oskaloosa, Iowa: Herald Printing Co., 1891), p. 14.
59. *Minutes of New York Yearly Meeting of Friends* (New York: John F. Trow and Son, 1876), p. 16.
60. See the article, giving full documentary evidence, in the *Friends' Review*, Vol. XLVII (October 12, 1893), pp. 186, 187. One of the questions asked was "Dost thou believe in the resurrection of the just and the unjust in the day of judgment; and that the wicked shall go away into eternal punishment, and the righteous into eternal life?" Joel Bean answered, "We would not be understood as subscribing to a construction to this question which would commit us to the belief that any portion of the human race, or any individual soul is condemned to endless punishment until the resources of God's infinite compassion and the means of his redeeming grace and power in Christ Jesus for their salvation have been exhausted without avail." Joel Bean concluded, "As my public preaching could never have been charged with any preaching on this point, and as I have always refrained from the assertion of positive belief regarding the purposes of God which are not clearly disclosed, this query enters the domain of my private opinion."
61. *Ibid.*, p. 187.
62. *The Friend* (Philadelphia), Vol. LXVII, No. 26 (Januray 20, 1894), p. 207. The editor commented, "We cannot approve of the course pursued by the officers of this meeting to which these Friends have been attached. This course seems to have originated in a desire to discipline those Friends because they did not unite in the progressive measures which Iowa Yearly Meeting has adopted."
63. "Editorial," *The Christian Worker*, Vol. XXIII (December 14, 1893), p. 793. *The Christian Worker* was first published in New Vienna, Ohio in 1871-1883, and then was published in Chicago from 1883-1894.
64. See "Minutes of College Park Association of Friends, 1889-1932," entry dated November 7, 1893. These unpublished minutes are located in the files of the College Park Monthly Meeting, San Jose. A further note was written by Lydia Bean Cox, the secretary: "S. J. Brun expressed a sense of discouragement in view of the abandonment of primitive Quakerism by many in our society. Others felt that the principles of Spiritual Christianity were now particularly needed and peculiarly satisfying."
65. Thomas Hodgkin was a leading English Friend and Quaker historian.
66. Letter of Helen B. Harris to Thomas Hodgkin, dated December 21, 1893. Original is in the Friends House Library, London. Typescript copy is located in Haverford College Library, Haverford, Pennsylvania.
67. Letter of Henry M. Wallis to Thomas Hodgkin, dated January 23, 1894. Original is in the Friends House Library, London. Typescript copy is located in Haverford College Library, Haverford, Pennsylvania.
68. Letter of Henry S. Newman to Thomas Hodgkin, dated November 27, 1893. Original is in the Friends House Library, London. Typescript copy is located in Haverford College Library, Haverford, Pennsylvania.

69. Letter of English Friends to Joel and Hannah Bean, dated January 1894, as a result of the petition circulated by Thomas Hodgkin. Copy located in Haverford College Library, Haverford, Pennsylvania.
70. Letter of Joel and Hannah Bean to Thomas Hodgkin, dated January 23, 1894. Copy is located in Haverford College Library, Haverford, Pennsylvania.
71. Letter of Henry S. Newman to Thomas Hodgkin, dated March 7, 1894. Original is in Friends House Library, London. Typescript copy is located in Haverford College Library, Haverford, Pennsylvania. See also the article by Joseph J. Dymond, "Friends in Iowa," *The Friend* (London), Vol. XXXIV, No. 6 (February 9, 1894), pp. 87, 88. Dymond reports his visits to Iowa and voices sympathetic concern for the problems of Iowa Yearly Meeting.
72. "Editorial," *The American Friend*, Vol. V, No. 44 (November 3, 1898), p. 1033.
73. *Ibid.*
74. "The Disownment of Joel Bean and Others," *The British Friend*, Vol. XLVI, No. 11 (November, 1898), p. 282. Disownment is something of a technical term among Friends and amounts to an excommunication.
75. *Ibid.*, one of the grandchildren was Anna Cox, who later married Howard Brinton and was influential in the formation of Pacific Yearly Meeting.
76. *Ibid.*
77. "Editorial," *The American Friend, op. cit.*, p. 1033.
78. Honey Creek Quarterly Meeting later rescinded this action, but not before Dover Monthly Meeting of New Hampshire, Joel Bean's old home Meeting, granted him membership.
79. "The Disownment of Joel Bean and Others," *The British Friend*, Vol. XLVI, No. 12 (December, 1898), p. 305.
80. *Ibid.*
81. See "Minutes of College Park Association of Friends, 1889-1932," *op. cit.*
82. Thomas and Thomas, *op. cit.*, p. 206.
83. See Chapter VIII.

Chapter VII—The California Yearly Meeting of Friends Church

1. Glenn S. Dumke, *The Boom of the Eighties in Southern California* (Los Angeles: Ward Ritchie Press, 1944), pp. 4, 5.
2. See the chapter on "Railroad Competition," Dumke, *op. cit.*, pp. 17-27. Dumke cites Joseph Netz, one of the historians of the boom, who said: "The result of this war was to precipitate such a flow of tentative migration, such an avalanche rushing madly to Southern California as I believe has had no parallel," p. 25.
3. Dumke, *op. cit.*, p. 11. For an excellent discussion of the period prior to the 1880s, see Robert G. Cleland, *The Cattle on a Thousand Hills: Southern California, 1850-1880* (San Marino: Huntington Library, 1951).
4. *Minutes of Iowa Yearly Meeting of Friends* (Oskaloosa, Iowa: Herald Book and Job Printing, 1880), p. 13.
5. *Minutes of Iowa Yearly Meeting of Friends* (Oskaloosa, Iowa: Herald Printing Co., 1886), p. 13.
6. *Ibid.*
7. Louis T. Jones, *op. cit.*, p. 118.
8. Evans, *Dictionary of Quaker Biography, op. cit.*
9. Louis T. Jones, *op. cit.*, p. 119.
10. *Ibid.*, p. 107.
11. *Ibid.*
12. See especially the account by Jennie Hollingsworth Giddings, *I Can Remember Early Pasadena* (Los Angeles: Lorrin L. Morrison, 1949). Jennie was a daughter of Lawson Hollingsworth and gives a vivid recollection of the Colony established by Colonel Jabez Banbury. See also Hiram A. Reid, *The History of Pasadena*, (Pasadena, California: privately printed, 1895), and J. W. Wood, *Pasadena, California, Historical and Personal: A Complete History of the Organization of Indiana Colony* (Pasadena, California: privately printed, 1917).
13. *Ibid.*, p. 25.

14. See the article, "Pasadena Friends," *The Christian Workman*, Vol. 5, No. 7-8 (August, 1897), p. 6.
15. *Ibid.*
16. *Ibid.*
17. Cora A. Sydnor, *A Chronicle of Pasadena Friends, 1884-1959* (Pasadena: The House of Printing, 1959), p. 7.
18. *Minutes of Iowa Yearly Meeting of Friends* (Oskaloosa, Iowa: Herald Printing Co., 1884), p. 9.
19. *The Christian Workman, loc. cit.*
20. *Ibid.*, p. 2.
21. *Ibid.* See also Henry E. McGrew, "A Brief History of the First Friends Church of Pasadena, California," unpublished manuscript located in the Quaker Collection, Whittier College Library, Whittier, California.
22. *Minutes of Kansas Yearly Meeting of Friends* (Wichita, Kansas: Journal Printing Co., 1886), p. 17.
23. "El Modena," *The Christian Workman, op. cit.*, p. 2.
24. In 1966, the El Modena Friends Church sold their property and began construction of a new sanctuary located several blocks from the original site.
25. For a discussion of the revival movement in Kansas, see Sheldon Jackson's chapter on "Revival and Transformation," *A Short History of Kansas Yearly Meeting of Friends, op. cit.*, pp. 50-66.
26. See the *Minutes of Kansas Yearly Meeting of Friends* (Wichita, Kansas: Journal Printing Co., 1887), p. 7. Cf. *Minutes of Iowa Yearly Meeting of Friends* (Oskaloosa, Iowa: Herald Printing Co., 1887), p. 2.
27. *Ibid.*, p. 5. See also the "Report of Iowa Yearly Meeting," *Friends' Review*, Vol. XLI, No. 8 (September 22, 1887), p. 122.
28. *Minutes of Iowa Yearly Meeting of Friends* (Oskaloosa, Iowa: Herald Printing Co., 1888), p. 6.
29. *Ibid.*, p. 9.
30. *Ibid.*
31. "Whittier," *The Christian Workman, op. cit.*, p. 8.
32. Dumke, *op. cit.*, p. 111.
33. Aquilla H. Pickering, "Story of the Beginning." A personal account quoted by Benjamin F. Arnold and Artilissa D. Clark, *The History of Whittier* (Whittier, California: Western Printing Co., 1943), p. 13.
34. *The Christian Workman, loc. cit.*
35. Dumke, *loc. cit.*
36. Some discrepancy appears in two accounts of the naming of the town of Whittier. *The Christian Workman* indicates that Elizabeth Grinnell of Pasadena first proposed the name of Whittier for the new colony, *loc. cit.* However, Aquilla Pickering's own account gives the credit to Micajah D. Johnson; see Arnold and Clark, *op. cit.*, p. 12.
37. Dumke, *loc. cit.* See also William W. Robinson, *Whittier: A Calendar of Events in the Making of a City* (Los Angeles: Title Insurance and Trust Co., 1942), p. 14.
38. "Whittier," *The Christian Workman, op. cit.*, p. 9.
39. *Ibid.*
40. *Ibid.*
41. *Ibid.*
42. *Ibid.*, p. 11.
43. *Ibid.*, p. 12.
44. See Chapter V.
45. "Alamitos," *The Christian Workman, op. cit.*, p. 10.
46. "Long Beach," *The Christian Workman, op. cit.*, p. 11.
47. *Ibid.*
48. Walter H. Case, *History of Long Beach and Vicinity*, Vol. I (Chicago: S. J. Clarke Publishing Co., 1927), pp. 454, 455.
49. "Minutes of the Organization and Official Actions of Long Beach Monthly Meeting of Friends at Long Beach, Los Angeles County, California," p. 3. Unpublished records located in the files of First Friends Church, Long Beach, California.
50. *Ibid.*, p. 4.

51. *Ibid.*, p. 11.
52. "Berkeley," *The Christian Workman*, *op. cit.*, p. 13.
53. *Ibid.*
54. "Minutes of Pasadena Quarterly Meeting," dated May 18, 1889. The records are kept in the vault of First Friends Church, Whittier, California.
55. John Henry Douglas, "Pastoral and Evangelistic Report for 1889 and 1890," supplement to the *Minutes of Iowa Yearly Meeting of Friends* (Oskaloosa, Iowa: Herald Printing Co., 1890), pp. 7, 8.
56. *Ibid.*, p. 5.
57. *Ibid.*, p. 1.
58. "Villa Street Meeting," *Friends Bulletin*, No. 7 (December, 1938), p. 8. T. S. Kenderdine compares visits in the 1890s to the two Friends Meetings in Pasadena in his book, *California Revisited* (Newton, Pennsylvania: Doylestown Publishing, 1898), pp. 173-177.
59. "Villa Street Meeting," *loc. cit.* This meeting continues to be the only Meeting of Conservative Friends in California.
60. "Minutes of the Organization and Official Actions of Long Beach Monthly Meeting," *op. cit.*, p. 7.
61. *Minutes of Iowa Yearly Meeting of Friends* (Oskaloosa, Iowa: Herald Printing Co., 1892), p. 4.
62. *Minutes of Iowa Yearly Meeting of Friends* (Oskaloosa, Iowa: Herald Printing Co., 1894), p. 11.
63. "Minutes of Whittier Quarterly Meeting, February 16, 1895-February 19, 1916," pp. 1-3. The minutes are located in the vault of First Friends Church, Whittier, California.
64. *Minutes of Iowa Yearly Meeting of Friends* (Oskaloosa, Iowa: Herald Printing Co., 1893), p. 8.
65. *Ibid.*
66. *Minutes of California Yearly Meeting of Friends Church* (Whittier, California: California Yearly Meeting, 1895), p. 9.
67. "California Yearly Meeting," *The American Friend*, Vol. II, No. 16 (April 18, 1885), p. 374.
68. *Minutes of California Yearly Meeting of Friends Church, 1895, op. cit.*, pp. 12, 13.
69. *Minutes of California Yearly Meeting of Friends Church* (Whittier, California: California Yearly Meeting, 1896), p. 14.
70. See "The New Yearly Meeting of California," *The Friend* (London), Vol. 34, No. 28 (June 8, 1894), pp. 374, 375; also "California Yearly Meeting," *The Friend* (London), Vol. 35, No. 18 (May 6, 1895), p. 284. Cf. "Philadelphia and California Yearly Meetings," *The American Friend*, Vol. II, No. 17 (April 25, 1895), p. 389.
71. "California Yearly Meeting," *The American Friend*, Vol. II, No. 16 (April 18, 1895), p. 375.
72. *Ibid.*
73. *Minutes of Iowa Yearly Meeting of Friends* (Oskaloosa, Iowa: Herald Printing Co., 1895), p. 7.
74. Nannie Arnold, "The Church of the New Era," *The Christian Workman*, Vol. III, No. 1 (January, 1895), p. 4.
75. See articles in *The Christian Workman*, Vol. 5, No. 7-8 (August, 1897), pp. 4-15.
76. "Minutes of the Owenyo Monthly Meeting, 1902-1905." These records are preserved in the vault of First Friends Church, Whittier, California.
77. *Minutes of California Yearly Meeting of Friends Church* (Whittier, California: The Register Press, 1901), p. 4.
78. San Diego Quarterly Meeting was established in 1911.
79. Long Beach Quarterly Meeting was established in 1953. A reorganization of the business proceedings of California Yearly Meeting in 1963, however, resulted in the disbanding of the three Quarterly Meetings in the Los Angeles area, i.e., Pasadena, Whittier, and Long Beach.
80. Present listing of the Monthly Meetings of California Yearly Meeting of Friends Church: Alamitos, Alhambra, Anaheim, Arcadia, Azusa, Bell, Berkeley, Capay Rancho, Citrus Heights, Denair, Diamond Bar, East Whittier, El Modena, Fresno,

Granada Heights, Inglewood, Lindsay, Long Beach, Midway City, Montebello, North Holtville, Pasadena, Phoenix (Arizona), Pico Rivera, Ramona, Rose Drive, Sacramento, San Diego, Spring Valley, Tucson (Arizona), Ventura, Walnut Creek, Whittier, Woodlake Ave., and Yorba Linda.

81. *Minutes and Proceedings of the Five Years Meeting of the American Yearly Meetings—1902* (Philadelphia: John C. Winston Co., 1903).

82. *Faith and Practice of California Yearly Meeting of Friends Church*, Part II (Whittier, California: California Yearly Meeting, 1967), p. 87. The fourteen constituent Yearly Meetings are: Baltimore, California, Canada, Cuba, East Africa, Indiana, Iowa, Jamaica, Nebraska, New England, New York, North Carolina, Western, and Wilmington. Ohio never joined the Five Years Meeting, while Oregon and Kansas withdrew in 1926 and 1937 respectively. These last three Yearly Meetings, together with Rocky Mountain, have formed the Evangelical Friends Alliance. See the article by Arthur O. Roberts in *American Quakers Today*, edited by Edwin Bronner (Philadelphia: Friends World Committee, 1966), pp. 58-69.

83. *Faith and Practice*, Part I, *op. cit.*, p. 4.

84. *Ibid.*

85. *Ibid.*, p. 5.

86. *Ibid.*

87. *Ibid.*, pp. 11-29.

88. Note the position that California Yearly Meeting takes here regarding the nineteenth century controversy with Joel Bean over the office and ministry of the "Inner Light." Cf. with his statement "That in *every* man there is the light and spirit of Christ" [italics mine], *The Friend* (Philadelphia), Vol. 58, No. 15 (April 11, 1885), p. 287.

89. Keith Sarver, *The Quaker Image* (Whittier, California: California Yearly Meeting of Friends, 1966), p. 19. Mr. Sarver is the General Superintendent of California Yearly Meeting and reflects the predominant view held by the members.

90. *Faith and Practice*, Part I, *op. cit.*, p. 19. The position taken here is mediating and doesn't go to the extremes warned of by Joel Bean. Cf. Joel Bean, "The Issue," *op. cit.*, p. 50.

91. *Faith and Practice*, Part I, *op. cit.*, p. 11. A distinct contrast can be noted in the views of Scripture as held by California Yearly Meeting and by Pacific Yearly Meeting; see Chapter VIII.

92. *Ibid.*, pp. 19, 20. This statement is in sharp contrast to Joel Bean's position, who could not believe that "any portion of the human race, or any individual soul is condemned to endless punishment. . . ." *Friends' Review*, Vol. XLVII (October 12, 1893), p. 187.

93. *Faith and Practice*, Part I, *op. cit.*, p. 7.

94. *Ibid.*, p. 30.

95. Sarver, *op. cit.*, p. 20.

96. "Minutes of Pasadena Quarterly Meeting of Friends," *op. cit.*, p. 5.

97. *Ibid.*, p. 8.

98. *Ibid.*

99. Cited by Herbert E. Harris, *The Quaker and the West* (Whittier, California: Whittier College, 1948), p. 17.

100. *Ibid.*, p. 20.

101. For a discussion of the collapse of the land boom of southern California, see Dumke, *op. cit.*, pp. 259-276.

102. *Minutes of Kansas Yearly Meeting of Friends* (Wichita, Kansas: Journal Printing Co., 1886), p. 17.

103. Harris, *op. cit.*, p. 25. For a general discussion on Quaker Education, see William W. Comfort, *The Quaker Way of Life* (Philadelphia: American Friends Service Committee, 1959), pp. 94-109.

104. *Ibid.*, p. 32. See also Harry W. Nerhood, "The Founding of Whittier College," *Bulletin of Friends Historical Association*, Vol. 41, No. 2 (Autumn 1952), pp. 104-120.

105. *Ibid.*, p. 33.

106. *Minutes of California Yearly Meeting of Friends Church* (Whittier, California: California Yearly Meeting, 1900), p. 53.

107. *Minutes of California Yearly Meeting of Friends Church* (Whittier, California: California Yearly Meeting, 1901), p. 34.

108. Harris, *op. cit.*, p. 37.

109. Of all the Quaker colleges in America, Whittier College bears perhaps fewer of the distinctive marks of Friends. It maintains friendly, but very loose, connections with California Yearly Meeting. For the most recent discussion of Whittier College, see Charles W. Cooper, *Whittier: Independent College in California* (Los Angeles: Ward Ritchie, 1967).

110. William P. Pinkham, a Quaker from Ohio Yearly Meeting, was one of the early leaders of the Training School. He also served for a time as associate editor of *The Evangelical Friend*, a periodical published in Cleveland, Ohio. See William P. Pinkham, *Lamb of God: Or, the Scriptural Philosophy of the Atonement* (Los Angeles: George Rice and Sons, 1895) and "The Doctrine of Sanctification," *The Evangelical Friend*, Vol. IX, No. 4-5 (April-May 1913), pp. 1-3.

111. *Minutes of California Yearly Meeting of Friends Church* (Whittier, California: California Yearly Meeting, 1902), pp. 48, 49.

112. *Ibid.*

113. See Chapter V. From the earliest days, the Quaker meetings took a stand against the excessive use of alcohol, but not until the late nineteenth century was total abstinence emphasized. See Brinton, *Friends for 300 Years*, p. 143.

114. For a discussion of the travels of Frances E. Willard, see Anna Gordon, *The Beautiful Life of Frances E. Willard* (Chicago: Women's Temperance Publishing Association, 1898), p. 106.

115. Ella C. Veeder was a recorded Friends minister and was later appointed as the first pastor of the Alamitos Monthly Meeting in 1890.

116. Arnold and Clark, *op. cit.*, p. 104.

117. *Minutes of California Yearly Meeting of Friends* (Whittier, California: California Yearly Meeting, 1895), p. 31.

118. *Ibid.*, p. 37.

119. See Lester Jones, *Quakers in Action* (New York: The Macmillan Co., 1929) for a full account of this work of American Friends Service Committee during this period. The report and action of California Friends can be found in *Minutes of California Yearly Meeting of Friends Church* (Whittier, California: California Yearly Meeting, 1918), pp. 37-40. See also William W. Comfort, *Quakers in the Modern World* (New York: The Macmillan Co., 1949).

120. Louis T. Jones, *op. cit.*, p. 235. See also the account of the Children's Home Society in the *Long Beach Press-Telegram*, December 6, 1964.

121. *Minutes of California Yearly Meeting of Friends Church* (Whittier, California: California Yearly Meeting, 1895), p. 28.

122. *Historical Sketch of the Missions of California Yearly Meeting of Friends* (Whittier, California: California Yearly Meeting, 1922), pp. 13-17.

123. *Ibid.*, pp. 27-33.

124. Russell, *op. cit.*, p. 463. For a full discussion, see Rayner W. Kelsey, *Friends and the Indians, 1655-1917* (Philadelphia: The New Era Printing Co., 1917).

125. *Ibid.*, p. 163, 172. For further information on William Nicholsen, see the account by Walter C. Woodard, *Timothy Nicholsen, Master Quaker* (Richmond, Indiana: The Nicholsen Press, 1927), p. 252.

126. *Minutes of California Yearly Meeting of Friends Church* (Whittier, California: California Yearly Meeting, 1897), p. 43. The first mention of California Yearly Meeting in *The Friend* (Philadelphia), as far as the author was able to discern, occurred ten years after its founding. A brief account of the work in Alaska at Kotzebue is given, with the following statement: "The best feature about the work at Kotzebue, the missionaries say, is that the people are really converted with very little emotion or excitement. Yet their lives are changed and remain changed." *The Friend* (Philadelphia), Vol. 79, No. 16 (October 16, 1905), p. 127.

127. *Historical Sketch of the Missions of California Yearly Meeting of Friends, op. cit.*, p. 18.

128. *Ibid.*, p. 19.

129. A missionary paper, *The Harvester*, was published in Chiquimula, Guatemala, by the Friends Mission from 1907-1956. The only complete set in existence is in the possession of Matilda Haworth, member of the Long Beach Monthly Meeting.

130. *Minutes of California Yearly Meeting of Friends Church* (Whittier, California: California Yearly Meeting, 1895), p. iv.
131. Russell, *op. cit.*, p. 422.
132. Jay, *op. cit.*, pp. 368-372.
133. These Friends were also present at the opening of California Yearly Meeting and are named by Walter Williams in a list of leaders of the revival movement in Quakerism; Williams, *op. cit.*, p. 198. For a further discussion of Amos Kenworthy, see Lydia M. Cammack and Truman C. Kenworthy, *Life and Works of Amos Kenworthy* (Richmond, Indiana: Nicholsen Printing and Mfg. Co., 1918).

Chapter VIII—The Pacific Yearly Meeting of the Religious Society of Friends

1. See the article written by Isabel H. Bliss, "Unaffiliated Friends Meetings," in *American Quakers Today*, *op. cit.*, pp. 85-92.
2. *Ibid.*, p. 87.
3. "Minutes of College Park Association of Friends, 1889-1932," *op. cit.*
4. See Howard H. Brinton, "The College Park Association of Friends," an unpublished manuscript presented to and approved by the College Park Association on June 19, 1927. The original typescript is in the possession of Howard H. Brinton, Wallingford, Pennsylvania. Samuel and Paul Brun, who worshiped at the College Park Meeting, were French Quakers; see Herbert C. Jones, *op. cit.*, p. 4.
5. Brinton, "College Park Association of Friends," *op. cit.*
6. *Ibid.*
7. *Ibid.*
8. William C. Allen, "College Park Association," *The Friend* (Philadelphia), Vol. 84, No. 23 (November 24, 1910), p. 165.
9. See the report of the leadership of Joel Bean in "College Park Association," *The Pacific Friend*, Vol. XVI, No. 21 (January 7, 1909), p. 6.
10. Allen, "College Park Association," *loc. cit.*
11. *Minutes of College Park Association of Friends, 1889-1932, op. cit.*
12. Brinton, "The College Park Association of Friends," *op. cit.*
13. "Minutes of the College Park Association of Friends, 1889-1952," *op. cit.*
14. Herbert C. Jones, *op. cit.*, p. 4. See a full discussion in Nellie Blessing-Eyster, *A Chinese Quaker* (New York: Fleming H. Revell Co., 1902).
15. "The Mooney Concern," *Friends Bulletin*, No. 4 (May 1, 1930), p. 6.
16. "Discipline of the College Park Association of Friends." Pamphlet printed and circulated by the College Park Association, n.d.
17. Otha Thomas, "Friends and Scriptures," *Friends Bulletin*, No. 3 (January 1, 1930), p. 2.
18. See the article by Walter E. Vail, "Charles Cox; In Memoriam," *Friends Bulletin*, No. 5-6 (March 1, 1931), p. 4.
19. *The Friend* (Philadelphia), Vol. 113, No. 19 (March 21, 1940), p. 327.
20. Cited by Rufus Jones, *Ibid.*
21. Herbert C. Jones, for example, served twenty-two years as a State Senator, having been first elected in 1913.
22. *Friends Bulletin*, No. 4 (May 1, 1930), p. 5.
23. Elizabeth H. Shelley, "Hannah Elliot Bean," *The Friend* (Philadelphia), Vol. 82, No. 44 (May 6, 1909), p. 347.
24. *The Friend* (Philadelphia), Vol. 86, No. 17 (November 28, 1912), p. 175.
25. Augustus T. Murray, "Joel Bean," *The Annual Monitor for 1915*, No. 103, edited by Joseph J. Gill (Gloucester: John Bellows, 1914), pp. 12-25.
26. *Ibid.* For a report of the memorial service, see William C. Allen, "In Memory of Joel Bean," *The Friend* (Philadelphia), Vol. 87, No. 36 (March 12, 1914), pp. 439, 440.
27. B. L. Weeks, *op. cit.*, p. 138.
28. *Friends Bulletin*, No. 1 (January 31, 1929), p. 1. In a later letter to Amy Post of Haverford College, dated December 18, 1937, Anna Brinton explained, "The first series of *The Friends Bulletin* was an effort of College Park Meeting in 1929-1931. It lapsed because most of the Friends in that meeting died and the editor of the series moved away. . . . A second series was begun in 1934, as a

supplement to the first." The original letter is in the Haverford College Library, Haverford, Pennsylvania.

29. Howard Brinton, "A Quaker Opportunity," *Friends Bulletin*, No. 2 (July 1, 1929), p. 3.
30. Bliss, *op. cit.*, p. 88.
31. Howard H. Brinton, *Seventy-five Years of Quakerism, 1885-1960* (Philadelphia: Philadelphia Yearly Meeting, 1960), pp. 20-21.
32. From a personal interview with Howard H. Brinton in Wallingford, Pennsylvania, on December 1, 1966.
33. William E. Lawrence, "The Pacific Coast Association of Friends," *Friends Bulletin*, No. 1 (January, 1934), p. 1.
34. The first Friends meeting was held in Riverside on May 8, 1928. After ten years of informal organization, the group was organized as a Monthly Meeting on November 12, 1939. See *Friends Bulletin*, No. 35 (May, 1947), p. 5.
35. The Berkeley Meeting had functioned since 1914, when Philadelphia Yearly Meeting expressed a concern for a meeting in the Bay area. See *Friends Bulletin*, No. 4 (May 1, 1930), p. 2.
36. Howard Brinton recalled in the personal interview, December 1, 1966, that the Orange Grove Meeting was one of the most enthusiastic and liberal supporters of the Pacific Coast Association.
37. *Friends Bulletin*, No. 25 (December, 1945), p. 5.
38. In an article on the problem of American-Japanese relationships, Floyd Schmoe of Pacific Coast Association wrote, "What the Japanese-American is now is largely the result of our influence, what he becomes in the future will depend almost entirely upon our attitude toward him. We not only have a real interest in this problem, but a real responsibility." *Friends Bulletin*, No. 11 (June, 1941), p. 3.
39. John Dorland, "Editorial," *Friends Bulletin*, No. 2 (August, 1934), p. 2.
40. Brinton, *Seventy-Five Years of Quakerism, 1885-1960*, p. 21. See also his essay, *How They Became Friends*, Pendle Hill Pamphlet No. 114 (Wallingford, Pennsylvania: Pendle Hill, 1961), for further personal insights.
41. Howard Brinton, "Do We Need a Pacific Yearly Meeting?" *Friends Bulletin*, No. 5-6 (March 1, 1931), p. 10.
42. Brinton, *Seventy-Five Years of Quakerism, 1885-1960*, p. 21.
43. Letter of Howard H. Brinton to Pearl W. McPherson and others, dated April 30, 1941. Copy of the original is in the files of Howard Brinton, Wallingford, Pennsylvania.
44. "Editorial," *Friends Bulletin*, No. 28 (May, 1946), p. 1.
45. Brinton, *Seventy-Five Years of Quakerism, 1885-1960*, p. 22.
46. Howard Brinton, "The Function of a Yearly Meeting," *Friends Bulletin*, No. 30 (July-August, 1946), p. 1.
47. Brinton, *Seventy-Five Years of Quakerism, 1885-1960*, p. 22.
48. *Friends Bulletin*, No. 29 (June, 1946), p. 3.
49. "Minutes of the Pacific Coast Association of Friends," *Friends Bulletin*, No. 32 (October, 1946), p. 3.
50. *Ibid.*
51. From a personal interview with Anna Cox Brinton on December 1, 1966, at Wallingford, Pennsylvania. The Pacific Coast Association functioned until 1958.
52. Virginia N. Barnett, "Why a Pacific Yearly Meeting?" *Friends Bulletin*, No. 35 (January 1, 1947), p. 1.
53. "Minutes of Pacific Yearly Meeting," *Friends Bulletin*, No. 43 (October, 1947), p. 5. Note the contrast in the establishment of California Yearly Meeting, which was officially authorized by Iowa Yearly Meeting and approved by other yearly meetings. Pacific Yearly Meeting was established independently, however, and not by an older, parent yearly meeting.
54. From a personal interview with Howard Brinton, December 1, 1966, at Wallingford, Pennsylvania.
55. Brinton, *Seventy-Five Years of Quakerism, 1885-1960*, p. 21.
56. *Friends Bulletin*, No. 79 (September, 1950), p. 7.
57. The reduction in monthly meetings from the previous year was probably due to the lack of information from China. The secretary reported, "We regret that mail

has been returned unclaimed from the Monthly Meeting in Shanghai." *Friends Bulletin*, No. 101 (September-October, 1952), p. 3.

58. *Friends Bulletin*, Vol. 28, No. 11 (November, 1960), p. 8.

59. *Friends Bulletin*, Vol. 29, No. 8 (September, 1961), p. 10.

60. From the report of the statistical secretary of Pacific Yearly Meeting, Mildred Burck, *Friends Bulletin*, Vol. 35, No. 1, (September, 1966), p. 3.

61. From a personal interview with Howard Brinton, December 1, 1966, at Wallingford, Pennsylvania.

62. *Discipline of the Pacific Yearly Meeting of the Religious Society of Friends* (Palo Alto: Pacific Yearly Meeting, 1965), p. 9.

63. *Ibid.*, p. 10.

64. *Ibid.*, p. 16.

65. *Ibid.*, p. 17.

66. This was substantiated by personal interviews with Howard Brinton on December 1, 1966, in Wallingford, Pennsylvania; with Herbert C. Jones on January 23, 1967 in San Jose, and with Madge Seaver, clerk of Pacific Yearly Meeting, on January 23, 1967 in San Francisco. An individual exception would be Ferner Nuhn, Claremont, who was closely associated with the development of the *Discipline*. In a letter to the author, dated May, 1968, Ferner Nuhn suggests that the concern of some Friends in Pacific Yearly Meeting is not for the formulation of a theological creed, but that "Quakers should be literate theologically. We should know how to say what we individually experience and believe, even though we do not ask conformity by everyone in a statement of faith."

67. Madge Seaver, "Friends and Theology," *Friends Bulletin*, Vol. 27, No. 1 (February, 1959), p. 1.

68. *Ibid.*, p. 2.

69. *Friends Bulletin*, Vol. 28, No. 11 (November-December, 1960), p. 8. Howard Brinton suggests that silent worship provides a basis of unity and understanding with other religions, in *Quakerism and Other Religions*, Pendle Hill Pamphlet No. 93 (Wallingford, Pennsylvania: Pendle Hill, 1957).

70. *The Discipline of the Pacific Yearly Meeting of the Religious Society of Friends*, *op. cit.*, p. 37.

71. Bronner, *American Quakers Today*, *op. cit.*, p. 94.

Chapter IX—The Past Is Prologue

1. William Comfort has described a similar situation in these words, "The evangelical heat has been turned off so long, that although there is still fire in the furnace, the radiators are cold," in "Are We a *Religious* Society?" *The Friend* (Philadelphia), Vol. 113, No. 33 (March 21, 1940), p. 329.

2. Howard Brinton suggests that Pacific Yearly Meeting is even more pacifistic than Philadelphia Yearly Meeting, primarily because most of its members did not merely inherit their convictions. From a personal interview, December 1, 1966, at Wallingford, Pennsylvania.

3. Bliss, *op. cit.*, p. 88.

4. See *Trends in American and Canadian Quakerism, 1925-1950* (London: Friends World Committee for Consultation, 1951). California and Pacific Yearly Meetings also illustrate the two varieties of belief in Quakerism noted by Albert Fowler. California Yearly Meeting is of the particular variety. Its concept of Christianity is "inseparable from the faith it possesses." Pacific Yearly Meeting, however, tends toward the universal variety, "Christianity in its Quaker interpretation is but one religion among many, all good and sufficient expressions of God's purposes." Albert Fowler, *Two Trends in Modern Quaker Thought*, Pendle Hill Pamphlet No. 112 (Wallingford, Pennsylvania: Pendle Hill, 1961), p. 2.

5. The first meeting was held in Whittier, California, on January 13, 1963. The ten representatives were: Bess Bulgin, Lloyd Halvorson, Warren Mendenhall, Gurney Reece, and William Wright from California Yearly Meeting; William Bruff, Jr., Rega Engelsberg, Edwin Morgenroth, Ferner Nuhn, and Margaret Simkin, from Pacific Yearly Meeting. Ferner Nuhn, "California and Pacific Yearly Meeting Dialogues," *Friends Bulletin*, Vol. 33, No. 11 (July-August, 1964), p. 8.

6. *Ibid.*

Index